AMERICAN PLURALISM
AND THE
JEWISH COMMUNITY

AMERICAN PLURALISM
AND THE
JEWISH COMMUNITY

Edited by

Seymour Martin Lipset

Transaction Publishers
New Brunswick (U.S.A.) and London (U.K.)

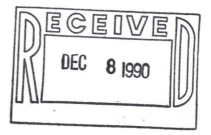

Library of Congress Catalog Number: 89-4725
ISBN: 0-88738-286-X
Printed in the United States of America

Library of Congress Cataloging-in-Publication Data

American pluralism and the Jewish community/ edited by Seymour Martin
Lipset.
    p.   cm.
    ISBN 0-88738-286-X
    1. Jews—United States—Politics and government. 2. Jews—United
States—Identity. 3. Jews—California—San Francisco—Politics and govern-
ment. 4. Raab, Earl. 5. United States—Ethnic relations. 6. San Francisco
(Calif.)—Ethnic relations. I. Lipset, Seymour Martin.
E184.J5A617   1989
305.8'924'073—dc19
                              89-4725
                                CIP
                                Rev.

19263601

Contents

Preface

This is a book of essays, about a peculiar people in an exceptional country, which is dedicated to a special man. To deal with the man first, my friend Earl Raab is a warm human being, a scholar who has produced books and articles, while working more than full time in the Jewish community. As a staff person and subsequently Executive Director of the Jewish Community Advisory Council of San Francisco, he played a major role in the affairs of that city in areas that went far afield from the interests of the Jews, particularly in civil rights and mental health. But his main concern has been for the security of Jews in the city, the nation, and the world. Bill Becker, a collaborator with him in civil rights activities, has written a chapter for this book, which supplies a glimpse of his life and activities.

When Raab's co-workers desired to honor him on his retirement, as members of the people of the book, they decided on a book of essays written by his friends and colleagues across North America. But knowing him, they felt that the kind that he would most appreciate would be a scholarly volume, one which would add to our understanding of the Jewish community in America. The results are before you—a collection of articles, analyzing different aspects of Jewish pluralism. All of them were written for this book, with the exception of one by Raab, "There's No City Like San Francisco." The article, written in 1950, represents the start of his involvement with the city. More importantly, it is still viable as an analysis and description of Jewish exceptionalism in San Francisco, and illustrates Raab's ability at sociologically analytical journalism.

Although as editor I am responsible for the selection of authors, a number of institutions and people made the book possible through commitment of institutional resources and time. These include the Hoover Institution of Stanford University, the Jewish Community Relations Council of San Francisco, and the Russell Sage Foundation. Sydnee Guyer and Janet Shaw gave generously of their time in providing editorial assistance and sage advice as to contents and style. I am indebted to them.

Finally, I would like to acknowledge a deep personal debt to Earl Raab. We have been friends and collaborators for over four decades. During that time, we have written books and articles, and worked together in various communal activities both within the Jewish arena and beyond. I have learned much from him about society; but, more importantly, he has taught me about people. His life has illustrated an old Jewish adage, that to be able to help yourself, you must be willing to give priority to helping others.

I

Jewry in North America

1

A Unique People in an Exceptional Country

Seymour Martin Lipset

To understand American Jewry, it is important to recognize that their experience on this continent differs qualitatively from those of their co-religionists in other countries. Jews won acceptance as fully equal citizens earlier here than elsewhere. They have faced much less discrimination in the United States than in any other Christian nation. Although never more than 3.7 percent of the population, now 2.5, they have been given one third of the religious representation. In many public ceremonies, there is one priest, one minister, and one rabbi. Currently (1989), there are thirty-one Representatives and eight Senators in Congress.[1] Many represent areas with few Jews in the population. Studies of national-origin and religious groups, using census and sample survey data, find that "Jews, regardless of ethnic ancestry, attain higher levels of education, occupation and income than all other sub-groups . . . "[2] A national survey of American Jews and non-Jews completed for the American Jewish Committee in April 1988 by Steven M. Cohen also leads to the conclusion that "Jews are among the wealthiest groups in America . . . [that] per capita Jewish income may actually be almost double that of non-Jews." More than twice as many Jews as non-Jewish whites report household incomes in excess of $50,000. At the other end of the spectrum, almost twice as many non-Jews as Jews indicate incomes of less than $20,000.[3] As Calvin Goldscheider and Alan Zuckerman note: "The pace of socioeconomic change and the levels attained are exceptional features of Jews compared to non-Jews."[4]

These generalizations have been abundantly documented for various high-level groups. An analysis of the 400 richest Americans, as reported by *Forbes* magazine, finds that two fifths of the wealthiest forty are Jews, as are twenty-three percent of the total list.[5] Jews are disproportionately present among many

3

sections of the elite, largely drawn from the college educated. Data gathered for an American Leadership Study in 10 major sectors in 1971-72 indicated that Jews "comprise[d] over 11 percent of the overall sample, compared to only 3 percent of the national population." No other group did as well.[6] An analysis of those listed in *Who's Who in America*, as of 1974, found 8.4 percent were Jewish, up from two percent in 1944-45. Jews have been over represented, as compared to all other ethnic groups except the English, from the early 1920s on. By the mid-1970s, they were far ahead of those of English descent as well.[7] More specialized studies point to their heavy presence among the top two hundred intellectuals (50 percent), American Nobel Prize winners in science and economics (40 percent), professors at the leading universities (20 percent), high level civil servants (21 percent), partners in the leading law firms in New York and Washington (40 percent), the reporters, editors and executives of the major print and broadcast media (26 percent), the directors, writers, and producers of the 50 top grossing motion pictures from 1965 to 1982 (59 percent), and the same level people in two or more prime time television series (58 percent).[8]

These achievements are related to the extraordinary scholastic accomplishments of American Jews. As of the beginning of the 1970s, four fifths of college-age Jews were enrolled in higher education, as compared to half that proportion, two fifths, for the population at large. And, like the faculty, they are heavily located in the more selective (higher academic standards) schools. An American Council on Education survey of college freshmen found that those of Jewish parentage had significantly higher secondary-school grades than their Gentile counterparts, in spite of the fact that a much larger proportion of all Jews than of others go on to college. Moreover, Jews seemingly perform better as undergraduates; by a considerable margin, they are disproportionately elected to Phi Beta Kappa.[9]

The Linkage with American Values

It has been argued that the ability of Jews to do so well in America reflects the fact that Jewish characteristics and values have been especially congruent with the larger culture, that they strongly resemble the modal national pattern. Writing in the 1920s, the sociologist Robert Park "suggested that Jewish history be taught in the schools so that Americans can learn what America is. Park argued that in their energy and drive for achievement Jews were quintessentially American."[10] Evidence in support of such assumptions may be found in Weber's analysis of the relationship between the Protestant ethic and the spirit of capitalism in America, East European Jews' reaction to Benjamin Franklin, and the contemporary links between a capitalist reformer, Margaret Thatcher, and British Jews. In his classic work, *The Protestant Ethic and the*

Spirit of Capitalism, Weber in explaining the economic success of the United States notes that the Puritans, Old Testament Christians, brought the religiously derived values conducive to capitalism—rationality, hard work, savings, a strong achievement drive—with them and, therefore, that "the spirit of capitalism . . . was present [in America] before the capitalistic order."[11] His principal examples of a secularized capitalist spirit are drawn from the writings of an *American*, Benjamin Franklin.[12] Weber quotes extensively from Franklin's works as prototypical of the values that are functional for the emergence of an industrialized system.

Franklin's values not only appealed to Americans, they found an enthusiastic audience in eastern Europe among Jews, to whom they also resonated as consistent with their religious beliefs and secular culture. Franklin's writings were translated into Yiddish around 1800, were read devoutly, and discussed in Talmudic discourse fashion by young Jews in Poland and Russia after they had completed their daily religious studies in yeshivas.[13]

Weber recognized the "actual kinship of Puritanism [Calvinism] to Judaism," and the way it played out in America. He noted: "Puritanism always felt its similarity to Judaism . . . The Jews who were welcomed by Puritan nations, especially the Americans . . . were at first welcomed without any ado whatsoever and are even now welcomed fairly readily . . . "[14]

The linkages of Protestant sectarian and Jewish values to the bourgeois or market ethic, and the classical liberalism of Americanism, are to be found in the closing decades of the twentieth century in the relationship of Margaret Thatcher to the Jews. She admires them as hard-working, self-made people who believe that "God helps those who help themselves." She has chosen to represent the most Jewish district in Britain, Finchley, and has appointed five Jews to Cabinet posts at different times, and has designated the Grand Rabbi, Immanuel Jakobovits, a member of the House of Lords. In commenting on the latter action, various British publications have noted that she much prefers the tough-minded, self-help, work-oriented values of the Grand Rabbi which also encompass commitment to personal philanthropy, to the soft Tory welfare emphases of the Archbishop of Canterbury.[15]

Unlike Thatcher's predecessors as leaders of the Conservative party, she is not a Tory, an orientation once described by one of them, Harold Macmillan, as "paternalistic socialism." She is a classical liberal; i.e., a supporter of the Hayek–Friedman–Reagan laissez-faire, antistatist, meritocratic view of the world. Basically the goal of the Thatcher revolution, whether consciously conceived of in these terms or not, is to create a country that sociologically resembles the United States; that is rid of its postfeudal status and mercantilist–Tory–socialist elements; that like America, is an achievement–oriented bourgeois liberal society. And she sees the British Jews as most like the kind of people she would prefer most of her compatriots to be, prototypically American, competitively oriented.

The Background

The United States began as a new society, formed by settlers in a wilderness. It is the most important country that is not postfeudal. The black situation apart, it lacks the experience of fixed social status groups, castelike structures that in English are sometimes referred to as estates or, to use the German word, *standen*. Feudal and aristocratic systems required the explicit exhibition of deference to superiors. They rejected the values linked to social mobility, and emphasized particularism, family, and ethnic and religious background as sources of status and citizen rights.

America, as Friedrich Engels and Max Weber, among many, emphasized, is the purest example of a bourgeois society, one that has followed capitalist market norms, uninterfered with by values derived from feudalism. These norms assume universalism, that every one is treated according to the logic of the market, will buy and sell at the best possible price from whoever will trade. Individuals should be hired because they are the most competent available, regardless of background, whether black or white, Jewish or Gentile. Ideally, discrimination linked to ascribed characteristics will injure the bigot in his competition with those who are not prejudiced. Perceiving America as the purest market society implies that it has been a meritocracy, an open society, open to talent, open to the most efficient, the most competent.

From its origins, America has been a universalistic culture, slavery and the black situation apart; and linked to universalism is an emphasis on equality. Equality in the American sense has not only meant equality of opportunity, but as important, it has implied equality of respect. Tocqueville noted that, in spite of enormous difference in economic position, the most important status that defines interaction is that of the person, in his time of course, a white male person. Everyone is entitled to respect, regardless of where he stands in the economic or power structure, or whether he is Christian or Jewish.

Beyond its beginnings in frontier societies, the United States is a new nation, created as the outcome of a victorious revolution which formulated a special ideology or creed, Americanism. As a new nation legitimated by an ideology, it differs from other countries, which take their identity from a common history, not a political doctrine, a national Creed. Americanism is an "ism" or ideology in the same sense that Communism, Fascism, or liberalism are isms. It can be subsumed in four words: anti-statism, individualism, egalitarianism, and populism.[16] As the self-conscious center of the liberal and increasingly populist revolutions (from 1776 to early in the twentieth century), from the point of view of her own people as well as others, the United States has been open to new members. One may become an American by joining the party, accepting the Creed. Conversely, one may be expelled, be proscribed as un–American, regardless of birth, by rejecting the doctrine, by accepting an alien one. Though immigrants may acquire citizenship almost everywhere, the meaning of being English, French, German, is predominantly a birthright status. Almost every country outside the United States, except for the Soviet Union (not Russia) is a historically defined one, united by a common history, not a political doctrine. And until relatively recently, citizen rights were associated with the dominant established religion, different Christian denominations in Europe and Latin American, and Islam, still, in most of the Moslem world.

The United States, however, does not have a state church. Tocqueville saw, in the voluntary character of religion in America the secret of its greater religiosity, as well as the stability of its democratic order. Voluntary denominationalism encourages allegiance and participation, and the formation of a host of mediating organizations, positioned between the citizenry and the state. It inhibits the tendency of the latter to monopolize power, which he believed, – and, according to 1988 opinion polls, most Americans still feel– is inherent in governmental institutions. But though America has remained the most devout country in Christendom (except for a few like Ireland and Poland, where religion and the struggle against national oppression are interlinked), no one is expected to adhere to any dominant denomination. For the first time in the history of the Diaspora, since the dispersal from Roman Palestine, Jews became free to partake in the polity as equals with every one else. As Edward Tiryakian presents the unique American environment:

> Briefly, at the heart of American exceptionalism concerning the Jewish experience in America, is that while the United States is to and cannot be affectively and spiritually "the Land" in the way that Israel is "the Land" (but is also more than "the Land"), it has been more of a rewarding *and accepting* home than any other setting outside the Holy Land itself . . . What makes the American case different from others?

> Jews in America have not been singled out as "wholly other" by virtue of religious culture and/or civil religion. In fact because of a "deep structure," affinity if not alliance between Calvinist–Puritanism and Judaism, it is in American that Jews have increasingly found full societal and cultural participation and acceptance symbolized by the term "Judeo-Christian."[17]

The special character of American pluralism, as it affects the position of Jewry, is discussed in chapter three by the Israeli sociologist, Shmuel Eisenstadt. As he notes, the encouragement to American Jewry to play a full role in society and the polity is endemic in George Washington's message to the Jews of Newport in 1790, that in the new United States "all possess alike liberty of conscience and immunities of citizenship." Even more significantly, he emphasized that the patronizing concept of "toleration . . . of one class of people . . . [by] another" has no place in America, that Jews are as much Americans, and on the same basis, as any one else.[18] He recognized that tolerance denotes second class-citizenship. The next three Presidents, Adams, Jefferson and Madison also noted that America was different from Europe, that the discrimination against Judaism prevailing there did not exist here, where, in Jefferson's words all are "on an equal footing." He "rejoiced over the presence of Jews in the country because they would insure that religious diversity which, in his judgment, was the best protector of liberty."[19]

The European democratic movements sought to free the Jews from the religious-based restrictions on their rights to citizenship and free movement. But their anticlericalism led them to denigrate Judaism as an obscurantist doctrine that should wither under the pressure of the Enlightenment. The French Revolution gave Jews all civic rights, but specifically limited their freedom to maintain an organized communal structure, explicitly denying them group rights.[20] Subsequently, Napoleon, who tore down ghetto restriction in countries he conquered, grew concerned about the seeming desire of French Jews to remain socially distinct from others. Such concerns were foreign to the Americans. They opposed church establishment, but welcomed religion.

The most dramatic indicator of the pluralistic character of religion in the first half-century of American independence is evident in one of the most interesting and peculiar pieces of legislation enacted by an American Congress, the Sunday Mails Law. Passed in 1810, it authorized the Postmaster-General to sort and deliver mail on Sundays. In 1825, postmasters were ordered to keep offices open for the entire day. Some churchmen reacted by forming a General Union for Promoting the Observance of the Christian Sabbath. In answer to such protests, a Senate Committee headed by Richard Johnson, a Kentucky Senator and head of a national Baptist group, authored a Senate Committee report on the Act, adopted by the full body in 1830, which explicitly said: "The Constitution regards the conscience of the Jew as sacred as that of the Christian," and concluded that the government was obligated to affirm to all its "institutions on *Sunday*, as well as every day of the week."[21]

The fact that leading politicians could openly advocate that the federal government must consider the rights of Jews and other non-Christians indicates the extent to which many believing Protestants of the early United States were able to accept religious diversity.[22] Richard Johnson, the author of the 1830 Senate Report, was nominated for the vice-presidency as Martin Van Buren's running mate on the Democratic ticket, supposedly because of his popularity stemming from the Report. The Sunday requirement lasted until the late 1880s, when it was dropped by the Postmaster–General.[23] It must be noted, however, that the situation was quite different in many states, which, under

Sabbatherian and later trade union pressure, preserved or reenacted colonial legislation requiring Sunday closing by business. By 1868, however, fifteen states had exempted Saturday observers, Jews, and Seventh Day Baptists and Adventists from the rule.[24]

In 1860, when Jews still could not hold office in most of Europe, the House of Representatives was opened with a prayer by a rabbi, thus acknowledging "the equal status of Judaism, with Christianity, as an American faith."[25] Congress was to reaffirm in 1861 the position that Jews were entitled to the same rights as Christians. It had passed a law concerning military chaplains, which stated that they were to be regularly ordained ministers of some Christian denomination. Objections from Jewish groups led to an amendment to allow rabbis to serve as well.

The position of the Jews in early America was not only a function of political developments, it related to the special character of American Christianity, the fact that the United States is the only Protestant sectarian country. The European and Latin American nations have been dominated by the churches the Anglicans, Catholics, Lutherans, and Orthodox. The overwhelming majority of Americans were and are adherents of the sects: the Baptists, Methodists, and hundreds of other smaller denominations. The churches have been established and hierarchical. The sects have never been state related; they have always been voluntary institutions, and most of them have been congregational.

As Tocqueville and latter–day students of American religion and society have emphasized, Protestant sectarianism, which stresses the personal relationship of individuals with God, unmediated by church or hierarchy has contributed to the strength of individualism in this country. The competitive relationship of the sects with other denominations has enabled the Jews to fit in, as one out of many, rather than as the only or principal deviant group. In any case, until relatively recently, most Protestant sectarians viewed the Roman Catholics harshly, more negatively than the Jews. Catholicism was seen by many Americans, not as a different set of religious beliefs, but as an alien conspiracy seeking to undermine the American Protestant way of life and, therefore, as outside the pale.

The American Jews adapted to the dominant Protestant pattern. They developed a congregational style, eschewing organized communal or hierarchical structures that once characterized Jewry in many European countries.[26] In the latter case, Jews were governed by *kehillahs*, communal organizations, which included all of them, and in a number of nations, by Grand Rabbis, whose status has resembled that of bishops or archbishops. Canadian Jewry, living in a country, that places greater emphasis on the solidarity of ethnic and religious communities than the United States, as Morton Weinfeld notes in chapter six, is organized in one group, the Canadian Jewish Congress, which is somewhat like a European *kehillah*. American Jewry has no Grand Rabbis or disciplined communal bodies. An effort to form a *kehillah* in New York before World War I failed.[27] Judah Magnes, who played a major role in creating the New York *kehillah* in 1909, was to note a decade later that the "European notion of a uniform . . . all-controlling . . . kehillah cannot strike root in American soil . . . because it is not in consonance with the free and voluntary character of American religious, social, educational, and philanthropic enterprises . . . "[28] The contemporary complex voluntary communal organization structure and the nature of the American Jewish polity are discussed in chapters eleven and twelve by Daniel Elazar and Lawrence Rubin.

Relations with the Larger Society

There were relatively few Jews in the United States before the Civil War. They only totaled 15,000 in 1825, increasing to 50,000 in 1848. Some were able to reach high places in the American military and political systems, including a number of Congressmen and local elected officials. The most prominent of the latter, Mordecai Noah, served, at different times between 1813 and 1841, as U.S. Consul to Tunis, High Sheriff of New York, Surveyor of the Port of New York, Associate Judge of the New York Court of Sessions, and editor of six different New York newspapers. He also headed a number of Jewish communal organizations.[29] August Belmont, a Jewish banker who had once represented the Rothschilds, was chairman of the Democratic National Committee from 1860 to 1872. In 1860, the Commander of the Mediterranean Fleet was Uriah Levy, an affiliated Jew. There were at least four Jewish Generals in the Union Army.[30] At a time when Jews were still barred from public office in almost all of Europe, two Jews, David Yulee of Florida and Judah P. Benjamin of Louisiana, were elected to the U.S. Senate. The former in 1844, and the latter in 1854. Benjamin is better known as Secretary of the Treasury and Jefferson Davis's closest advisor in the Confederacy during the Civil War.[31]

On the other hand, there were a few anti–Semitic occurrences during the Civil War. In the North, Jewish cotton speculators and traders were stigmatized as helping the South economically. The most noteworthy action against them was Ulysses S. Grant's order, barring Jewish peddlers from the area under his command.[32] Abraham Lincoln promptly countermanded it. The president did not object to penalizing individuals whose actions were aiding the enemy, which, as he told Grant, presumably "was the object of your order, but . . . it is . . . [the] terms [which] proscribed an entire religious class," that were objectionable. Grant, it may be noted, was to quickly indicate regret, and to say the order was penned "without reflection." He informed the War Department a day later, that it would never have seen the light of day had it not been telegraphed immediately after he signed it. More significantly, he told his wife that Congressional censures against him had been deserved since he "had no right to make an order against any special sect." As President, he "proved himself a friend of the Jews and appointed many to posts at home and abroad. He offered a Jew, Joseph Seligman, the post of Secretary of the Treasury, which he declined." Grant supported the Jews in the "controversy raised by . . . the A.S.P.C.A. over the alleged cruelty practiced by Jews in the [kosher] slaughtering of animals."[33]

Concern for the welfare of Jews in other parts of the world has been characteristic of western Jewry since Roman times, and American Jews have obviously conformed to the rule. What is particularly notable about the phenomenon in the past two centuries is the extent to which they have been able to get support form the larger political system. In 1840, the United States protested the persecution of Jews in Turkish-controlled Syria; in the 1880s, pogroms in Czarist Russia were officially condemned. In the first case, the Secretary of State wrote to the American Minister to Turkey to do what he could to mitigate the oppression. His letter noted that the United States places "upon the same footing the worshipers of God, of every faith and form, acknowledging no distinction between the Mahomedan, the Jew and the Christian."[34] The American government frequently sought to intervene on behalf of the Jews of Romania, demanding that American and native Jews be accorded equality before the law. In 1879, in writing to the American Minister dealing with Romania, Secretary of State Evarts notes: "As you are aware, this government has ever felt a deep interest in the welfare of the Hebrew race in foreign countries, and has viewed with abhorrence the wrongs to which they have at various periods been subjected by followers of other creeds in the East."[35]

In the period between the Civil War and World War I, protests against anti-Jewish policies and pogroms in Czarist Russia occurred repeatedly. Some stemmed from an 1832 commercial treaty, which provided that local laws applied to nationals of each power in the other country. However, when these provisions were used by the Russians to legitimate restrictions on American Jews, the State Department and Congress objected. From Garfield on, every administration complained about American Jews not having equal rights. Resolutions were passed by Congress calling for the abrogation of the treaty. In 1908, the platforms of both major parties, denounced it, and it was cancelled in 1911.

In 1881, Garfield, in denouncing a pogrom, inaugurated a pattern of protests about the treatment of Russian Jews. From then through World War I, American governments often expressed sympathy with them and voiced complaint to the Czarist government. Such actions were frequent from 1903 to 1906, when over 300 pogroms occurred, reflecting the tumultuous revolutionary times.[36]

There were limits to the willingness of the American government to intervene on behalf of Jews abroad, which may convey a message for contemporary times. It is easy to win games in which you are the only major player, but you can lose against a strong opponent. In 1858, Jews in America and Europe rallied to protest the kidnapping and forced conversion to Catholicism of an Italian Jewish youngster, Edgardo Mortara, an action which the Vatican refused to reverse. Although American Jews put as much pressure on the national administration as they could, and there are many supportive editorials in the public press, this time the State Department did not react. The failure may have reflected the weakness of President James Buchanan, but more importantly, Jewish pressure was countered by Catholic efforts, and the Democratic politicians apparently did not want to alienate a large group of supporters.[37]

Anti-Semitism

The seemingly philo–Jewish behavior on the part of nineteenth– and early twentieth–century American political elites did not imply the absence of hostile attitudes or behavior. Anti–Semitism, of course, existed in America, sometimes on a large scale. It is a disease endemic in the long–term competitive relationship between Judaism and its daughter religion(s). Antagonistic beliefs and negative stereotypes are part of the folk mythology of Christendom. The original settlers and subsequent groups of immigrants brought them to the New World. The special economic skills in finance and commerce, which Jews developed in Europe to survive in societies that denied them access to ownership of land (the principal form of capital and investment), made them especially vulnerable to blame and persecution in periods of economic malaise and other severe crises.

The United States has not been an exception, even if the anti-Jewish outbreaks here have been much less virulent than in other countries. Comparing the phenomenon in nineteenth-century Europe and America, Leo Ribuffo concludes, "Anti-Semitism in the United States was relatively less violent, less racist, and less central to the world views of those who accepted it."[38] Conversely, nativism—hostility to immigrants—was a recurrent phenomenon in America, particularly active during periods of economic and political crisis. Jews sometimes were included as a secondary target, but the most extreme forms of nativism were to be found among the more fundamentalist Protestants, and took the form of anti-Romanism, of opposition to supposed conspiracies and real immigration waves that seemingly threatened the Protestant character of the country.[39]

Significant anti-Semitism showed up in the late nineteenth century, directed against the growing affluence of the German Jews, at a time when the Jews numbered about 250,000. As of 1889, " . . . bankers, brokers, wholesalers, retail dealers, collectors, and agents accounted for 62 percent of their occupations. In addition, 17 percent were professionals."[40] In the post–Civil War period, a number of Jews of German origin developed the leading banking houses of the country. They, together with New England scions of the Puritans, dominated investment banking.[41]

Although socializing and marrying largely with themselves, these extraordinarily successful people were opposed to social separatism. Some were among the founding members of the high–status social clubs formed in many cities immediately before and after the Civil War. But as the number of the first–generation or otherwise affluent Jews grew, wealthy Gentiles began to look for ways to deny them social access. Status strains endemic in a rapidly expanding and changing society upset people at different levels of the social structure. Those descended from the old wealthy of the pre–Civil War era found their claims to superior status threatened by the newly wealthy, some of whom were Jews. The Gentile *nouveau riche,* in turn, discovered that wealth alone was not sufficient to earn them admission to high society, and sought to differentiate themselves from the Jews. There was open resistance to allowing Jews into the social elites, into their neighborhoods, into their clubs and resorts and, ultimately, efforts to hold down their numbers in high-ranking universities and professions.[42] But it "is important to stress the fact that this caste line was only drawn at the end of the nineteenth century, when . . . the members of the upper class were setting themselves apart in other ways."[43] As John Higham describes the background:

> At every level so many successful people clamored for admission to more prestigious circles that social climbing ceased to be a simple and modest expectation . . . In order to protect recently acquired gains from later comers, social climbers had to strive constantly to sharpen the loose, indistinct lines of status. With a defensiveness born of insecurity, they grasped at distinctions that were more than pecuniary, through an elaborate formalization of etiquette, the compilation of social registers, the acquisition of aristocratic European culture, and the cult of genealogy.[44]

East European Jews

The late nineteenth century also witnessed the steady mass immigration of poor Jews from eastern Europe, which, by World War I, produced a population of over three million, mostly concentrated in the tenement districts of the major northern cities. Although much poorer than their German origin coreligionists, they were much better prepared for the life and economy of American cities than other immigrants. Almost all Jews came from urban environments.

"Between 1899 and 1914, fully two-thirds of the Jews entering the United States had been engaged in manufacturing and mechanical pursuits in Europe, more than three-fourths as skilled workers." This background provided them with "an enormous structural advantage over other immigrants in the pursuit of occupational integration and social mobility."[45] Although able to obtain employment in their traditional skills, most were poor. They worked mainly in the garment industries or in trade, often initially as peddler, the lowliest form of self–employment.[46] Living in crowded slums, in areas marked by high crimes rates and red–light districts, speaking Yiddish, frequently looking unkempt and outlandish, they helped to produce new anti–Semitic stereotypes. These fed nativist prejudices. Considerable tensions developed between the Jews and other immigrant groups, which presaged some of the more serious working–class–based anti–Semitic movements of the 1930s.

Poverty and bad housing conditions did not stop these East European Jews from moving up. The skills and values they brought with them enabled them to quickly outdo even those at their starting socioeconomic level in rates of upward social mobility. "For each wave of immigration from Russia bringing penniless and green immigrants into the slums, there was an exodus by immigrants who after five or ten years or so had managed well enough so they could leave the squalor of those slums."[47] They advanced through self-employment and education, particularly the latter. "Jewish children were in school longer than other immigrant groups . . . and accounted for relatively high percentages of those who attended schools and universities in the large cities of the Northeast . . . In comparison to most other immigrant groups, as well as to native-born Americans, Jewish children were more likely to reach and finish high school and more likely to enroll in college preparatory course."[48]

The most significant aspect of the American Jewish experience, prior to the Great Depression, was not its religious, organizational, and political diversity, but the improvement in its circumstances, as the children of the immigrants acquired substantial education and skills. Without going into further detail on the specific patterns of upward mobility, it should be noted that the East European Jews have been able to become, first, the best educated; then, the most middle–class; and, ultimately, the most affluent ethnoreligious group in the country; other than their coreligionistsof German origin.[49] As Lucy Dawidowicz notes, no "other immigrant group evinced such rapid and dramatic success."[50] From a concentration in the garment and other skilled trades, East European Jews moved toward heavy involvement in the professions.

The desire to attain a first–class education at the best universities led to crises in the 1920s, as the major eastern private colleges and professional schools found the proportion of Jews among their students rising into the double-digit percentiles (40 percent at Columbia). Arguing that these developments were undermining the character of their institutions and professions, that concentrations of Jews in particular places would result in anti–Semitism (*sic*), they covertly or openly restricted Jewish enrollment, through use of quotas or special forms of preference, for which few Jews could qualify. Although these restrictions kept down the number at the Ivy League and other elite private colleges, they did not stop young ambitious Jews from securing higher education. They flooded the public institutions, such as City College in New York.

Limited in the proportion who could become physicians, many who could not get into medical school became dentists or pharmacists. Others who were not admitted to major law schools went to less prestigious ones, or studied for other business–related professions, such as accounting. During the 1930s, when economic adversity limited support for prolonged professional education and opportunities for employment in private industry, many young Jews became teachers or civil servants. And self–employment, the most traditional way for Jews to escape restrictions, probably absorbed the greatest proportion of the ambitious.

To analyze the sources of Jewish achievement would take this essay too far afield. Suffice it to say that students of the subject have stressed: (1) a religiously inspired drive for education, which, secularized, has been linked to disproportionate intellectual contributions since the early Middle Ages; (2) the fact that Jews have been the urbanites *par excellence*, a background that has advantaged individuals in succeeding in the centers of business, professional, and intellectual life; (3) a greater socialization in middle–class norms and habits than any other less–privileged group, including a strong achievement drive, "the habits of care and foresight," and the capacity to defer gratification[51]; and (4) greater rootlessness, the ability to form new social relations in different ecological and class environments, one in which Jews show up as having more than other American ethnic groups.[52] In discussing these issues, Glazer notes:

> Judaism emphasizes the traits that businessmen and intellectuals require, and has done so since at least 1,500 years before Calvinism. We can trace Jewish Puritanism at least as far back as the triumph of the Maccabees over the Hellenized Jews and of the Pharisees over the Sadducees. The strong emphasis on learning and study can be traced that far back, too. The Jewish habits of foresight, care, moderation probably arose early during the two thousand years that the Jews have lived primarily as strangers among other peoples.[53]

The restrictions on Jewish entry into elite institutions, which, in part, reflected the competitive concerns of the non-Jewish middle–class and elites, were paralleled by increasingly negative reactions among the less–affluent mass population; particularly, but not exclusively, fundamentalist and evangelical Christians in rural areas and smaller urban centers. The latter dominated the country numerically until the start of the twentieth century, but massive non-Protestant immigration—Catholic, Orthodox and Jewish—and the steady growth of metropolitan areas were undermining their cultural and religious supremacy. American society was becoming cosmopolitan, secular, and urban. The census of 1920 reported that for the first time in American history urban dwellers were in a majority. Symbolically, large cities had become the centers Jewish and Catholic influence.

Evangelical Protestantism, as noted earlier, had long formed the base for opposition to Catholic immigration, while ignoring or even accepting the Jews for the most part. But in reaction to their massive infusion and economic success, the largely urbanized Jewish population also became a target, starting in the second decade of the century. In 1914, Tom Watson, a former leader of the People's party, and subsequently intellectual Godfather of the revived Ku Klux Klan, stimulated a lynching of Georgia Jewish businessman, Leo Frank, "for the death of a working–class Gentile" girl, a crime of which he was innocent. Watson continued a vitriolic anti–Semitic campaign for years thereafter. The outpouring of hate against Catholics, Jews, and Negroes contained in Watson's nationally circulated newspaper took an institutionalized form in the multimillion member Ku Klux Klan of the 1920s, although Watson himself never joined, as far as is known.[54]

The Klan, which documentably represented a form of evangelical Protestant backlash, was supported disproportionately by lower–status rural and small urban-community white sectarians. It attacked Catholics, Negroes, Jews, radicals, and "immoral" people — divorcees, adulterers, prostitutes, and the like. Although much less concerned with Jews than with Catholics and personal immorality, Klan publications were replete with elaborate Jewish conspiracies. They reprinted *The Protocols of the Elders of Zion*, which they found in another 1920s' focus of anti–Semitic agitation, Henry Ford's *Dearborn Independent*.[55]

Religious and Political Activity

The changing composition of American Jewry, and the diverse impact of world events, led to deep divisions in the community. The older German strand accommodated to their late nineteenth-century environment by modifying their religious practice. They developed Reform Judaism, whose practice and doctrine resembled the liberal Protestantism and Unitarianism of the non-Jewish middle- to upper-classes.[56] The more successful among the East Europeans—coming, if they were religious— from more Orthodox backgrounds, helped to create a more Americanized religious movement, the Conservatives. The Orthodox retained strength among the poorer and less-assimilated elements.[57]

But many Jews in eastern Europe had rejected religion entirely. Facing anti–Semitic regimes and societies, they could not simply enter the majority cultures. Barred from being members of conservative parties, they supported radical or revolutionary movements. They came to America as socialists and tried to remain such as workers. The major Yiddish newspaper, the *Forward*, was socialist. The predominant Jewish unions in the garment and other industries, joined in the United Hebrew Trades, backed the Socialist party.[58] The only two Congressmen the party elected before World War I—Meyer London, from the East Side of New York, and Victor Berger, from Milwaukee—were both Jewish. The Socialists were second to the Democrats in many Jewish districts in New York until the New Deal, when most of their supporters voted for Franklin D. Roosevelt; often on a third, American Labor, party line.

Zionism constituted the second-largest secular political strand among Jews in eastern Europe and North America. (The religiously Orthodox opposed the movement, believing that only God could redeem the promised land for the Jews.) It was, however, weaker than socialism until World War II, and, in any case, included a large socialist wing.[59]

To iterate the obvious, the period from the start of the Great Depression and the rise of Nazism has witnessed the greatest transformation in world Jewry since the destruction of the second Temple. The prolonged economic collapse stimulated the growth of extremist movements, some of which in Germany, the United States, and elsewhere, focused on blaming the Jews for all that went wrong. The German developments led to the Holocaust and the murder of six million Jews, one–third of the world's population. Ironically, the chain of events set in motion by Nazism also resulted in increased emigration to Palestine, and to the rebirth of the state of Israel in 1948. Thus, the most terrible and the most triumphant moments of Jewish history since the second Exile are intimately interlinked.

In the United States, assorted anti–Semitic right–wing movements, the most important of which was Father Coughlin's National Union for Social Justice, as well as a number of smaller ones which appealed to evangelical Protestants, gained strength. There is no reliable estimate of their support; they failed miserably at the ballot box. On the other hand, national opinion polls suggest that as much as one-quarter of the population approved of the racist demagogue, Charles Coughlin, who broadcast every Sunday on a national radio network. That support dropped to one-seventh by 1940. Assorted surveys designed to estimate the degree of anti-Semitism among the American public by responses to various prejudicial statements about Jews, conducted by Jewish defense groups, reported that roughly one out of two could be classified as anti–Jewish. This pattern lasted through World War II.[60]

Although the presence of protofascist movements and the increase in anti-Semitism did not have much effect on the personal or economic lives of

American Jews, they clearly affected governmental policy towards Germany and the Holocaust. Franklin Roosevelt, though strongly anti-Fascist and supportive of American participation in a war against Germany, consciously refrained from linking such concerns to the plight of the Jews, for fear of losing support. America turned refugees from Europe away. Anxiety about public sentiments continued to affect American policy during the war, helping to block efforts to help Jews in extermination camps.

The Depression stimulated growth of anti-Semitism and the country's shameful response to the plight of Jewish refugees, and then to the Holocaust clearly challenge the assumption that the Jewish experience in America is qualitatively different from that in other countries, that the United States is exceptional. All that may be said is that if the United States behaved badly, many others—such as Canada, which refused to take in any Jews—did worse; that the government and the large majority of Americans were for doing all that was necessary to defeat Nazism. Very few people, including the great majority of American Jews, could bring themselves to believe that the Nazis were, in fact, trying to physically annihilate the Jews of Europe.

For whatever reason, the situation changed dramatically almost as soon as the war was over. Opinion polls documented striking drops in bigoted attitudes; not only toward Jews, but to other minorities as well.[61] The United States strongly supported the creation of the state of Israel. Although most Americans lacked enough knowledge of the Middle East to voice opinions, the large majority of those who did backed Israel against the Arab states that were trying to annihilate her.

On the behavioral level, dramatic changes developed as well. Almost all the restrictions against Jews, such as limited access to advantages or restrictive quotas, began to decline or disappear. This was particularly evident in academe, both with respect to admission and hiring. The greater numbers of Jews trained in elite institutions were able to secure employment commensurate with their academic background. By the end of the 1980s, it is hard to find any area of American life in which discrimination is still a problem.[62] Public opinion has changed in tandem with behavior, although a declining minority, sometimes as much as 25 percent, will still voice agreement with anti-Jewish statements when put to them by pollsters. Without going into a methodological discussion, it may be noted that the significance of these opinions is reduced when considered in light of reactions to the same statements about excessive power, choice of neighbors, and intermarriage posed for other groups. Viewed in comparative ethnic context, Jews do extremely well.[63]

There are seven developments that are crucially relevant to an understanding of contemporary American Jewry: commitment to and activities in support of Israel; Israel—Diaspora relations; differentiated religious involvements, demography—including extremely low birth rates, increasing intermarriages, immigration, and assimilation, continued social mobility, communal organiza-tion; and political participation. Most of them are dealt with in the various essays in this volume. The concerns about and links to Israel are not treated separately, since they constitute the most important underlying issues that have determined the nature of American Jewry since the formation of the state. As Nathan Glazer once noted, Israel has become the religion of the American Jews. It is the center of Jewish life, the cause to which more Jews are deeply dedicated than any other. The story of Jewish philanthropy and political activity on behalf of the Jewish state has been covered in a myriad of books and articles and need not be reiterated here. It is alluded to in various chapters, particularly in Arnold Dashevsky's analysis of contributors in chapter 13.

Philanthropy is particularly important. According to Barry Kosmin, director of research for the New York Council of Jewish Federations, Jews contributed $3.5 billion to assorted causes in 1986.[64] Perhaps one-quarter of this went to Israel, of which less than $400 million were via the United Jewish Appeal. Jews now give about the same amount to non-Jewish causes as they do to those of their own community.

The emphasis on giving, which has its roots in the need that the secure and prosperous help the less affluent and persecuted in medieval Europe, carries over to contributions to politics as well, much more to Democrats than Republicans, but in significant amounts to the latter also. The leading student of campaign contributions, Herbert Alexander, reports that Jewish PACs (Political Action Committees) "played a significant role in transferring control of the Senate from the Republicans to the Democrats" in 1986 by their extensive donations to six victorious challengers for Republican held seats in 1986.[65]

Although the special political orientations of American Jews are discussed in chapters seven, eight, and nine by Irving Kristol, Carl Sheingold and Alan Fisher, it may be noted that the results of the 1988 elections, as reported in many opinion polls, confirm their generalizations that while Jews earn more than any ethno-religious group for whom data exist, (including Episcopalians), they are more liberal to left in their opinions than other white groups, and vote like Hispanics. In November 1988, according to most exit polls, over 70 percent of the Jews supported Dukakis. Republican presidential voting among them has declined slightly—but steadily—since 1980, when Ronald Reagan secured just above one-third of the ballots. Close to 80 percent of the Jews backed Democrats for Congress in 1988. The only identifiable subset that is disproportionately conservative and Republican is composed of the Orthodox, particularly the more extreme and less affluent among them. But a majority of the Orthodox voted for Michael Dukakis.[66]

In reporting on the results of two extensive national questionnaire surveys that he conducted on the political attitudes of American Jews and non-Jews in

April 1988 and January 1989, Steven M. Cohen's findings reiterate those reported by Fisher in chapter nine on California Jews in 1986. Cohen concludes: "Jews are more liberal than non-Jews. In no [opinion] area are Jews significantly more conservative than non-Jewish whites, and in many areas, Jews are substantially more liberal than Gentiles . . . [I]n many issue domains, the Jewish center is well to the left of the Gentile center." Black mayoralty candidates—such as Bradley in Los Angeles, Green in Philadelphia, and Washington and Sawyer in Chicago—received a much higher proportion of votes among Jews than from any other definable white group other than academics. Jewish liberalism even extends to policies that go against their interests as well-to-do people. Thus, according to Cohen, "more Jews than whites or blacks endorse raising taxes as a way of cutting budget deficits."

Conversely, the much publicized discussion of a supposed shift of Jews to the right which has appeared in recent years is largely by left intellectuals, who cite the appearance of an allegedly predominantly Jewish group of neoconservatives as evidence of Jewish behavior generally. The proof is very weak, as an indicator of Jewish increased conservatism, for a number of reasons: The number who have been so identified is a tiny proportion of the total group of Jewish intellectuals; Jews are also to be found in disproportionate numbers among those associated with various left-wing journals and causes; and, in any case, the majority of those labeled neoconservatives are still Democrats, and have never backed Ronald Reagan or George Bush.[67] More generally, the studies of Jewish elites, by Stanley Rothman and colleagues (referred to earlier), indicate that "elite Jews are even stronger supporters of the Democrats than the general Jewish population." They have "consistently supported the Democratic candidate [for president] by margins of more than four to one." Close to one third, "31 percent of elite Jews think that the U.S. should move towards socialism."[68]

Most American Jews have remained adherents of the social democratic values of their parents, as is evident in the results of a national telephone survey taken by the *Los Angeles Times* in April, 1988. As Irving Kristol notes in chapter seven, when asked which among three "qualities do you consider most important to your Jewish identity," over half (59 percent) replied "a commitment to social equality," while under a fifth (17 percent), chose "support for Israel" or "religious observance." When queried in the same poll as to whom they preferred in the then-upcoming Israeli elections, "Peres, the Labor candidate" won out by over two and one half to one over "Shamir, the Likud candidate" among those with opinions. As with their behavior in American politics, the Orthodox were the only denominational group to prefer Shamir— by two to one. There is relatively little difference among the others related to religious preference, or degree of affiliation.

Extant survey data also indicate how American Jews react to the two Israel–related issues that have become salient, the question of the religious legitimacy of conversions performed by non-Orthodox rabbis, the "who is a Jew" question; and the policy debate as to whether Israel should negotiate giving up control of the West Bank and Gaza as part of a peace settlement, and deal with the Palestine Liberation Organization. Given that over 90 percent of American Jews are not Orthodox, and that intermarriage with non—Jews has become very common, as Chaim Waxman documents in chapter five, it is not surprising that American Jews strongly oppose a change in Israeli law. Cohen found in both April 1988 and January 1989, that they overwhelmingly opposed the proposal that "Israel change its laws so as to recognize only those conversions performed by Orthodox rabbis," by twelve to one. Nine months before Arafat agreed to recognize Israel and reject the use of terrorism in December 1988, both the *Los Angeles Times* and Cohen's surveys indicated that more American Jews would support an agreement, which involves giving up territory for peace, than believe that the country should hold on to them indefinitely. By a plurality, 41 to 31 percent, they favored "territorial compromise . . . in return for credible guarantees of peace." Cohen also found that in 1988 and 1989, two-thirds agreed with the statement: "If the PLO recognizes Israel and renounces terrorism, Israel should be willing to talk with the PLO," while only one-sixth disagreed.

The explanation for Jewish adherence to liberal-left politics, while having become astonishingly affluent, is obviously complex. Earl Raab and I have tried to deal with it elsewhere, as do contributors to this volume.[69] Without anticipating their analyses, it may be noted that Raab and I suggest the behavior is linked to the continued effect of leftist political values imported from eastern Europe, noted above; deep concern about anti-Semitism, still linked in the minds of many American Jews much more to the political right than to the left; and the impact of norms underlying *tzedekah*, the obligation on the fortunate, the well-to-do to help individuals and communities in difficulty. As noted earlier, the latter norm became general among European Jews during the Middle Ages, when it was literally a condition for survival, given that some communities were generally experiencing severe persecution, while others were doing well. The political values derived from *tzedekah* are communitarian, implying support for the welfare state. Beyond this, historic experience with discrimination seemingly leads many Jews to favor civil rights legislation for other minorities. Whether for these reasons or not, a plurality, by 44 to 31 percent, told Cohen that "Jewish values, as I understand them, teach me to be politically liberal."

More surprising, given the extent to which the United States has been open to Jews, and the clear evidence of a sharp fall-off in social and economic restrictions on them since World War II, they remain fearful of anti-Semitism.

Only one out of seven of those responding to Cohen's questionnaires agreed: "Anti-semitism in America is currently not a serious problem for American Jews." An overwhelming majority, over three-quarters (76 percent), replied that it is a serious problem; two-thirds disagreed with the statement: "Virtually all positions of influence in America are open to Jews." The fact that they feel this way contributes to an identification with the left against the right. Cohen found in 1988 that, when asked what proportion of a number of groups in the United States is anti-Semitic, three times as many (20 to 7 percent) said that many or most Republicans are, as thought the same of Democrats. The replies for "few are" were 32 percent for Republican and 47 percent Democrats. The pattern was similar with conservatives and liberals, 23 to 9 percent, for "many or most are," and 32 to 51 for "few are."

The reluctance of most Jews to accept evidence that anti-Semitism has declined or to shift their image as to the relative contribution of the left and the right, given the reality of their progress in American society and the strong efforts on behalf of Israel by Republican administrations, is striking testimony to the role of historical experience and memory. San Francisco provides strong evidence of how some Jews can totally ignore reality. Polls taken among contributors to the San Francisco Jewish Community Federation have found that one third agree that a Jew can not be elected to Congress from San Francisco. A poll reported such results in 1985 when all three members of Congress from contiguous districts in or adjacent to the city were Jewish, as were the two State Senators, the mayor, and a considerable part of the city council.

The lack of confidence in the larger community goes beyond concern with anti-Semitism. A national survey taken in 1964 by the National Opinion Research Center produced evidence that Jews are very much less trustful of others on a personal level than the members of seven other white ethnic groups, Irish, Scandinavian, Slavic, German Protestant, German Catholic, Italian and WASP. On a scale, created from answers to six questions, running from plus 4 (total trust) to minus four (total distrust), Jews scored on the average minus 3. *No other group was in the minus range.* The questions included items such as "Do you think most people can be trusted?" and "If you don't watch out, people will take advantage of you?"

But if Jews are more distrustful than others, they are more self-confident and less self-deprecatory than any of the other ethnic groups. And congruently, they are highest on the scale measuring "inner-direction", self-reliance, and lowest on "other-direction," need for approval.[70] These orientations contribute to the anti-establishment stance of the astonishingly successful Jews, their willingness to be highly participatory critics of their society, and their upward mobility.

The obvious question with respect to these findings about Jewish attitudes and behavior is to what extent do these continue to hold for new generations, those coming of age. The evidence from a number of national studies and analyses conducted by Steven Cohen, Alan Fisher and William Helmreich, as well as examination of the *Los Angeles Times,* April 1988 survey and Election Exit Polls by various newspapers and networks, is consistent with respect to politics. Younger Jews (under 30, or under 45) are more likely to vote Republican and to identify as Republicans than older cohorts, by 10 to 15 percent. Age is also related to concern over anti-Semitism, identification with Israel, and contributions to Jewish philanthropy. Such findings are to be expected, since the younger Jews are more distant in time from the experiences which led older generations to act as they do. Seemingly, success is an open society, characterized by less anti-Semitism than at any time in the twentieth century, and growing up with Israel as an established fact, should produce differences.[71] However, as Alan Fisher notes, the lead among Jews of Democrats and liberals has *"remained surprisingly stable over the last decade."*[72] Even though, more conservative behavior by young Jews has been reported over a number of elections, the next older generations (defined as over 30 or 45) repeatedly turn out to be more Democratic than they were when younger.

The lack of an identifiably more conservative group to emerge among the post-youth cohorts suggest that as Jews move into mature adult status, sink roots in the community, some may drop their more conservative youthful orientations and absorb the dominant community pattern towards American politics and Israel. New substantive issues may eventually make a difference, but it will require an emotional wrench, or more generational difference, to eliminate the Democratic party's advantage in Jewish voting or the overwhelming commitment to Israel.

Conclusion

Can we still speak of American exceptionalism for the country at large, and the position of the Jews in it? In another paper, dealing with the first half of the question, I answer yes. The country remains the most classically liberal one in the industrialized world—lacking a socialist party, with one of the smallest trade union movements in proportion to the labor force; considerably wealthier in per capita real income terms; having expanded the number and proportion of jobs, since World War II and in the 1980s, more than other developed countries; and having elaborated its populist political system.[73] As in the nineteenth century, it continues to give more support to Jewish causes abroad than any other country by far. This is evident in its extensive and often isolated support of Israel, politically and financially; and the aid to the cause of Soviet Jewry, in terms of pressure on the government of the USSR, the admission of the Jewish emigres, and the financing of their settlement costs in America and Israel.

American Jews continue to do extraordinarily well in the economic, political and social structures of the country. They not only contribute liberally to Israel and communal institutions, but to many others as well, particularly including politics, Democrats much more than Republicans, but significantly to the latter as well. "Jewish support of hospitals, museums, symphonies, and universities [as well as the United Funds] across the country now appears disproportionate not only to their numbers but also even to their proportion of the wealthy."[74]

At the same time, as Waxman's analysis indicates, Jewish success contains within it the seeds of decline. Close to 90 percent of all Jewish youth attend universities, disproportionately, as noted, the very best. These institutions are liberal politically and socially. They not only reinforce the propensity to back left causes, but press the newer generations of Jews to live by universalistic criteria, which disparage particularistic ethnic loyalties, not only with respect to dating and mating, but unquestioning support of Israel as well. The very high rate of intermarriage, now approaching 50 percent, and the low birth rate are closely linked to the level of university enrollment.

The fears concerning demographic decline may be counterbalanced in part by the continued attractiveness of America to foreigners, including Jews. The United States is still by far the world's largest receiver of refugees and other immigrants. The upswing from the 1970s on has included a renewed Jewish influx, a phenomenon not generally publicized, since it involves a rejection of Israel as a place to settle or live. According to HIAS (Hebrew Immigrant Aid Society) reports, between 1967 and 1980, the agency assisted in settling over 125,000 Jews in the United States. HIAS records do not include the large number of Jewish immigrants from Latin America, Canada, South Africa, and Iran. Nor do they list the well over one hundred thousand Israelis who have come here.[75]

Clearly, the story of American and Jewish exceptionalisms, closely intermingled as they are, is not over. But the tale bears telling for it is one of the better sagas in human history. It is hoped that the chapters in this book will provide some insights and data for the chroniclers.

Notes

1. As of 1987, close to two-fifths of the Jewish House members served on the Middle East Subcommittee of the Foreign Affairs Committee. Peter Y. Medding, *New Directions in American Jewish Politics* (New York: American Jewish Committee, forthcoming, 1989).
2. David L. Featherman, "The Socioeconomic Achievements of White Religio-Ethnic Subgroups: Social and Psychological Explanations," *American Sociological Review* 36 (1971), p. 207.

3. Steven M. Cohen, *The Political Attitudes of American Jews, 1988: A National Survey in Comparative Perspective* (New York: American Jewish Committee, forthcoming, 1989). A decade earlier, Andrew Greeley concluded from National Opinion Research Center data that Jews are "the most successful group in American society." Andrew M. Greeley, *Ethnicity, Denomination and Inequality*, (Beverly Hills: Sage, 1976), p. 39.

4. Calvin Goldscheider and Alan S. Zuckerman, *The Transformation of the Jews* (Chicago: University of Chicago Press, 1986), p. 183.

5. Data from Gerald Bubis as reported in Barry A. Kosmin, "The Dimensions of Contemporary Jewish Philanthropy," (unpublished paper, North American Jewish Data Bank, Graduate School, City University of New York, 1988), p. 13.

6. Richard D. Alba and Gwen Moore, "Ethnicity in the American Elite," *American Sociological Review* 47 (June 1982) p. 377.

7. Stanley Lieberson and Donna K. Carter, "Making It in America: Differences Between Eminent Black and White Ethnic Groups," *American Sociological Review* 44 (June 1979), pp. 349-352.

8. For an overview and references on intellectual and artistic activities, see Charles E. Silberman, *A Certain People. American Jews and Their Lives Today* (New York: Summit Books, 1985), pp. 143-156. For the top intellectuals, see Charles Kadushin, *The American Intellectual Elite* (Boston: Little Brown, 1974), pp. 19-32; on American Nobel Laureates, see Harriet Zuckerman, *Scientific Elite: Nobel Laureates in the United States* (New York: Columbia University Press, 1977), p. 68. The data for professors are from Seymour Martin Lipset and Everett Carl Ladd, "Jewish Academics in the United States: Their Achievements, Culture and Politics," *American Jewish Year Book*, 72 (1971), pp. 92–93. For the other elite groups see Stanley Rothman, Robert Lichter and Linda Lichter, *Elites in Conflict: Social Change in America Today* (forthcoming).

9. The references for these findings are in Lipset and Ladd, "Jewish Academics . . . ," p. 99.

10. Henry L. Feingold, *A Midrash on American Jewish History* (Albany: State University of New York Press, 1982), p. 189. Robert E. Park, *Race and Culture* (Glencoe, ILL: The Free Press, 1950, pp. 354-5. For excellent discussions of this congruence see Arnold M. Eisen, *The Chosen People in America. A Study in Jewish Religion Ideology* (Bloomington: Indiana University Press, 1983), pp. 25-52 and Joseph L. Blau, *Judaism in America From Curiosity to Third Faith* (Chicago: University of Chicago Press, 1976), pp. 7-20.

11. Max Weber, *The Protestant Ethic and the Spirit of Capitalism* (New York: Scribner, 1935), pp. 54–55.

12. Ibid., pp. 48–50.

13. Hillel Levine, personal communication. Anita Libman Lebeson, *Pilgrim People* (New York: Minerva Press, 1975), p. 178; Blau, *Judaism in America*, p. 113. Nissan Waxman, "A Neglected Book," (Hebrew) in *Shana Beshana: Yearbook of Heichal Shlomo* (Jerusalem: 1969), pp. 303–315.

14. Max Weber, *Economy and Society* (Berkeley: University of California Press, 1978), I, pp. 622-23. For an elaboration of the links between Puritanism and Judaism, particularly in America, see Edward A. Tiryakian, "American Religious Exceptionalism: 'Protestant, Catholic, Jew' Revisited." *Social Compass* (forthcoming, 1989).

15. Anthony Blond, "The Jews and Mrs. Thatcher," *The Sunday Telegraph*, December 11, 1988, pp. 14-15.
16. For an elaboration of this analysis, see Seymour Martin Lipset, "American Exceptionalism Reaffirmed," in Byron Shafer, ed., *Still Different: A New Look at American Exceptionalism* (New York: Oxford University Press, 1989, forthcoming).
17. Tiryakian, "American Religious Exceptionalism."
18. "Washington's Reply to the Hebrew Congregation in Newport, Rhode Island," *Publications of the American Jewish Historical Society* No. 3 (1895), pp. 91–92.
19. John A. Hardon, *American Judaism* (Chicago: Loyola University Press, 1971), pp. 32–33. Lebeson, *Pilgrim People*, pp. 165-7.
20. Ludy S. Dawidowicz, *On Equal Terms. Jews in America 1881–1981* (New York: Holt, Rinehart and Winston, 1982), pp. 68–69; Arthur Herzberg, *The French Enlightment and the Jews* (New York: Columbia University, 1968), p. 360; Silberman, *American Jews*, pp. 39–41.
21. Seymour Martin Lipset, *The First New Nation: The United States in Historical and Comparative Perspective* (New York: W.W. Norton, 1979, Second Edition), pp. 164–5; for the report see Richard Mentor Johnson, "Sunday Observance and the Mail", in George E. Probst, ed, *The Happy Republic* (Glouster, Mass: Peter Smith, 1968), pp. 247–255.
22. James R. Rohrer, "The Sunday Mails and the Church-State Theme in Jacksonian America," *Journal of the Early Republic* 7 (Spring 1987), pp. 53-115.
23. Herbert A. Gibbon, *John Wanamaker* (New York: Harper and Bros, 1926), I, p. 321.
24. Manfred Jones, "The American Sabbath in the Gilded Age," *Jahrbuch fuer Amerika Studien* 6 (1961), pp. 89-114.
25. Bertram Wallace Korn, *Eventful Years and Experiences. Studies in Nineteenth Century American Jewish History* (Cincinnati: The American Jewish Archives, 1954), pp. 98–9.
26. Seymour Martin Lipset, "The American Jewish Community in Comparative Perspective," in *Revolution and Counterrevolution, Change and Persistence in Social Structures* (New Brunswick, NJ: Transaction Books, 1988, Third Edition), pp. 141-153. Blau, *Judaism in America*, pp. 51-72.
27. Arthur A. Goren, *New York Jews and the Quest for Comunity. The Kehillah Experiment, 1908–1922* (New York: Columbia University, 1970).
28. Ibid, p. 252.
29. Peter Wiernik, *History of the Jews in America* (New York: Hermon press, 1972, Third Edition), pp. 128–34.
30. Ibid, 229–40.
31. Henry L. Feingold, *Zion in America* (New York: Hippocrene Books, 1974), pp. 89–90.
32. Joakim Isaacs, "Ulysses S. Grant and the Jews," in Jonathan D. Sarna, ed., *The American Jewish Experience*, (New York: Holmes and Meier, 1986), pp. 62–4.
33. Wiernik, *History of the Jews*, pp. 270–1.
34. Cited in Morris U. Schappes, ed., *A Documentary History of Jews in the United States, 1654–1875* (New York: Schocken Books, 1971), p. 209.
35. Wiernik, *History of the Jews*, pp. 345–6. For a detailed account of such interventions which I only found after this book was in press, see Cyrus Adler and Aaron M.

Margalith, *American Intercession on Behalf of Jews* in the *Diplomatic Correspondence of the United States 1840–1938,* (New York: American Jewish Historical Society, 1943).

36. Feingold, *Zion in America*, pp. 239–49.

37. David Biale, *Power and Powerlessness in Jewish History* (New York: Schocken Books, 1986), p. 124. Bertram W. Korn, *The American Reaction to the Montara Case 1858-1859* (Cincinnati: The American Jewish Archives, 1957), pp. 88–92.

38. Leo P. Ribuffo, "Henry Ford and The International Jew," *American Jewish History* 69 (June 1980), p. 437. For a review of the historical literature see Leonard Dinnerstein, "The Historiography of American Antisemitism" in his *Uneasy at Home, Antisemitism and the American Jewish Experience* (New York: Columbia University press, 1987), pp. 257–67.

39. Seymour Martin Lipset and Earl Raab, *The Politics of Unreason: Right Wing Extremism in America, 1790–1977* (Chicago: University of Chicago Press, 1978, second edition), pp. 47–8, 89–90.

40. Goldscheider and Zuckerman, *The Transformation*, p. 166. For details see Nathan Glazer, "Social Characteristics of American Jews, 1654–1954," *American Jewish Year Book* 56 (1955), pp. 9-10. Arthur A. Goren, *The American Jews* (Cambridge: The Belknip Press of Harvard University Press, 1982), pp. 34–6.

41. Barry E. Supple, "A Business Elite: German-Jewish Financiers in Nineteenth-Century New York," *Business History Review* 31 (Summer 1957), pp. 143–78; Vincent P. Carosso, "A Financial Elite: New York's German–Jewish Investment Bankers," *American Jewish Historical Quarterly* 66 (September 1976), pp. 67–87.

42. Lipset and Raab, *The Politics of Unreason*, pp. 92–5.

43. E. Digby Baltzell, *The Protestant Establishment* (New York: Random House, 1964), p. 138.

44. John Higham, "Social Discrimination Against Jews in America, 1830-1930," *American Jewish Historical Society* 47 (1957), p. 10; "Anti-Semitism in the Gilded Age: A Reinterpretation," *Mississippi Valley Historical Review* 43 (1957), p. 566. For these and other essays see Higham, *Send These to Me . . .* (New York: Atheneum, 1984).

45. Goldscheider and Zuckerman, *The Transformation*, pp. 166–7.

46. Chaim I. Waxman, *America's Jews in Transition* (Philadelphia: Temple University Press, 1983), pp. 49–51.

47. Dawidowicz, *On Equal Terms*. p. 51; Silberman, *American Jews*, pp. 125-7, 132–4; and Dinnerstein, *On Equal Terms*, pp. 15-40.

48. Goldscheider and Zuckerman, *The Transformation*, p. 168.

49. Nathan Reich, "The Role of the Jews in the American Economy," *YIVO Annual* 5 (1950), pp. 197-205; Nathan Glazer, "The American Jew and the Attainment of Middle-Class Rank: Some Trends and Explanations," in Marshall Sklare, ed., *The Jews, Social Patterns of an American Group* (Glencoe, IL: The Free Press, 1958), pp. 138–146; Sidney Goldstein, "Socioeconomic Differentials Among Religious Groups in the United States," *American Journal of Sociology* 74 (May 1969), pp. 612–631; Simon Kuznets, *Economic Structure of the Jews* (Jerusalem: Institute of Contemporary Jewry, Hebrew University, 1972); Marshall H. Medoff, "Note: Some Differences Between the Jewish and General White Male Population in the United States," *Jewish Social Studies* 43 (Winter 1981), pp. 75–80.

50. Dawidowicz, *On Equal Terms*, p. 51. See also Goren, *The American Jews*, pp. 73–76.

51. Glazer, "Social Characteristics . . . ," pp. 30–1. See also Silberman, *American Jews*, pp. 137–8.

52. Fred L. Strodtbeck, "Family Interaction, Values and Achievement," in Sklare, ed., *The Jews*, pp. 162–3; and Lipset and Ladd, "Jewish Academics . . . ," pp. 96–9.

53. Glazer, "Social Characteristics . . . ," p. 31; Blau, *Judaism in America*, pp. 112–15.

54. Lipset and Raab, *The Politics of Unreason*, pp. 97–9.

55. Ibid, pp. 110–40, esp. p. 139 for discussion of anti-Semitism.

56. Moshe Davis, *The Emergence of Conservative Judaism The Historical School in 19th Century America* (New York: The Jewish Publication Society of America, 1963), pp. 149-228.

57. Marshall Sklare, *Conservative Judaism. An American Religious Movement* (New York: Schocken Books, 1972), pp. 43–82; Hardon, *American Judaism*, pp. 119–146.

58. For the evidence see Lawrence H. Fuchs, *The Political Behavior of American Jews* (Glencoe, IL: The Free Press, 1956), pp. 121–30, 151–70. See also Ronald Sanders, *The Downtown Jews*, (New York: Dover Publications, 1987), pp. 56–180; Melech Epstein, *Jewish Labor in U.S.A.* (New York: Trade Union Sponsoring Committee, 1950).

59. Glazer, *American Judaism*, p. 71; Goren, *The American Jews*, pp. 57–9.

60. Lipset and Raab, *The Politics of Unreason*, pp. 171-189. For a detailed review of opinion polls about Jews from the 1930s to the 1960s, see Charles H. Stember and others, *Jews in the Mind of America* (New York: Basic Books, 1966), pp. 60–76, 82–5, 116–62.

61. Ibid.

62. Dawidowicz, *On Equal Terms*, pp. 131–2.

63. Seymour Martin Lipset, "Blacks and Jews: How Much Bias?", *Public Opinion* (July/August 1987), pp. 4–5, 57–58. For a review of the most recent findings on attitudes and behavior, see Leonard Dinnerstein, "Antisemitism in the United States Today," *Patterns of Prejudice* 22 (Autumn 1988), pp. 3–14.

64. Kosmin, "Jewish Philanthropy . . . ," p. 19.

65. Herbert L. Alexander, "Pro-Israel PACs: A Small Part of a Large Movement," (Unpublished paper, Department of Political Science, University of Southern California, 1988). For comprehensive documentation, see Michael J. Malbin, "Jewish PACS: A New Force in Jewish Political Action," in Daniel J. Elazar, ed., *The New Jewish Politics* (Latham, MD: University Press of America, 1988), pp. 51–55.

66. William B. Helmreich, "American Jews and the 1988 Presidential Elections," *Congress Monthly* 56 (January 1989), pp. 3–5; and Peter Steinfels, "American Jews Stand Firmly to the Left," *New York Times*, "News of the Week," January 8, 1988, p. E7.

67. Seymour Martin Lipset, "Neoconservatism: Myth and Reality," *Society* 25 (July/August 1988), pp. 29–37.

68. Robert Lerner, Althea K. Nagai, and Stanley Rothman, "Martinality and Liberalism Among Jewish Elites," to be published in the Summer or Fall 1989 issue of *The*

Public Opinion Quarterly. The basic report on this study is in Rothman, Lichter and Lichter, *Elites in Conflict*.

69. Seymour Martin Lipset and Earl Raab, "The American Jews, the 1984 Elections, and Beyond," in Elazar, ed., *The New Jewish Politics*, pp. 33–51; see the other essays in the Elazar volume as well. See also Stephen D. Isaacs, *Jews and American Politics* (Garden City: Doubleday, 1974), pp. 149–59, 196–7; Milton Himmelfarb, *The Jews of Modernity* (New York: Basic Books, 1973), pp. 65–116; Charles S. Liebman, *The Ambivalent American Jew* (Philadelphia: The Jewish Publication Society of America, 1973), pp. 135–73; Leonard Fein, *Where Are We? The Inner Life of America's Jews* (New York: Harper and Row, 1988), pp. 227–35; Stephen J. Whitfield, *Voices of Jacob, Hands of Esau. Jews in American Life and Thought* (Hamden, CT: Archon Books, 1984), pp. 73–112; Silberman, *American Jews*, pp. 345–56; Fuchs, *The Political Behavior*, pp. 149–59, 196–7; and Werner Cohn, "The Politics of American Jews," in Sklare, ed., *The Jews*, pp. 614–26.

70. Andrew M. Greeley, *That Most Distressful Nation. The Taming of the American Irish* (Chicago: Quadrangle Books, 1972), pp. 149–55. The original data were collected by Melvin Kohn and reported on in his book, *Class and Conformity* (Homewood, IL: Dorsey Press, 1969). See especially pp. 61–5. For other data on Jewish self-confidence and mental health see Silberman, *American Jews*, pp. 140–2.

71. For the most detailed analysis by age, see Alan M. Fisher, "Where the Jewish Vote is Going," *Moment* 14 (March 1989), pp. 41–3.

72. Ibid, p. 42 (emphasis, S.M.L.)

73. Lipset, "American Exceptionalism Reaffirmed"

74. Kosmin, "The Dimensions . . . ," p. 16.

75. Drora Kass and Seymour Martin Lipset, "Jewish Immigration to the United States from 1967 to the Present," in Marshall Sklare, ed., *Understanding American Jewry* (New Brunswick, NJ: Transaction Books, 1982), pp. 272–94.

2

American Jewry or American Judaism

Nathan Glazer

Between "American Jewry" and "American Judaism" there exists a peculiar tension of which most American Jews, I believe, are not aware. By "Jewry" I mean simply the body of American Jews and everything they do and are. As noted in the previous chapter, they are predominantly businessmen and professionals; their children overwhelmingly go to college; they are concentrated geographically in major cities, and retire very often to Florida; their average income is high; and they vote Democratic, and even when they vote Republican they vote for Republican liberals. By "Judaism" I refer to something more specific—the religion of the Jews, not just any religion that Jews defined by descent practice, but a historical complex, one that has evolved and become different things at different times and that is still evolving, but that can be transformed to the point where, although it may still be the religion of Jews or of Jewry, it is no longer Judaism.

Arguments over just what that point is can be intense. Without settling that matter, we can generally agree what is "closer to" or "farther from" the Judaism of our fathers and grandfathers, or from normative, traditional Judaism.

A related distinction is that between "Jewishness" and "Judaism." "Jewishness" is what Jews do; but suggests, as against "Jewry," some connection with a distinctive Jewish past, a culture, some involvement in activities with a specific Jewish component, social, cultural, political, or religious. Thirty years ago, I entitled one chapter in my book, *American Judaism*, "Jewishness and Judaism."[1] The chapter dealt with American Jewish life between the two world wars, and in it I described the very vigorous Jewish life of the areas settled by immigrants in the big cities in the 1920s and 1930s. I pointed out how much of that life was specifically antagonistic to Jewish religion, to Judaism,

31

while it was positive about some other aspects of Jewish life. This seems strange to us now, but in the 1920s and 1930s one could find, for example, anti-religious Zionists, secular Jewish schools that were anti-religious, Yiddish culturalists, anarchist, socialist, and communist Jewish organizations for different age groups and with varied objectives, all of which could have been described as atheist and anti-Judaist.

Things are very different today. It is assumed—and is indeed true—that those who support one manifestation of Jewish life tend to be supportive of all the others. We do not find, as we did fifty years ago, Reform synagogues that are strongly anti-Zionist, or Jewish organizations of whatever kind that are strongly anti-religious or anti-Judaist. In the chapter following "Jewishness and Judaism" in my book, I described the very different situation that emerged after World War II, as Jews moved to the suburbs, as the dense Jewish immigrant quarters of the big cities were broken up, and as the synagogue became, from only one Jewish institution struggling against others, the central Jewish institution of the new Jewish communities. Great numbers of synagogues were built, Jewish schools became part of the synagogue complex, the synagogue became the place where every Jewish issue found a home.

This chapter was entitled "The Jewish Revival." In view of the weight I am putting on the distinction between Jewishness and Judaism, could it not have been entitled "The Judaist Revival?" But that would not have been quite right; there was an ambiguity to this Jewish revival. The religious element was rather thin, despite that institutionally the synagogue was the bearer of the revival. But I argued—as did others at the same time—that what we were seeing in the building boom of new synagogues was less an expression of religiosity than ethnicity. Jews wanted to remain Jews, wanted their children to remain Jews, wanted them to marry other Jews, but one would have been hard put to find a strong overtly religious impulse.

The Jewish revival, it hardly need be said, had nothing in common with the kind of "revivalism" we are familiar with from the history of American Protestantism. There were no radio rabbis, no mass conversions, no fervent public commitments at mass revival meetings to observe the commandments. What we saw was something like an institutional explosion. Will Herberg had made the argument in his *Protestant–Catholic–Jew* [2] that the religious revival which, of course, affected more than Jews, in the United States in the 1950s, had little to do with faith and religious impulses and it seemed primarily concerned with ethnicity; that is, with the desire of people to maintain communities based on ethnic attachment. In the America of the 1950s, this required taking the institutional form of religion. Ethnicity then was embarrassing and backward-looking; religion was respectable and American. I agreed, at least as far as Jews and the Jewish revival were concerned. I quoted one rabbi who wrote: "[The congregants] invariably imply, and often explicitly state, 'We need you as our representative among the non-Jews, to mingle with them, to speak in their churches to make a good impression. We do not need you for ourselves. Well, for the old people, perhaps, and for the children, yes, once a week, but for the Gentiles most of all.'" It seems that Jews did not need rabbis for religious purposes. I wrote that the common feeling "among large numbers of Jews was that the institutions of the Jewish religion were useful because they contributed to the continued existence of the Jewish people. The ancient notion that Israel existed to serve the law was here reversed: it was argued the law existed to serve Israel."[3]

But that is all in the past. Secular Jewishness in almost all its institutional forms has declined almost to the vanishing point. Even nonreligious Jewish institutions have become in terms of observance more Judaist: They do not meet on Friday night or Saturday, serve kosher food, or give an honored place to prayers and rabbis. One would think the story of this conflict, this tension, is at an end. Why bring it up now? But it has revived in a somewhat different form in the last few years to lead a most vigorous life in dispute and controversy that has given rise to new and confusing dichotomies. After all, the argument between Jewishness and Judaism was how would the Jews survive in the United States: as a people simply bearing the ethnic label, Jews, or as a religion? The conclusion of the argument in the 1950s was that the Jews would survive as a religion. The new conflict is over what kind of religion is surviving as the vehicle of survival? Further, if the only function the religion is serving is survival, what kind of religion is that? Indeed, if the only content of the religion becomes survival, can it even serve that single function?

We saw the argument flare up a few years ago in discussions and reviews of Charles Silberman's *A Certain People*.[4] It comes up again in a group of books published in 1988: Leonard Fein's *Where Are We? The Inner Life of America's Jews*,[5] Charles S. Liebman's *Deceptive Images: Social Science and the Study of American Jews*,[6] Steven M. Cohen's *American Assimilation and Jewish Revival*.[7]

A cluster of dichotomies ask the same questions, and point to the same problem. What is the nature of Jewish life in the United States; and how, and in what form, will it continue? To put it more crudely, will the Jews survive in the United States, and if so, how? But I must point out that neither I nor these writers mean continuation in a physical form. None of the writers I have referred to see any danger to the physical existence of Jews in the United States. While the word "survive" reminds us, properly, of the Holocaust and of the permanent threat to the security of Israel—and of the survival of Jews there—that is not the problem for the Jews of the United States.

These writers are speaking of a corporate survival carrying a Jewish identity, and even more, carrying a religious identity and a religious meaning. When Leonard Fein, Charles Liebman, and Steven Cohen ask what is the future of

American Jews, will they survive, and how, they are asking, what will be the content of Jewish life? They divide between what we may call an optimistic view, a pessimistic one, and something in between—and all three positions are of interest.

Steven Cohen, from whose earlier work Charles Silberman drew heavily in his optimistic book, *A Certain People*, I will put forth as the representative of optimism. He has allies—perhaps more optimistic than even he is—in Calvin Goldscheider and Alan Zuckerman.[8] The optimist tells us, to begin with, and recall that, first of all, the Jews will survive physically because neither intermarriage nor low fertility will substantially reduce what is now the largest Jewish community in the world. Further, he tells us—and on this point all agree—that the expectation of straightline assimilation held by Jewish sociologists of an earlier day, the expectation of a steady weakening of Jewish identity, commitment, loyalty, and observance with each passing generation, was exaggerated. Previously, Will Herberg made great use of Marcus Hansen's essay on the return of the third-generation immigrant.[9] He turned this provocative thesis into "Hansen's Law," which said: "what the children want to forget, the grandchildren want to remember." Hansen's thesis is a great support of optimists. Indeed, those of us who grew up in immigrant homes, and who are aware of how far we typically moved away from Jewish knowledge, tradition, and religious observance have been surprised—or at least some of us have—that our children have not moved the same distance from our practices and beliefs, but have, to some extent, "returned." The empirical data shows some signs of "return," in the form of greater regular observance of some religious rites (seder, Passover, and Hanukkah candles), and no decline in synagogue membership in the third generation.

But the most controversial element of the optimistic scenario deals not with these empirical points, but with interpretation. The Jewish commitment continues, the optimists tell us; Jewish religion continues. Jewish schools continue to teach, and children go to them. The pessimists say, hold on. Charles Liebman calls his book *Deceptive Images*, and before I read it, I wondered where the deception was. The deception that he is talking about is this claim that American Judaism is healthy. To present this picture of health, one must accept whatever Jews do as Judaism. If they have become increasingly remote from tradition, if they observe only two commandments out of the 617, and these mostly for the children, why that is alright. Jews are still Jews, Judaism survives, it is only that it has become transformed. Liebman dubs those who give the healthy interpretation of the condition of American Judaism, "transformationists." They argue Judaism has always changed through the ages. The Judaism of the first century would have been unrecognizable in the tenth, as that of the tenth century would have been unrecognizable in the nineteenth; and so, in the twentieth century of American life, moving into the 21st, Judaism is something else again, but Jews are still Jews. This is a somewhat crude view of the "transformationist" position, but it gets to the essence of the controversy.

One of our difficulties in coming to terms with this controversy is that Jews do not speak easily about religion; that is, religion as it is understood in divinity schools. Indeed, Jews find something a little Christian and un-Jewish or un-Judaist in such things as a catechism of beliefs, confession of faith, fervent prayers to a living god; they are happier with practices. Indeed, as they move further from tradition it is not, I would hazard, that their *beliefs* change; it is that their *practices* change. When the Orthodox criticize most Jews for straying from tradition, they refer to their practices, not their beliefs.

This characteristic of Judaism makes it easy for us to take the position that nothing essential has changed in Judaism, it is simply adapting to American life and to modernity, as it once adapted to Mesopotamia, to Spain, or to Poland. But I think this is too simplistic; Judaism has indeed changed. Its change is of sufficient gravity to at least raise the question of continuity. But perhaps a more important question is what role can Judaism play for Jews and Jewish life when its religious content is radically reduced?

That reduction is indicated, for example, in some of the data on recent surveys Leonard Fein presents in his book, *Where Are We?* Consider: In a recent survey, 91 percent of Jews agree that "Without Jewish religion, the Jewish people could not survive." On the other hand, two-thirds disagree with the statement: "To be a good Jew, one must believe in God."

But even to ask such a question in a survey is rare. Surveys of Jews, as we know, ask about practices, not beliefs. "We know considerably more about ritual practice than about religious belief . . . Two out of five do not fast on Yom Kippur, four of five don't observe the dietary laws, only 10 percent attend services more than once a month. But 84 percent attend a seder, 82 percent light Hanukkah candles."[10]

We have known for at least twenty years, since Marshall Sklare and Joseph Greenblum's studies of Lakeville,[11] that, to the average American, a good Jew is someone who does good things: contributes to Jewish causes, aids the poor, doesn't lie and steal, obeys the law, and the like. He is certainly a good man, but is he a good Jew?

Fein quite properly worries about this. If the meaning of a Jew is to be good, then what do we tell our children, and what is the point to a Jewish corporate survival?

As we know, there is an answer to this, but it is not one that satisfies the pessimist (Liebman) or Fein, whom I will place between the pessimists and optimists. The answer is that the Jews survive in order to survive. "Survival" has become the rallying cry not only to the Jewish people—and for a people, there is no more important one—but also of the Jewish religion, and that does raise a problem. Surveys and experience suggest that the content of the Jewish religion—as a system of belief, as an orientation to the world—is remarkably reduced. If we examined what Jews wrote in their magazines, books, and newspapers, what they were told from the pulpits in sermons, and to what they responded in their synagogues, temples, and organizations, one would conclude that Judaism now deals with only one overwhelming concern, the physical survival of the Jews. First, of course, is the Holocaust: the outpouring of books and educational materials, and the building of museums and memorials. The themes addressed in this huge effort vary: "Never again"; "Our children must be taught"; "The world must be taught"; "We must not let the world forget"; or "We cannot allow the reality of what happened to be denied." In the wake of the Holocaust, nothing arouses Jews as much as the denial that it occurred, or agitates them as much as the fear the denial will be believed. As Leonard Fein writes, " . . . we engage in a veritable orgy of Holocaust museum construction—and learn that it is far easier to raise money for the construction of such museums than it is, say to offer higher wages to the scandalously underpaid teachers in Jewish schools . . . the Simon Wiesenthal Center for Holocaust Studies, in Los Angeles, an institution that at the time of its creation was widely viewed as being entirely redundant with existing efforts, has become (by far) the most successful solicitor of contributions of any domestic Jewish organization."[12]

Linked with the Holocaust is the other great survival concern, the overwhelming fear for Israel's safety, the threat of the destruction of the Third Commonwealth. And there are the lesser survival concerns to which we have referred: intermarriage, low fertility, the assimilation of Russian or American Jews.

The Jewish religion, Judaism, has become the religion of survival. It has lost touch with other values and spiritual concerns. No one has to argue in favor of survival; there is nothing else if one does not survive. We do not have to ask further, if we are in Israel, why Israel wants to survive; or ask further, if one is a Jew in the United States, why the Jews want to survive. But we should ask why the corporate community of Jews in the United States want to survive, and why it wants to do so in the form of a religion, when the traditional content of that religion, it would seem to me (and to any observant Jew), has been quite reduced. What has replaced it? On the one hand, the common content of a universal ethic, which has nothing distinctively Jewish about it, and on the other, survival—remember the Holocaust and save Israel. That is what Judaism comes down to if we question Jews about it, and that is what the pessimists— Liebman calls them the "traditionalists"—find inadequate. The "transformationists," on the other hand, by discovering what Judaism has become, see good reasons for the singular focus of Judaism. Judaism maintains a distinctive identity for Jews. What more is needed?

Leonard Fein probably would not want to be grouped with the "traditionalists," but he is certainly critical of the transformationist view. "Here we have one of the world's great religious civilizations," he writes, "yet if a child comes home and asks his/her parent, 'What does it mean that we are Jews?', odds are the answer will not be about belief, or about ritual, or about shared language or shared culture or even shared history. Odds are the answer will one way or another focus on our shared fate, on the horrid prospect that when 'it' happens again, we will all again be lined up together."

"What happens," he writes further, "when Jewish identity is reduced to a response to anti-Semitism? What happens is this: those embattled few who have made the welfare of the Jews their mission look out upon a Jewish community whose members are Jewishly available only to protect a right they themselves do not (and do not want to) enjoy, only to defend a way they do not (and would not) walk . . . And so anti-Semitism becomes a motive, perhaps the motive, for Jewish life."

Fein insists that there must be more than the warmth of ethnic ties to Jewish life. It must have a meaning, because he wants to regard "the Jewish community . . . as a means rather than an end in itself." [13]

I would modify this conclusion somewhat. The Jewish people does not need a purpose, just as an animal species does not need a purpose. It has evolved through nature and history, and life is an ultimate value. But the Jewish religion is another matter. That can only be an end if we truly believe it is the word of God; but how many of us believe that? If we do not, the religion has to be a means to an end. It has to carry values, to lead to something of worth; can that value, that worth, for a transcendental religion, be the maintenance of the Jewish people?

It seems problematic that this transcendental and universal religion has become the chief workhorse and ally of national survival: good enough if one has a purely instrumental attitude to religion. But a religion does not survive on instrumental value alone. If one stands outside of religious faith, one can see its instrumental value and support it for that reason alone. Religion, in general, helps maintain families; keeps children from drugs, crime, and premature sexuality; and, in the case of the Jews, as we know, religion is a major mainstay of the state of Israel (also a major trouble for the State). The more religious American Jews—that is, the Orthodox and the devout Conservatives—are more committed to Israel's defense, care more about it, may go to live there, despite that Israel is still somewhat more secular than religious. But if one stands within religion, one cannot see it as simply instrumental: "I believe because it is useful." There is a paradox about religion's instrumental value. Religion has to be believed, for its own sake, to serve instrumentally. If it is not believed, it loses even its instrumental value. Yet, the element of noninstrumental faith in American Judaism is now radically reduced.

There are two proposals to give American Judaism some transcendent value, something of the power of the traditional faith. Neither of these two proposals is new. Leonard Fein makes a powerful plea in his book for a Judaism of liberal concern. Judaism is meant, he says, to repair the world—not solely to save Jews. Repairing the world means helping the poor, the deprived, and the welfare state. It also means attention to the non-Jewish poor and the deprived, as there are certainly immeasurably more non-Jews in the world than there are Jews.

He almost answers his own proposal; rather, he agonizes over his own answer, and is not fully satisfied with it. The main reason he is not fully satisfied is that liberalism (along with its variants to the left) has come into conflict with the other crucial aspect of Judaism, its particularism, its concern for the Jewish people and the state of Israel. I need not go into this increasing split between what liberals and progressives consider right, and the interests and fate of the state of Israel and the Jews who live there. Nor is this conflict simply one with the present government; even if the government were to take the most liberal position that is compatible with Israel's survival, that would not satisfy most of those who criticize it from what generally is called the left. There is the deep suspicion among Jews that many of those who criticize the state of Israel from the liberal–left–progressive position are not much concerned with its survival. Fein's aim of replacing part of the lost traditional content of Judaism with a universalistic liberalism comes in many variants, from that of classical Reform to various kinds of Jewish radicalism, to Leonard Fein's new formulation.

And then there is the second great answer—traditionalism, or Orthodoxy. Charles Liebman, in *Deceptive Images*, seriously considers the Orthodox alternative, because Orthodoxy has shown a strength in the last thirty years that is, indeed, surprising.

One of the chief pieces of evidence against the old thesis, that assimilation was inevitable among American Jews, is that Orthodoxy has not declined in the past thirty years and, indeed, by various measures, has become stronger. Liebman makes the interesting point that this generation is the first in two hundred years in which Orthodoxy has not declined. The relationship of this to our general problem is complicated: On the one hand, the resistance of Orthodoxy would seem to give strength to the optimists, the transformationists; on the other hand, Orthodoxy not only survives and grows stronger, it also becomes increasingly resistant in its consideration as an intrinsic part of a variegated Jewish community, the great majority of whom do not observe the commandments. It is increasingly ready to cut itself off from connection with the greater part of American Jewry. In other words, Orthodoxy rejects the Judaism to which the transformationists point to support their claim that American Judaism is healthy.

But even Orthodoxy, on examination, does not escape the radical reduction of the religious element in Judaism. If the Orthodox Jew tries to account for his distinctiveness, there is not much that we would consider spiritual, referring to higher values, to transcendent values, or even to God. We will once again hear only one thing—survival. Fein argues: Concerning "the rationale of the Jewish endeavor," the "what for?" "the sobering truth is that even the Orthodox, in making their case, are not very likely to argue from God: like almost all others, they rest their case on the idea of survival itself . . . when young people are asked to 'stay' Jewish, . . . they are not asked to do so for God's sake or for their own but in the name of Jewish survival."[14]

I believe that is true. Another recently published work, Jeffrey Gurock's interesting history of Yeshiva University, *The Men and Women of Yeshiva*, can be searched in vain for what we might consider a spiritual element to the Orthodox revival. Perhaps I define "spiritual" and "religious" too narrowly, or perhaps I am influenced by Christianity and by American Protestantism. I may be looking for something in American Judaism that is not there because it is not Jewish. The dominant theme in the history of Yeshiva is survival; of course, that is the dominant theme in the history of any college, university, or institution. I do not refer to Yeshiva's survival; rather, Yeshiva's argument for its own survival is that it helps in the survival of the Jews.

Consider: In describing the University's extension into fields of social work and communal service, which created some controversy as it was against the classic and essential mission of educating rabbis, Gurock tells us, "it was assumed that these workers would use their combination of professional training and 'deep appreciation of spiritual values' learned at Yeshiva to promote positive Jewish identity among their clients. An unspoken but implicit additional agenda was that these social workers would promote, with the lightest touch, interest in Orthodoxy." One struggles to give content to the phrase— which is quoted from some official document—"deep spiritual values." The only content one can give it is the maintenance of some of the distinguishing observances of Orthodoxy, but it is not clear just what their spiritual content is. The only clear content we can give these observances was that they preserved the distinctiveness of the Jews and their separation from others, and, in the contemporary context, their own separation from other branches of Judaism. But Gurock himself struggles with the question of what was being served: " . . . was Yeshiva's overwhelming concern, however lofty, with the problems of survival of their particular religious or ethnic group, appropriate for an American university?"[15] Samuel Belkin, president of Yeshiva, found the justification of this primary insistence on survival in the philosophy of cultural pluralism as developed by Horace Kallen and used by his predecessor Bernard Revel. Ironically, the philosophy that justified the maintenance of the distinctive Orthodox strand had to come from what was really a secular sociology.

Charles Liebman, exploring in a hardheaded manner the reasons for Orthodoxy's success—let us be reminded it is a modest success, an institutional success, and it has not transformed the faith or practice of American Jews, among whom only 10 percent or less can be considered Orthodox—also cannot find what I would call religious or spiritual reasons. "Orthodoxy's current influence is due to a number of factors. The most important one . . . is the sense of many non-Orthodox Jews that Orthodoxy is the voice of Jewish authenticity . . . the sense of many Conservative and Reform Jews (including rabbis) and at least some leaders of secular Jewish organizations . . . that although they are not Orthodox and don't want to be Orthodox, the Orthodox are better Jews . . .

"The sense that Orthodoxy is the voice of Jewish authenticity may stem from the fact that Orthodoxy is a legitimate expression of the Jewish tradition by everyone's standard whereas Orthodoxy denies that status to Conservatism and Reform . . . Most important is that Orthodoxy speaks with a sense of confidence about its Jewishness that the non-Orthodox lack . . .

"The influence of Orthodoxy may also be attributable to the feeling among many non-Orthodox that the Orthodox are the real Jewish survivors. They are the ones least likely to assimilate."[16]

Survival has become the theme of Jewish life, and the theme of Jewish religion. Leonard Fein finds it not enough, and indeed most thoughtful observers of American Judaism find it not enough. But what else is there? Liberalism is a weak reed. It was not enough for classical Reform, which has returned to particularism even while it tries to maintain its weak attachment to general social reform. I don't think it will be enough for American Jews. There are too many contradictions between a political stance, even a good and compassionate one, and the particularistic interests and needs of the Jewish people. Orthodoxy is increasingly confident, but its religious content has become to my mind ossified, and if it has a living motive, that motive is also survival. "We survive better than you do," the Orthodox tell us; indeed, on the basis of what I see around me, in a hundred years only a fragment of American Orthodox Jews will survive; while American Jews, in general, affected by intermarriage and a secular society not easily influenced by religious themes, will preserve only a hazy identity as Jews.

In the debate between the transformationists and the traditionalists, I believe the transformationists are correct about what is happening to American Jews and American Jewish religion; but I believe the traditionalists are also correct in asserting that it is very far from traditional Judaism, and whatever its distance it is not enough to maintain commitment and identity.

The Holocaust and Israel are the contents of American Judaism forty years after the establishment of the state and the end of the Holocaust. Can one imagine that they can continue to play this role and maintain American Judaism forty years from now? Or that they can be supplemented with a stronger general liberalism and progressivism? Or that that can be replaced by a renewed traditionalism? Those are the alternatives available. But when one reviews them it seems that earlier sociological projections of the Jewish future in America had a substantial measure of truth. Jews will assimilate; however, that assimilation will not take the form of the disappearance of Jewish identity. The identity, without much content, of Jews will continue. But neither traditional religion—Orthodoxy—nor the transformed religion, whose major theme is survival and liberalism, seem strong enough or appropriate enough to our conditions to be sustained. What sustains them now is the fear of physical destruction, a reality in the past, and a reasonable possibility in the future. That gives us our agenda today, and perhaps for many years to come. But it is a different agenda, I believe, from that of two-thousand years of Jewish history, and not one that has the staying power of the religion of the past.

Notes

1. Nathan Glazer, *American Judaism* (Chicago: University of Chicago Press, 1957).
2. Will Herberg, *Protestant–Catholic–Jew* (New York: Doubleday, 1955).
3. Glazer, *American Judaism*, pp. 125–6.
4. Charles E. Silberman, *A Certain People: American Jews and Their Lives Today* (New York: Summit Books, paperback edition 1988).
5. Leonard Fein, *Where Are We? The Inner Life of America's Jews* (New York: Harper and Row, 1988).
6. Charles S. Liebman, *Deceptive Images: Social Science and the Study of American Jews* (New Brunswick, NJ: Transaction Books, 1988).
7. Stephen M. Cohen, *American Assimilation and Jewish Revival* (Bloomington, IN: Indiana University Press, 1988).
8. Calvin Goldscheider and Alan S. Zuckerman, *The Transformation of the Jews* (Chicago: University of Chicago Press, 1984); Calvin Goldscheider, *Jewish Community and Change: Emerging Patterns in America* (Bloomington, IN: Indiana University Press, 1986).
9. Marcus Lee Hansen, "The Problem of the Third Generation Immigrant" (Rock Island, IL: Swenson Swedish Immigration Research Center and Augustana College Library, 1937). This is a republication of the 1937 address bearing the same title.
10. Leonard Fein, p. 51.
11. Marshall Sklare and Joseph Greenblum, *Jewish Identity on the Suburban Frontier: A Study of Group Survival in the Open Society* (New York: Basic Books, 1967).
12. Fein, p. 69.
13. Fein, pp. xvi, 147, 178.
14. Fein, p. 45.
15. Jeffrey S. Gurock, *The Men and Women of Yeshiva* (New York: Columbia University Press, 1988), pp. 150, 151.
16. Charles S. Liebman, pp. 57, 58.

3

The American Jewish Experience and American Pluralism: A Comparative Perspective

Shmuel N. Eisenstadt

The Jewish experience in the United States exhibits unique features in the panorama of Jewish historical experience, and at least some of these are closely connected with specific characteristics of American pluralism. The problem to be addressed here is what are some of these salient features that characterize Jewish life in America, and to which aspects of American pluralism are the most closely related.

We will not deal at any length with some of the well-known features of American Jewish life, such as the unusual educational and occupational mobility and advancement, and the impact of these processes on the possibilities of assimilation. Rather, we focus on what seems the most distinguishing aspect of the American Jewish experience—the incorporation of Jews into all the arenas of American life, and the effects of such incorporation on structuring of Jewish life and self-perception.

The incorporation of Jews in the United States has been manifest above all in the burgeoning of Jewish institutions and in their public visibility and acceptability; in the Jewish definition of their collective identity, and in their participation in the general institutional, especially political and intellectual, aspects of American society.

The common denominator of these tendencies has been the open public display and acceptance of the communal Jewish experience and activities, defined not only in religious terms, but also in broader "ethnic" national terms, or in terms of "peoplehood." Combined with this is the perception by the Jews of themselves, which is accepted by their host societies, as full, emancipated citizens of those societies, not just (as happened in Eastern Europe between the wars) as one national minority group among other such groups.

Thus, instead of restricting Jewish identity and collective endeavors to semiprivate religious and philanthropic spheres, as was the case in nineteenth-century Western and Central Europe, this new attitude accepted, and even emphasized, the combination of the communal, "ethnic," and political components of Jewishness, and of their peoplehood, even if it was religious organizations that have long served as the major bases of such communal organizations. At the same time these activities were perceived by the Jews, and seemingly also by the general population, as legitimate ways of participation in society.

This incorporation of Jews into American society became visible from the late 1960s, but had its beginnings in the nineteenth century even before the great immigrations of the 1880s. The more general acceptance of Jewish distinctiveness was connected with the transformation, beginning in the late 1950s, of the American scene, especially with the weakening ideology of the melting pot and the upsurge of ethnic pride in general.

During this period a rapid process of educational and occupational advance took place. Major universities, which until this time had had *de facto* quotas for Jews, allowed open enrollment. Jews entered these universities, graduated from them, and moved on to become prominent in professional, academic, cultural, and mass-media fields. Though many sectors, such as banking and top industry, remained closed to most Jews until the late 1960s or early 1970s, from about the mid-1970s many additional economic areas opened their doors to them.

For a large proportion of the Jewish community, the progression of economic and occupational mobility gave rise to an expanding scope of collective Jewish ventures and the growth of Jewish education on both the local and national levels. Although this process became stronger after the early 1970s, the roots could be traced back twenty years.

By the mid-1950s, there was already a burgeoning of collective Jewish political activities closely connected with the state of Israel, which provided a central focus for Jewish endeavor. The image of Israel, based as it was on the myth of a pioneer conquering of the waste land, rooted in a biblical vision, was very close to some basic components of the American myth and helped greatly to legitimize these undertakings. Later on, organized action on behalf of Soviet Jewry became another central focus of Jewish political life.

Closely related to internal Jewish organization and the self-definition of Jewish collective identity has been the participatory nature of the Jews in not only the occupational and economic but also political and cultural, but the general aspects of American life.

Although many individual Jews became active in politics, Jewish lobbies developed, and Jews were politically organized (particularly on behalf of Israel and Soviet Jewry), no Jewish parties developed, and no specifically Jewish representatives were elected to Congress. This is in direct contrast to the orientation in Eastern Europe. Similarly, major Jewish writers—Saul Bellow, Bernard Malamud, and others—did not create, as in Eastern Europe, a Yiddish or Hebrew literature for Jewish audiences.

However, unlike most of their counterparts in Western and Central Europe, these writers and intellectuals did not aim at assimilation; they did not deny or reject their Jewish heritage or concerns. Indeed, very often it was quite the opposite. In their works they stressed Jewish themes and Jewish personalities as part of the broader American scene; many of them closely identified themselves with Jewish activities, and their connections with political or communal Jewish groups were often very close.

There developed among the Jews an aspect of culturalism sponsored by Jewish organizations but oriented to a large degree to the general problems of American society. The developments combined Jewish themes with open participation in the intellectual life of America, attempting to provide a specific Jewish dimension to the more general discussion of American problems. *Commentary*, the independent monthly published by the American Jewish Committee, is indicative of this focus.

Jews also developed unique patterns of political participation. In addition to the numerous political activities of Jewish organizations on behalf of strictly Jewish causes, noted above, Jews and Jewish leaders were active in general political movements. The civil rights movement is the single most important illustration. Unlike the participation of Jews in European radical movements, this was openly presented as a Jewish contribution to American political life.

From the late 1970s, Jews became more mobile in political life, nationally as well as locally. Recently there has been a parallel emergence of Jewish study centers in many universities and their placement in general academic departments or schools.

Even when various black organizations turned against the Jews, and when the experience of Jewish students and young radical activists in the 1960s and 1970s became problematic given the strong anti-Israel stand of these movements, the feeling of Jews that as Jews they are perhaps adding a special dimension to American political life has not abated.

It is interesting to note that the Jews have begun to move away from the left or liberal sector of the American political, social, and intellectual scene toward the more center- or right-wing one. This is evident in the general ambience of *Commentary* and in the relative prominence of Jewish intellectuals, many of whom (such as those close to *Commentary*) were members of leftist movements in their youth in the twenties. This was not just a case of individual Jews adopting conservative tendencies, or of being center- or right-wing ideologists (as could be found to some degree in Eastern Europe, for instance, Walther

Rathenau). What is significant here is that a fairly large proportion of Jewish intellectuals and journalists moved to the right—signaling, as it were, that their full participation in American public policy need not only take the form of protest from the left against the conservative or traditional center, but may also embrace the values of the (American) center.

It was against the background of these various trends that there developed among the Jews and, to a lesser degree, also among their host nations, the consciousness of a new vision of collective Jewish perception. The major characteristic of this new vision was the definition of the problem of Jewish experience in the modern world in terms of different ways to express Jewish identity and Jewish peoplehood in the Diaspora. The search stressed not only the religious dimensions, but also the political and civilizational dimensions of Jewish identity. At the same time, however, the Jews still saw themselves as full members of their respective nationalities.

Despite many misgivings and fears about an ultimate lack of viability of Jewish existence in the Diaspora, the vision took for granted the existence of a Jewish collective distinctiveness as a part of the general society while searching for different ways to express that identity. The feeling became increasingly prevalent among American Jews that it was possible for them to see themselves as both Americans and Jews. Unlike in Europe until very recently, American Jews seemingly did not see any contradiction between the two identities, even as they emphasized the collective, historical, and political dimensions of their Jewishness.

Closely related to this vision is the development by the various Jewish communities to articulate patterns of Jewish life. The dichotomy of living as an American or as a Jew no longer held. Many Jews were continuously changing their paths and did not lead lives that were primarily Jewish, but they did not want to lose their Jewishness. This led to a reformulation and a restructuring of their identity, and an increasing attachment to different elements of the Jewish tradition.

There was a strong return to religious customs that had become symbols of a collective peoplehood—candle lighting on Hanukkah and on the Sabbath; and the celebration of circumcision, bar mitzvah, marriage, and funerals. While this return to tradition did not necessarily signal the acceptance of the halakha as the basic framework of Jewish life, such a process took place to some extent. The upsurge of orthodoxy and neoorthodoxy constituted a closely connected process.

As already noted, another element that developed in the period after World War II was the emergence of collective Jewish political activity within the political framework of the host society. For the first time in exilic history, Jewish communities throughout the world became politically active and conscious as Jews. The pinnacle of this development was, of course, the establishment of the state of Israel.

The most interesting aspect of this process is that no simple relationship between attachment to Jewish customs and commitment to Jewish identity developed. Even within the orthodox circles, there has been increasing participation in the last two decades in some of the "general" spheres of life, such as higher education and political activities, which would have been anathema to the older Eastern European traditionalists.

What are the reasons for this unique modern Jewish experience? Some are closely related to central aspects of post-World War II history, especially the Holocaust and the establishment of the state of Israel. The impact of these traumatic and dramatic events could be discerned not only on the Jewish community in the United States, but also in various Jewish populations in Europe, particularly in England and France. In all these countries we find development not only of economic advancement, but also more open and widespread Jewish communal organization.

On the American scene, these developments appear most far-reaching. The concern and political action with respect to problems in Israel or to Soviet Jewry, as well as the participation of Jews in the arenas already noted, have been much more universal in the United States than in any other country of the postwar Western Diaspora. In this context, it is significant that some of these characteristics—the relatively open, nonapologetic, public concern with Jewish matters—could be found in aspects of the Jewish experience in America in the early part of the nineteenth century, even if they were then couched in religiosocial terms.[1]

The ideology of American (Jewish) reform was based on the assumption that religious reform was something common to all Americans. Although the extreme derivatives of this ideology were followed by many congregations, the ideal of becoming part of the American scene, without losing a sense of Jewishness, was quite widespread. It is perhaps not surprising that it was from within this reform movement that some of the most ardent Zionist leaders later emerged.

In the tradition of the American melting pot the movement became submerged, but it has reappeared in a new and much more diversified way in the last twenty or thirty years.

Seemingly, we should look for the reasons for this reappearance in various features of the American scene, possibly in the nature of American pluralism, since the developments in Jewish life are paralleled by a general ethnic revival in the United States. But the Jews have long lived in pluralistic societies. The entire modern Eastern European Jewish experience, especially before World War I, was shaped in the framework of pluralistic societies. What is it, then, in the particular nature of American pluralism that has shaped the modern sense of Jewish identity?

It might be worthwhile to look at some of the basic premises of American civilization as distinct from other pluralistic societies, especially as they have applied to Jews. It is natural to begin with the birth of the United States, and, thus, with George Washington's message to the Hebrew Congregation of Newport, Rhode Island, in 1790:

> The citizens of the United States of America have a right to applaud themselves for having given to mankind examples of an enlarged and liberal policy—a policy worthy of imitation. All possess alike liberty of conscience and immunities of citizenship.

> It is now no more that toleration is spoken of as if it were the indulgence of one class of people that another enjoyed the exercise of their inherent natural rights, for, happily, the Government of the United States, which gives to bigotry no factions, to persecution no assistance, requires only that they who live under its protection should demean themselves as good citizens in giving it on all occasions their effectual support.

> May the children of the stock of Abraham who dwell in this land continue to merit and enjoy the good will of the other inhabitants—while every one shall sit in safety under his own vine and fig tree and there shall be none to make him afraid.[2]

In 1810, Congress passed the Sunday Mail Law, which decreed that mail should be delivered on Sundays. As Seymour Martin Lipset notes, twenty years later, in 1830, "a Senate committee report . . . endorsed by a majority of that House, stated . . . laws proclaiming that the government should not provide services on Sunday would work an injustice to irreligious people or non-Christians, and would constitute a special favor to Christians as a group." The report was written by a deeply religious active Baptist:

> The Constitution regards the conscience of the Jew as sacred as that of the Christian, and gives no more authority to adopt a measure affecting the conscience of a solitary individual than that of a whole community . . . If Congress shall declare the first day of the week holy, it will not satisfy the Jew or the Sabbatarian. It will dissatisfy both and, consequently, convert neither . . . It must be recollected that, in the earliest settlement of this country, the spirit of persecution, which drove the pilgrims from their native homes, was brought with them to their new habitations; and that some Christians were scourged and others put to death for no other crime than dissenting from the dogmas of their rulers . . . If a solemn act of legislation shall in one point define the God or point out to the citizen one religious duty, it may with equal propriety define *every* part of divine revelation and enforce *every* religious obligation, even to the forms and ceremonies of worship; the endowment of the church, and the support of the clergy.

. . . It is the duty of this government to affirm to *all*—to the Jew or Gentile, Pagan, or Christian—the protection and advantages of our benignant institutions on *Sunday*.[3]

Thus, the attitude that developed in America was not simply religious tolerance in the European sense, based on the limitation or disestablishment of an established Church, although the expressions of such tolerance were often still couched in European terms.

The full nature of this behavior must be examined in the framework of a distinctively American ideology and basic political ideology. This new collective identity and its political expression was not based (as was the case in Europe) on historical tradition. Although it derived from religious premises, it was transformed into what Robert Bellah[4] called "civil religion"; future-rather than past-oriented, and based on the separation of church and state.

Though formulated in terms of the predominant Protestant tradition, the American way of life has been described in terms of a common political ideology with religious overtones and an emphasis on Christian heritage, rather than a combination of religious tradition with historical, ethnic, or national identities. In Samuel Huntington's words: "For most people national identity is the product of a long process of historical evolution involving common conceptions, common experiences, common religion. National identity is thus organic in character. Such however is not the case in the United States. American nationality has been defined in political rather than organic terms. The political ideas of the American creed have been the basis of national identity . . . The United States thus had its origins in a conscious political act, in assertion of basic political principles and in adherence to the constitutional agreement based on those principles . . . "[5] The crucial fact here is that American collective identity is described in terms of political ideology, with almost no territorial or historical components. Though it shared an orientation to the Bible with Zionist movements, the new territory was not sanctified in terms of primordial attachment to a land of the Fathers, or as the natural locus of a long history.

Similarly, the separation of church and state in the United States developed not as an outcome of struggles against a history of tension between the two, but from the basic fact that America was formed by members of various Protestant sects.

Because of these basic characteristics, America is accepting of religious, political and ethnic diversity so long as members of the different groups accepted the American political creed. Accordingly, immigrants, including the Jews, have not had to struggle to gain full citizenship rights. The question of Jewish emancipation never arose.

The legitimation of ethnic diversity is never achieved without some struggle. The American ideology of the melting pot and the way of life stressed in schools and in the media have been a homogenizing influence. Seemingly, the development of more particularistic identities is possible only in the private sphere. In Washington's address to the Jewish congregation in Newport, the expression "Children of Abraham" could have been interpreted as going beyond the purely religious connotation, while the use of biblical terms indicated an affinity to all people of the Bible.

There have been, of course, religious and social tension. Anti-Semitism manifested itself in the exclusion of Jews from many economic sectors. At times, there has been strong resentment among certain groups at the Jew's economic advances and growing cultural visibility. From the late 1960s on, the great upsurge of ethnicity in the United States also gave rise to growing anti-Semitism among some minority groups, and the demands for positive discrimination, for quotas, often *de facto* were directed against Jews. But the expressions of anti-Semitism in the United States never assumed the intensity or scope of their nineteenth- and twentieth-century parallels in Europe, nor have they impeded for any length of time the occupational advance of the Jews, and their growing public collective visibility.

American anti-Semitism, though often widespread and sometimes quite rampant and virulent, has differed in crucial ways from European. In the United States, it has not been connected with nationalism, nor has been an integral part of an historical ideology. Nor has anti-Semitism been a particular focal point of American hate groups. In Jonathan Sarna's words, American anti-Semitism had "to compete with other forms of animus, Racism, anti-Quakerism, Anglophobia, anti-Catholicism, anti-Masonry, anti-Mormonism, anti-Orientalism, nativism, anti-Teutonism, primitive anti-Communism— these and other waves have periodically swept over the American landscape, scarring and battering citizens. Because hatred is so varied and diffused, no group experiences for long the full brunt of national odium. Furthermore, most Americans retain bitter memories of days past when they or their ancestors were the objects of malevolence. At least in some cases, this leads them to exercise restraint. The American strain of anti-Semitism is thus less potent than its European counterpart, and it faces a larger number of natural competitors. To reach epidemic proportions, it must first crowd out a vast number of contending hatreds . . . The Founding Fathers, whatever they personally thought of Jews, gave them full equality. Hence, in America, Jews have always fought anti-Semitism freely. Never having received their emancipation as an 'award' they have had no fears of losing it. Instead, from the beginning, they made full use of their right to freedom of speech . . ."[6]

It is a moot question to what extent these tendencies make invalid the basic Zionist tenets about the inevitability of assimilation, demographic decline or, in the extreme, of anti-Semitic persecutions and perhaps destruction. Indeed, visions of the Holocaust have become prevalent in the collective memory of American Jewry. It is also difficult to assess the impact on the Jewish community of the growing political importance of the black population, or of a possible rift between the U.S. and Israeli governments, although many rather problematic indications can be seen.

Despite all these possibilities, those among the Jews who are concerned with such matters apparently were able to combine historical communality with full participation in American society. Seemingly, the many American Jews—especially those who uphold their Jewishness—refuse to see any contradiction to view anti-Semitism as a threat to their incorporation as Jews into the society.

They pointed out that even intermarriage could have unexpected results. Fairly often—certainly much more frequently than in Europe—assimilated Jews who marry Gentile women are brought back to some Jewish framework by their wives, who want to uphold tradition. Thus, instead of the "classical" problem of physical and cultural survival in the modern world, the crucial question for Jews becomes how to find new ways of authenticating their Jewishness in this new setting.

Here a paradoxical picture emerges. The movement to small communities, and the general demographic decline of the Jews—that same decline that, at least, partially accounts for their economic advancement—may make the maintenance of Jewish communalities and activities more difficult. Growing participation in general areas of life may deplete the reservoir of leadership for specific Jewish activities, as shown by the influx of Orthodox Jews within them. The attraction of Jewish college youth in the 1970s to various religious sects, like the Moonies, may have a similar influence. As noted above, the impact of black political power, increasingly disdainful of Jews and Israel, must be taken into account.

Perhaps most important is the possibility of gradual, painless Jewish assimilation, which is facilitated because it is not demanded. Paradoxically, such possibility may be reinforced by the ability to maintain a minimum of individuality within the mainstream of American Jewish life and, hence, to many, it may seem that no specific efforts are needed in this direction. Demographic trends reinforced such possibilities. Recent studies predict "a long-term" reduction in the number of Diaspora Jews, from 10.7 million in 1970 to 9.7 million in 1980, to a projected 7.9 million by the year 2000—due to immigration, secularization, modernization, and assimilation.[7]

Indeed, these processes that enable the Jewish activities and organizations to intensify, helped by the demographic trends noted above, may also encourage a relatively fast and smooth assimilation, simply because such absorption can take place without demands for changing religion or denying the sense of Jewishness.

These processes may lead to the development of three sectors of Jewish people. The first would be composed of various Orthodox communities that would continually move into a narrow, sectarian direction, abandoning the more universalistic orientations of the Jewish heritage. The second sector would be a small, hard core within the non-Orthodox majority that would attempt, mainly through attachment to Jewish education, to maintain a strong Jewish identity while continuing to participate in the general society. This sector, however, could be threatened both by the Orthodox group and by the third sector, the great majority who will, after a few generations, move into a painless, drifting assimilation.

The success of the Jews in being accepted in the United States, the development of numerous Jewish activities, and the diversified patterns of participation in various spheres of American life do not, by themselves, assure the continuity of Jewish collective life and creativity. Rather, this success—if unchanged by societal developments, or by changing relations among Jewish communities, in general, and within Israel, in particular—together with demographic decline, may lead to a fatal weakening of Jewish identity and collective cohesion.

Notes

1. Nathan Glazer, "Social Characteristics of American Jews, 1654–1954," *American Jewish Yearbook* (1955).
2. From *Publications of the American Jewish Historical Society*, No. 3 (1895; second edition 1915), pp. 91–2.
3. S.M. Lipset, *The First New Nation* (New York: W.W. Norton, 1979, second edition), pp. 164–5.
4. R.N. Bellah, *The Civil Religion in America*, in idem, *Beyond Belief* (New York: Harper and Row,), pp. 168–93.
5. S.P. Huntington, *American Politics: The Promise of Disharmony* (Cambridge, MA: Harvard University Press, 1981), p. 23.
6. J. Sarna, "Antisemitism and American History," *Commentary* (March 1981), pp. 46–7.
7. R. Bachi, in an interview with Yosef Goell, *Jerusalem Post* (August 11, 1983).

4

The Rhetoric of Chosenness and the Fabrication of American Jewish Identity[1]

Arnold M. Eisen

For at least the past half century, the religious thought of American Jewry has been dominated by a single issue, its rhetoric focused on a single theme: the chosenness of the Jewish people. Rabbis of the "second generation" (ca. 1930–1955) made election and associated ideas of mission, exclusivity, and covenant the central topic of their sermons and tracts. Theologians of the current "third" or "fourth" generations have implicitly and explicitly confirmed Arthur Hertzberg's dictum that "the essence of Judaism is the affirmation that the Jews are the chosen people: all else is commentary."[2] That emphasis is doubly puzzling: Why should one theme have provoked such an outpouring of interpretation, while others (exile, messiah, revelation) were virtually ignored? Why should this particular theme have been highlighted, when it urged a distinctiveness that most Jews wished to abandon, and presumed theological beliefs that they no longer shared? The discourse of American Jewry, it would seem, contradicted the beliefs and aspirations of rabbis and congregants alike. Yet, that rhetoric was not only articulated, but awarded pride of place.

The reason, as I have argued elsewhere,[3] lay in the functions that the theme of chosenness served, both for those who employed it and those who listened. Students of the other major American religious group[4] for whom chosenness was the focal thesis—the Puritans—have shown us how "rhetoric functions within a culture," and "reflects and affects a set of particular psychic, social and historical needs."[5] Those needs, in the Puritan case, focused on the formation of identity, the definition of self as opposed to the "nonchosen" others outside one's gates, and the multitude of possibilities confronting the chosen. Chosenness, I believe, served precisely the same function in the lives

53

of twentieth-century American Jews as they sought to make their way, yet remain distinct in the country that the Puritans first pronounced heir to the chosenness of Israel. This was not the only function performed by the ideology of mission and election (I have detailed others in previous research),[5] nor was it the sole determinant of American Jewish identity, whether collective or personal. It did, however, play a decisive role. The conviction of election enabled relatively secular American Jews to "make themselves holy" through the artifice of their words—to weave a definition of self from the fabric of tradition.

First, I will sketch the various interpretations of chosenness offered by American Jewish thinkers in the past fifty years; Second, I define, in greater specificity, the two key terms on which our analysis turns—rhetoric and identity; I also note several ways in which the rhetoric of chosenness has affected and shaped the fabrication of American Jewish identity in this period. Finally, I consider the intrinsic connotations and resonances that helped the image of "the chosen people" to perform the task assigned it in the face of considerable obstacles.

I.

The interpretations of election offered by particular American rabbis and theologians generally have varied with the movements to which they belonged. Orthodox thinkers have tended to be the least concerned with chosenness for two reasons. First, they do not need to discuss explicitly a doctrine that they affirm daily. Unlike rabbis in other movements, they have little difficulty with traditional beliefs in a personal God or His revelation of the Torah at Sinai; if Jews are bound by a halakha (law) not given any other people, it follows that God has chosen them for a unique role in perfecting His creation. Chosenness remains the "unformulated dogma,"[6] as it has been for centuries. During the 1930s and 1940s, moreover, Orthodoxy remained largely an immigrants community, and, thus, felt no need to accommodate inherited doctrine to a Gentile world and culture that it had not yet entered. In our generation, a large segment of the Orthodox community has come to resemble Conservative and Reform counterparts in its degree of integration into America, and chosenness has received somewhat more attention.

The Reform movement already had discarded chosenness in nineteenth-century Germany on the grounds that it prejudiced the achievement of Jewish emancipation. The German rabbis had substituted in its place, a more acceptable notion: the Jewish mission to the nations derived from the prophet Isaiah. Jews were to be a "light unto the nations"; a teacher and exemplar of monotheism and high ethical standards. In America, this, too, proved problematic. It was not tactful to point to the "darkness" of one's neighbors, nor was it logical to claim a moral superiority over those one sought to emulate. Thus, when the Reform movement adopted the statement of principles known as the Columbus Platform in 1937, it proclaimed that Israel's mission was to "witness to the divine in the face of every form of paganism and materialism," a witness to be accomplished by cooperation "with all men" rather than through teaching or example.[7] God's choice of Israel had given way to the belief that "Israel chose God."[8]

Regardless of who chose whom, however, the association of chosenness with special persecution remained, reinforced in the minds of this generation by the Nazis. "From the slave pens of the Pharoahs to the gas chambers of Hitler, the Via Dolorosa of this people of the immemorial crucifixion has stretched long and desolate through the weary centuries."[9] Thus spoke Abba Hillel Silver, perhaps his movement's most accomplished orator, in a masterful polemic entitled "Where Judaism Differed." Yet, as one Reform critic noted, Silver's notion of the Jewish mission seemed to lack any substantive content outside of martyrdom. American Jews were not called upon to do anything in particular, except to be ethical and support humanitarian causes.[10]

By the second generation's close, this hollow "mission" was no longer a favored theme, and Silver's own son and successor is typical of the third generation's thinkers in disavowing the idea in favor of a renewed emphasis upon chosenness.[11] He cannot literally believe in God's choice of Israel, but he affirms it nonetheless, and in this has been joined by theologians such as Emil Fackenheim and Eugene Borowitz.[12]

Mordecai Kaplan and his followers would have none of this in the Reconstructionist movement. Kaplan dismissed "mission" as pretentious bombast lacking any basis in Jewish tradition, and refused to "revaluate" or reinterpret chosenness as he had many other ideas and practices of Judaism. In *Judaism as a Civilization* (1934), he provided three reasons for this repudiation of the doctrine. First, Jews needed "some new purpose in life" that, unlike chosenness, would direct their energies into "such lines of creativity as will bring [them] spiritual redemption." Chosenness was no longer viable. Second, the claim to election was incompatible with participation in American life, for the interests of a "chosen people" surely would take precedence over those of America, precluding the Jews' "complete self-identification with the state." Third, the Jews no longer could believe in election, having lost faith in "supernaturalism," and no longer should believe in it, because it was ethically reprehensible to perpetuate ideas of "race or national superiority."[13] Kaplan proposed that Jews replace election with an idea of vocation. The notion of "calling" could "fulfill the legitimate spiritual wants" supplied by the idea of election without the latter's "invidious distinctions," all vocations being putatively equal.[14] This suggestion, though ingenious, met with little enthusiasm.

Conservative thinkers found themselves in the middle. Like Orthodoxy, they sought maximum continuity with tradition, but they experienced some of the same doubts as Reform colleagues, and also were subject to Kaplan's constant criticism from within their own movement and its seminary. Thus, in 1927 Louis Finkelstein wrote that "we say He chose Israel in the sense that Israel was more keenly aware of His being than other peoples" but followed this with the affirmation, "It is therefore literally true that the inspiration of the Torah and the Prophets is the expression of God's choice of Israel as His people."[15] A second rabbi argued in a series of essays and sermons that "all peoples had vocations, as did all individuals," but that God revealed "more or less of Himself, or unique aspects of Himself, as He chooses," thereby allowing for significant variation in vocation.[16] The movement's prayer book, in an extended apologia for retaining the doctrine, cited the link between election and Torah as well as the "psychological" indispensability of chosenness to Jewish survival. If Jews were to remain loyal to their faith despite the disabilities involved, they had to be convinced that "the Jewish people has played and yet will play a significant role in the world." The instinct of self-preservation would not suffice.[17] The current generation of Conservative thinkers has joined colleagues in other movements in affirming election as a "mystery" and a "scandal" defying human comprehension. This affirmation has come despite concepts of God and revelation woefully inadequate to belief in any traditional notion of election.

II.

It should be apparent from this schematic summary that few rabbis from the past fifty years engaged in setting forth systematically the rigorously defined concepts that we understand as theology. Rather, as I emphasized elsewhere,[18] they relied on imagery, metaphor, hyperbole, or even self-contradiction—all standard rhetorical devices—to reach affirmations that their theology did not enable them to grasp. Religious ideology, as we may call it, permitted them to draw on the intrinsicly powerful resonances of the word "chosen"—the special love of a parent, a place at the center, the ability to serve—to evoke and maintain loyalties threatened by the gap between traditional doctrines and contemporary disbelief.

Such a reliance upon the devices of rhetoric should not surprise us. The rabbis' efforts, whether in sermons, debates, tracts, essays, or longer works, were all "language designed to persuade"—the classical definition of rhetoric offered by Cicero.[19] Kenneth Burke, in a more precise formulation, stipulates that "rhetoric is the use of words by human agents to form attitudes or to induce actions in other human agents." It is fundamental to all human intercourse, for the use of language is a "symbolic means of inducing cooperation" in beings that, by nature, respond to symbols.[20] The greater the distance between two human beings (that is, between speaker and audience), and the less inclined one side is to the position of the other, the greater the need for rhetoric to step in and bridge the gap. However, unless the two groups already share a language and, at least, part of a world view, rhetorical appeals will be unsuccessful. Moreover, in a case where one party is in a position to coerce the other, rhetoric will be superfluous. Distance, relation, and the freedom of the actors to disagree are all essential prerequisites, leading Burke to postulate that the paradigm of rhetoric is courtship. For in courtship one being—one sort of being—tries to persuade another that their persons and interests are really one, and should be joined. Theology, Burke adds, is a similar enterprise: The attempt to speak to, and about, the being most different from ourselves, and to convince Him and ourselves that His interests and will are or should be identical to our own.[21]

One sees, then, why identification has always been a favored rhetorical strategy, for it is a means for one person (or interest or group) to persuade another that the audience or its interest is identical to the speaker or his interest. The two are identified with one another. American rabbis, attempting to persuade Jews and Gentiles alike of the Jews' rightful place in America, seized on the idea of the chosen people, common to both, as a means of furthering the partnership.

Identification can also link an audience with an ideal entity or an idealized aspect of themselves, bringing them to see themselves in its reflection. Thus, the Puritans' sense of self was shaped by sermonic identifications of their mission and land with those of God's original Israelites.[22] Identification, in both senses, presupposes identity even as it is shaped. In order for me to identify with you, I must have a sense of who I am and what I am; otherwise, I lack criteria that will lead me to accept or decline the identification that is proposed to me. Once having been identified, I will come to see myself in a new light, or to accord prominence to aspects of myself previously recognized but not made central. Puritans might leave their preachers' election-day addresses further convinced that their travails had been prefigured in the biblical saga of Israel. Jews might leave their synagogues convinced that America, unlike the countries from which parents or grandparents had come, was a place where Jews could call home. In each case, the rhetoric, primarily through a strategy of identification, provided the audience with a new or enhanced sense of who they were in contrast and relation to others.

III.

I will turn momentarily to the particular definitions of Jewish peoplehood in America that the rabbis' reinterpretations of chosenness served to strengthen, and how those definitions of the communal self were accomplished. First, however, we need to clarify the notion of identity, which has already been used here, as in the literatures on American Jews and American Puritans, with varying degrees of precision.

Most generally, the term identity connotes a sense of who and what an individual or group is, as opposed to what others are, and to all that it might be or might have been. Thus Sacvan Bercovitch calls the Puritan device of the halfway covenant a "high-point in the formulation of American identity."[23] It rendered the chosen people a wider and ascriptive category that included individuals who personally had not achieved the regenerative experience of God's grace. "We" came to include many who did not strictly speaking belong to "us, the elect," but whom one did not wish to relegate to the status of "them, the non-elect." Henceforth, Bercovitch argues, the category of the "chosen" grew steadily to include wider and wider circles of individuals: first, the children of the elect; then, all of New England; and finally, all of America—while tacitly excluding those who "clearly" did not belong—Indians, heretics, blacks.[24]

Before proceeding, we should note, that such a notion of collective identity rests, to a degree, on metaphor. A group is never "one" as a person is "one"—hence, the need for extraordinary efforts by every group to retain the identification of its members. However, contemporary philosophical work on personal identity,[25] psychological research into personality, and Plato's classical analogies between the polis and the individual all remind us that the individual self is no less a set of selves than the group; likewise, rent by conflict among warring factions and capable of becoming other than it is. The metaphor built into notions of collective identity is, therefore, both powerful and appropriate. That does not mean, of course, that individual and collective identity can be conflated, even in the case of a homogeneous primitive society. We need to pay attention to the ways in which personal identity is altered by changes in the collective identity of a group, and how groups seek to impose notions of self on individuals. We will find that chosenness is such a useful rhetorical aid to "the fabrication of identity" precisely because it seems to confer ultimate meaning, and impose a regimen of conduct, upon each and every individual who enjoys (ascriptive) membership in the elect group. The individual is defined out of anonymity and into a unique fate through identification with the chosen people.

The process begins with a given core that has the status of the self-evident and seems invulnerable to change. Unless we "know" who we are, in some sense, a speaker cannot persuade us that we are like someone or something else. Erikson has dubbed this core "what one is never not," around which one grows into that which one uniquely is.[26] The Puritans, we might say, were "never not" a group separated from their homes and the civilized world by an ocean, surrounded in their new land by a wilderness and hostile Indians; they were "never not" a group called by God to special work of cosmic importance. American Jews were "never not" a minority separated from its surroundings to some degree by group pride, historical consciousness, a distinct sensibility, folk customs, and religious rituals. Both groups became what they became, in part, by dressing in a borrowed wardrobe: the Puritans in the garb of ancient Israelites, the Jews in both that same garb and the clothing of modern, Gentile America. Again, the analogy of group to individual is rather exact. The task of formation of identity in the self is to coordinate its many outfits, new and inherited, thus making the patchwork all of a piece.

The social psychologist, Herbert Kelman, building on this notion of a core around which identity is fashioned, has usefully distinguished three dimensions of the identity thus provided: stability over time and across situations; integration of the various elements of identity with each other; and authenticity of relation to the personal and cultural "core" with which the self begins.[27] All three factors, we note at once, are rendered problematic in a pluralist and secular society such as that of contemporary America. For if culture, in Philip Rieff's words, is "a design of motives directing the self outward" and faith "a compelling symbolic of self-integrating communal purpose,"[28] no single symbol in America is compelling and no one purpose automatically claims our allegiance. Commitments compete in the marketplace; they do not enjoy immediate, long-lasting, or society-wide assent. Therefore, stability is imperiled. A firm set of given affirmations and rejections is lacking; thus, the self's resistance to the many facts that disconfirm the claims of any faith or commitment (what Rieff calls the "strain of observation and the assault of experience")[29] is weakened. The "never not" of the self, by definition, must be firm enough to withstand such challenges, but what is "never not" in a society open to changing commitments, where one's very sex—a fundamental component of identity, surely—can be altered? Integration, once a normative unification of the self that enabled us to speak of "integrity," gives way to the successful coordination of roles in a "role set," and of their performance before our varying audiences. Too often, as Lionel Trilling has observed,[30] the character ideal of sincerity or honesty to others has been superceded by that of authenticity, understood as lack of deception of oneself. We must know when we are playing roles and why we play them. Authenticity comes to connote the harmony of the various elements in our "wardrobe" with the core of self around which we have fashioned an identity, a harmony often difficult to achieve.

This relation of self to audience brings us to a final elaboration of the notion of identity, provided by social psychologist Simon Herman: the distinction among "objective public identity" (the pattern of individual or group traits as they appear to others), "subjective public identity" (the self's perception of how these traits appear to others), and "self-identity" (the self's vision of the pattern of traits as they "really are."[31] The term "objective" is, of course, a misnomer, since "others" are a diverse group with varied perceptions; how they perceive one is determined by a complex bundle of their own needs, prejudices, ideals, and self-perceptions, in which the perception of the "self," in which we are interested, may play a crucial role. Yet, as we shall see, the distinction is crucial to understanding the fabrication of American Jewish identity. For the subjective public identity, consisting of Jews' perceptions of how Gentiles viewed them, was decisive in their negotiation of a Jewish self-identity—their view of how Jews really are and should be.

Our discussion on how the rhetoric of chosenness has helped to shape American Jewish identity will conceive of this definition of self as a process that builds on a given core, interacting with other selves similarly engaged, and thus achieves a unique self characterized by stability, integration, and authenticity. I now consider four ways in which the rhetoric of chosenness has figured in that process among American Jews:

- by setting boundaries between themselves and Gentile America, through the definition of their community as a "religious civilization";
- by providing content to that limited distinctiveness, and to the identities of individual Jews, despite their abandonment of Israel's traditional covenant with God;
- by overcoming the challenge posed to this self-definition by the historical events of the Nazi era; and
- by provoking, and then coping with, several dangers to communal and personal identity that are inherent in the very notion of a chosen people, no matter the circumstances by which it is affirmed.

In conclusion, I reflect upon the intrinsic connotations and resonances that enabled the theme of chosenness to "bear" the tremendous burden placed upon it by American Jews—the weight of their fabricated identities.

IV.

The situation of American Jews in the 1930s and 1940s was not propitious for the appropriation of any traditional affirmations, least of all chosenness. A second-generation community—concerned largely on rising from the middle class, moving out of immigrant neighborhoods, and earning the acceptance of Gentile Americans—could hardly affirm without qualification that Jews were meant to live apart and destined to suffer persecution. Sharing the values of liberal Gentile neighbors and professing the creed of American democracy, Jews could not claim credibly a mission to bring those neighbors the truth. A people that had, by and large, cast off the "yoke of mitzvah" and shunned voluntary observance of the commandments could hardly wear the mantle of a "kingdom of priests and holy nation." "We cannot help ask ourselves," observed Rabbi Felix Levy in 1927, "if missionaries can flourish in the soil that produces department store and factory owners, corporation lawyers, labor leaders, itinerant professional propagandists and high-salaried rabbis?"[32]

This distance between daily reality, as known by Jews, and the traditional reality, conjured up by the rhetoric of their rabbis, posed dilemmas that become clearer if the three components of identity, specified by Kelman, are recalled. Milton Steinberg's expressed doubt, in 1934, that acrobats could retain their footing on as a narrow tightrope as Jews walked between their two worlds of tradition and America,[33] pointed to the problem of stability, graphically enacted: what to stand for and where to stand, so as to withstand the challenge of an all-too-accepting world. Would a notion of mission provide the right balance of distance from, and closeness to, one's Gentile neighbors and Jewish ancestors, and convey it to one's children? Would a notion of vocation? Would symbolic acceptance of chosenness, despite disbelief in revelation, messiah, and personal God? Jews searched for integration of their experience as a part of modern America, with the root-images of self associated with the consciousness of standing in the stream of Jewish history. One simply could not banish the images of a mother lighting Sabbath candles; a grandfather's tallis and tephillin; the centuries of martyrs; the pride in the Bible and the prophets; and, since World War II, the reaction to the Jews killed in the Holocaust or the building of the state of Israel. Yet, one simply could not assume that legacy for oneself, and there was little authenticity and little guilt in sloughing off large portions of the inheritance, the accumulated core of one's identity—the "never not" of previous generations of Jews. Small comfort that one could successfully play the roles of both Jew and American, and know the extent of one's self-deceptions as one played.

However, as noted, this gap between reality and tradition only served to provoke rhetorical strategies designed to bridge it, chiefly through the device of identification. Jews still were what the tradition pronounced them, despite appearances, and if they could no longer literally believe what Jews had once believed—particularly the theological presuppositions of chosenness—they could affirm traditional doctrine, nonetheless, as symbolic ideology. In this fashion, all parties to the second generation's debate on the desirable degree of separation from Gentile America invoked chosenness to supply and legitimate their positions. Julian Morgenstern, the president of the Reform movement's seminary, argued, in an address entitled "Nation, People, Religion—What Are We?" (1943), that "the true genius and destiny of Israel find expression only in its role as a religious people, the bearers of a spiritual heritage."[34] His colleague, Samuel Goldenson, drew the logical conclusion: "If we insist, as I believe we should, upon the moral basis and universal validity of democracy, we should at the same time emphasize less and less the particularisms in our Jewish heritage . . . that separate us from others, and stress the universal concepts and outlooks more and more."[35] Not surprisingly, advocates of an ethnic definition of American Jewry (by Mordecai Kaplan or Horace Kallen) rejected the Jewish mission out of hand, stressing instead a peoplehood demarked by distinctive customs, diet, history, and culture. Mission, Kallen wrote, was but "the most insidious of all pretenses, that of altruism . . . the lupine nature under the wool,"[36] while Kaplan repeatedly historicized, psychologized, and simply ridiculed the idea of chosenness—all strategies of disidentification that stressed the distance between reality and tradition, rather than seeking to overcome it. In the end, however, all sides were forced to give way: the Reform Jews, to a reacceptance of Jewish peoplehood, expressed in the definition of Judaism as "the historical religious experience of the Jewish people"[37]; Kallen, to the realization that Jews needed more than "kitchen traditions" to guarantee their survival[38]; and Kaplan, to recognition of the unique "vocation" of Judaism. All civilizations, by definition, had a religion, and all religions were, in theory, equal in their ability to provide salvation. But, Kaplan conceded, at present Judaism (for historical reasons, to be sure, and not any divine choice) was able to provide uniquely self-fulfillment to its adherents.[39] Thus, while all vocations were equal, one was more equal than others. Appeals to an instinctive "will to live" as Jews, Kaplan had learned, would not suffice. Difference had to be undergirded with transcendent significance. In this way, a moderate claim to chosenness won the assent of all parties, and served to define a modest degree of Jewish separation from Gentile neighbors.

This particular debate on Jewish exclusivity and chosenness was especially important, because the drawing of boundaries between self and others—the fundamental task of formation of identity—had been rendered difficult for this generation by their lack of visible markings such as dietary laws or fringes on their garments. It was further complicated by the lack of "others" who could remind Jews every day of who they were not. American Puritans, writes historian Michael Zuckerman,

> had to have those they scorned— the blacks, the Indians and all the idle, dissolute, and damned—to maintain the boundaries of their increasingly brittle identities. Precisely because they found themselves, and in truth created themselves, in their counteridentities, they required for their very sense of selfhood the outcasts they purported to abhor.[40]

One finds a remnant of these dynamics in stereotypes of the Gentiles whom Jews did not abhor, but rather, strove to emulate. One could not trust Gentiles: They were drunkards; they were sexually licentious; their moral standards were lax; they were not as smart as Jews.[41] Philip Roth could have been speaking for many American Jews when he wrote, in 1963, that while the Jewish culture transmitted to him by his parents was at best fragmentary, he had "received whole" a psychology that could be expressed in three words: Jews are better.[42] One sees the importance and difficulty of boundary maintenance in these circumstances in the Jews' deeply felt opposition to intermarriage and in hostility towards Jewish converts to Christianity. Watchfulness on the border is necessary when crossing is easy, when, indeed, Jews can go back and forth daily and so incorporate elements of the other into themselves. The rabbis of the Talmud sought to blame the golden calf on "the mixed multitude," who had accompanied the Israelites out of Egypt. Their modern counterparts similarly have attributed rising rates of crime and divorce among American Jews to assimilation, rather than to failings intrinsic to the community or its religion. Both explanations met apparently with some success, although neither is especially convincing; in each case, the required demarcation of Jews from the guilty Gentile party is lacking. The rhetoric of chosenness, given this fluidity of boundaries, served to reinforce such separations as remained. Jews were distinguished from Gentiles even if they looked, believed, and lived like Gentiles—for God or historical destiny had eternally set them apart.

Nothing less than God, or a "godlike-term," such as destiny, could have accomplished the task, and this necessity to invoke God posed two problems for Jewish thinkers: First, as we noted previously, they did not have the requisite belief; second, Jewish persecution made invocation of the "Lord of History" problematic. Reform rabbis who explained that Israel had chosen God (and not the reverse) continued, nonetheless, to speak of Israel's "mission as the servant people of the eternal" and its "messianic goal." In ascribing an activist mission to Jews listening passively to their sermons, they employed a rhetorical device, described by Burke, as a "kind of elation in which the audience feels as though it were not merely receiving but creatively participating in the speaker's assertion."[43] Other rabbis did the same, especially during the war years. Yet, as a Conservative rabbi observed in the late 1920s, Jewish suffering was "futile and gratuitous" unless it was motivated by the belief that Jews had a unique contribution to make to mankind, and that their survival represented the "finger of God in history."[44] Vague appeals to a universalist mission, and the argument that "the Jews chose God," were inadequate to the circumstances. When Rabbi Simon Greenberg was asked, in 1939, what sense it made for a Jewish mother to bring children into the world, he responded that Israel's place on the "battlefield" had been chosen by God as well as by previous generations of Jews, and so Jews had no choice but to remain "the mark at which every arrow poisoned throughout the ages."[45] Such a stark contrast (the "battlefield") between Jews pursuing justice and mercy, and a non-Jewish world succumbing to base appetites ("lust" and "thirst") reinforced the boundaries between Greenberg's audience and their Gentile neighbors, even if his reference was to a them overseas by whom all Americans abhorred. Persistence in the Jews' unhappy lot, somewhat masochistic if the reason lay only in the choice of previous generations, attained transcendent purpose if the battle lines were drawn by God.

Yet—the question was inescapable—why would God punish any of His children in this fashion, let alone His chosen? One suspects that Jews were led to the dialectic of "psychic uncertainty" and "rhetorical self-assertion" that historians have observed in the Puritans.[46] The more the facts failed to confirm election, the more "outlandish" the "aspiration" of the rhetoric.[47] Puritans, afraid that their "errand in the wilderness" might prove to have been an error in reading the text of God's involvement in history, were all the more determined that the consciousness of election survive in themselves and their children. Their preachers feared the "gulf of desperation" as much as, if not more than, the "rocks of presumption."[48] Kaplan and Kallen repeatedly point to the Jews' sense of inferiority as the stimulus to belief in election,[49] and the Conservative movement, we recall, even included the psychological need for the doctrine in its list of reasons for retaining chosenness in the prayer book. The more frequent recourse to this theme in sermons during the years of World War II strengthens our suspicion that the heights scaled by the rhetoric were inversely proportional to experienced depths of doubt and despair. The Jews' faith in their own identity was in jeopardy.

Two problems further plagued the assertion of election. First, as we have seen, the extension of an identity, once validated by specific activities, to individuals unable to point to such acts in their own lives had watered down the idea of election. The Puritans' halfway covenant, although it offered only provisional membership in the elect, served to blur the boundary between the saints and all others,[50] allowing ambitions to be cloaked in the mantle of chosenness. This led to guilt that the claim was undeserved, and the suspicion that one's existence was unjustified, lacking the mission that could legitimize it. It also could lead to the enlargement of individual ego in the absence of traditional constraints imposed by the group. Traditionally, chosenness strengthened both identities at once. The self was enlarged through the aggrandizement of the group ("Jews are chosen, so I am, too"), while achievements of individual Jews redounded to the credit of the group as a whole. Conversely, if an individual lacked confidence that he or she was living up to the terms of the collective calling, he nevertheless remained part of a group that plausibly could claim to be observing the covenant faithfully. Once the ties binding individuals to the chosen group have been attenuated, however, neither of these dynamics can function. The individual's guilt remains unassuaged; his or her ambition is neither contained nor ennobled. The energy generated by the claim to election, and the need to demonstrate it, is channeled into personal achievement—for example, success in the Jews' chosen callings of business and the professions—and no longer serves the calling of the group as a whole, although it does, of course, continue to foster group pride (the classic Jewish count of Nobel prizewinners). Integration and authenticity—difficult enough in such circumstances, as observed previously—are further threatened by the invocation of a collective calling to legitimize individual achievement.[51]

Finally, there is the problem that assertiveness of the collective Jewish self against its larger world would lead to tension, with Gentiles left out of the claim to chosenness. The Puritan's proclamation of self reechoed harmlessly off the trees of their wilderness, and came at the expense of a nonelect from whom they were separated by an ocean. American Jews, however, lived among neighbors whose resentment of Jewish pretensions to election could only be assuaged (and even then only partially) by rhetorical appeal to America's own election. You also are a chosen people, the rabbis repeatedly told America: the more we stress the original chosenness, the more well-founded your derivative claim will be. Hence, the chorus of rabbinic hymns of praise to America was heard, and the identification of Judaism with democracy, especially during the war years, when both the Jews and democracy seemed imperiled. Such arguments, resting on the identification of Jewish with American interests, could never be entirely persuasive. However, the problem that an identity founded on chosenness posed to Jewish acceptance in America has been mitigated by appeal to that very same chosenness—enlarged to include all America.

Thus, it is two ideas, "objective" and "subjective public identity," that shape the Jewish view of self. Jews responded to negative, Gentile images of Jews as clannish, elitist, or simply alien. They sought to exploit approbation extended to God's chosen people. They acted to mute or expunge prayers or declarations that might be offensive to Gentiles or became unacceptable to Jews who internalized the "objective" viewpoint of the outsider. The process is nicely highlighted in a debate between Mordecai Kaplan and the Christian theologian Franklin Littell. When the latter insisted that the Jews were God's chosen people, Kaplan replied that such a belief precluded acceptance of Jews by Gentile Americans, and so was unacceptable.[52] The third and fourth generations could move to reemphasize beliefs regarded as offensive in the second generation, because the pressure from the outside had been removed. In other words, Jews became less sensitive to Gentile criticism, because Gentiles had proven to be less offended by Jewish particularism than Jews had feared.

In sum, then, the favored theme of chosenness, sounded in countless sermons and debates, enabled the Jewish community to define and legitimate itself as a somewhat separate religious and ethnic entity. The rhetorical strategy of identification was employed to minimize the disparity between such claims to election and the reality of daily life. Doubts that the Jews were chosen by God, or that God could have chosen them for suffering, were met with reassertions of the doctrine and assurances that both the doubt and the persecution were experienced by previous generations of Jews. In this way, even nonobservant Jews were able to share in the pride and confidence conferred by belief in election, perhaps stimulating individual achievement outside the sphere of collective activities mandated by the traditional covenant. Belief in the choosing God was abandoned, the historicity of the moment of choosing (described in the Bible) was denied, traditional observances were ignored, and yet individual Jews remained Jews and so chosen. Identity had been fabricated from an inherited core, and could be transmitted.

V.

The complexity of these dynamics is bewildering, leading us to wonder how a single set of associations, conjoined in the single image of a chosen people, could provoke and contain such a variety of social and psychological effects. Moreover, if the Puritan case so resembles that of American Jews (despite the many differences between the situations of the two groups), we are further inclined to suspect that the symbol of chosenness that was shared by the two claimants to divine election may itself contain the elements that give rise to the dynamics that we have observed. The symbol itself, then, deserves our attention.

One source of its power, surely, as well as its usefulness in the fabrication of identity, lies in the connotation that the chosen one is defined out of the mass or totality. That is, chosenness stands against nonexistence rather than mere nonelection. The alternative is not merely anonymity, but the chaos of the void. This idea of individuation, implicit in the very notion of a transcendent personal God, makes it seem virtually inevitable that His distinctiveness be complemented and reflected in that of a distinctive people removed from the lot of all nations into a unique fate. Thus, Deuteronomy invokes the chosenness of Israel to argue for centralization of the cult, stating implicitly that the one God could be worshipped properly by the one people only at one central site—a plurality of altars would not do. To be is to be one; to be one is to be distinct from all others and know oneself to be so—at the essence, at the center.[53]

Yet, if one has been chosen by God, the choice must be a blessing—the result of unfathomable love rather than of caprice. The word "chosen" is used sparingly in the Bible, to convey the passion of the choosing. Its antonym is not "considered impartially" or "ignored," but "despised."[54] Choices are momentous. Precisely for that reason, it is all the more difficult to live up to the promise that the choice implies—to earn one's election, as it were. How does one earn existence, let alone existence at the center, the special love of the Creator? What can one do? What is enough? Only if the Chooser has specified His demands one can hope to live with a sense of suffering. The demands having been specified, however, our inability to meet them is manifest.

Notes

1. The title is borrowed from Michael Zuckerman, "The Fabrication of Identity in Early America," *William and Mary Quarterly* 34 (1977), pp. 184–5.
2. "The Condition of Jewish Belief" [reprinted from *Commentary* (August 1966)] in *Being Jewish in America* (New York: Schocken, 1979), p. 20.
3. See Arnold Eisen, *The Chosen People in America: A Study in Jewish Religious Ideology* (Bloomington: Indiana University Press, 1983).
4. Ibid., ch. 3–6.
5. Sacvan Bercovitch, *The American Jeremiad* (Madison: University of Wisconsin Press, 1978), p. xi.
6. Solomon Schechter, "Election of Israel," in *Aspects of Rabbinic Theology* (New York: Schocken Books, 1969), p. 57.
7. See the *Yearbook of the Central Conference of American Rabbis*, 1937, pp. 97–9.
8. Cf. Frederic A. Doppelt, "Are the Jews a Chosen People?" *Liberal Judaism* (February 1942), pp. 6–8; Samuel S. Cohon, "The Doctrine of the Chosen People," *Liberal Judaism* (May 1946), pp. 31–8, 48; Abba Hillel Silver, *Where Judaism Differed* (Philadelphia: Jewish Publication Society, 1957), pp. 1–5.
9. Silver, ibid., p. 82.
10. Jakob J. Petuchowski, "Where Judaism Differed," *Commentary* (August 1957), pp. 153–9.
11. Daniel Jeremy Silver, "Beyond the Apologetics of Mission," *Journal of the Central Conference of American Rabbis* (October 1968), pp. 55–62; "A Lover's Quarrel with the Mission of Israel," *JCCAR* (June 1967), pp. 8–18.
12. Eugene Borowitz, "On Celebrating Sinai," *JCCAR* (June 1966), pp. 12, 16; "The Chosen People Concept as It Affects Jewish Life in the Diaspora," *Journal of Ecumenical Studies* 12 (1975), pp. 553–68; Emil Fackenheim, *Quest for Past and Future* (Boston: Beacon, 1968).
13. Mordecai M. Kaplan, *Judaism as a Civilization* (New York: Schocken Books, 1967), pp. 7, 15, 22–4, 36–43.
14. Mordecai M. Kaplan, *The Future of the American Jew* (New York: Macmillan, 1948), pp. 226–9.
15. Louis Finkelstein, "The Things That Unite Us" *Rabbinical Assembly of America* (1927), p. 43; see Louis Ginzberg's less equivocal defense of chosenness in *PRAA* (1932), p. 306.
16. Ben Zion Bokser, "Doctrine of the Chosen People," *Contemporary Jewish Record* (June 1941), pp. 243–52; "The Election of Israel," *Conservative Judaism* (July 1947), pp. 17–25; "The Future of the American Jewish Community," *PRAA* (1948), pp. 194–9, 226–7.
17. Preface, *The Sabbath and Festival Prayer Book* (New York: United Synagogue of America, 1946), pp. vi–ix. The preface was written by Robert Gordis.
18. Arnold Eisen, "Theology, Sociology, Ideology: Jewish Thought in America, 1925–1955," *Modern Judaism* 2 (1982), pp. 91–103.
19. Kenneth Burke, *A Rhetoric of Motives* (Berkeley: University of California Press, 1969), p. 49.
20. Ibid., pp. 41, 162.

21. Ibid., pp. 177–9, 208; see also p. 111: "In this sense, even the most theological of terms can be implicitly modified by very accurate nontheological meanings which, though they may not show through the expression itself, were clearly felt by the persons using it"—as were the implications of Israel's election. For more on identification in general, see pp. 19–29.

22. Cf. Bercovitch, *American Jeremiad*, ch. 1–3; Sacvan Bercovitch, *The Puritan Origins of the American Self* (New Haven, CT: Yale University Press, 1975).

23. Bercovitch, *Puritan Origins*, p. 94.

24. Bercovitch, *American Jeremiad*, ch. 4–5, especially pp. 152–4.

25. See Derek Parfit, "Personal Identity," *Philosophical Review* 80 (January 1971), pp. 3–4; "Later Selves and Moral Principles," in Alan Montefiore, ed. *Philosophy and Personal Relations*, (London: Routledge Kegan Paul, 1973).

26. Erik Erikson, *Gandhi's Truth* (New York: W.W. Norton, 1969), p. 266.

27. Herbert C. Kelman, "The Place of Jewish Identity in the Development of Personal Identity," a working paper prepared for the American Jewish Committee's Colloquium on Jewish Education and Jewish Identity (November 1974).

28. Philip Rieff, *The Triumph of the Therapeutic: Uses of Faith after Freud* (New York: Harper Torchbooks, 1968), pp. 2–5.

29. Philip Rieff, *Fellow Teachers* (New York: Delta, 1972), p. 73.

30. Lionel Trilling, *Sincerity and Authenticity* (London: Oxford University Press, 1974).

31. Simon Herman, *Jewish Identity: A Social Psychological Perspective* (Beverly Hills: Sage Publications, 1977), p. 30. The distinction is based on work by psychologist D. R. Miller.

32. Felix Levy, "The Uniqueness of Israel," in Sefton D. Temkin, ed. *His Own Torah: Felix A. Levy Memorial Volume* (New York: Jonathan David, 1969), pp. 161–73.

33. Milton Steinberg, *The Making of the Modern Jew* (New York: Behrman House, 1948), p. 247.

34. Julian Morgenstern, "Nation, People, Religion—What Are We?" (Cincinnati: *Union of American Hebrew Congregations*, 1943).

35. *Yearbook of the Central Conference of American Rabbis*, (1939), pp. 331–48.

36. Horace M. Kallen, "On the Impact of Universal Judaism," in Kallem, *Judaism at Bay* (New York: Bloch, 1932), pp. 21–2.

37. The Columbus Platform: see endnote 7.

38. Horace M. Kallen, "The Dynamics of the Jewish Center" (1930), *Judaism at Bay*, pp. 232, 237, 245; "Jewish Education and the Future of the American Jewish Community" (1943), in Judah Pilch, ed., *Of Them Which Say They are Jews and Other Essays on the Jewish Struggle for Survival* (New York: Bloch, 1954), pp. 191–2; "To Educate Jews in Our Time" (1933), Ibid., p. 176.

39. Mordecai M. Kaplan, *The Meaning of God in Modern Jewish Religion* (New York: Reconstructionist Press, 1962), pp. 188–94, 303; *Judaism Without Supernaturalism* (New York: Reconstructionist Press, 1958), pp. 28–33.

40. Zuckerman, "Fabrication," p. 211.

41. For a discussion of these stereotypes see Eisen, *Chosen People*, ch. 6.

42. Philip Roth, comments in a symposium on "The Jewish Intellectual and Jewish Identity," *Congress Bi-Weekly* (Sept. 16, 1963), pp. 21, 39.

43. Burke, *Rhetoric*, p. 58.

44. Israel Goldstein, "Are People More Religious Than They Admit," *The Definition of a Good Jew* (New York: Congress B'nai Jeshurun, 1927), p. 13.

45. Simon Greenberg, "The Birthright" in Greenberg, *Living as a Jew Today* (New York: Behrman, 1940), pp. 3–4, 21–2.

46. Bercovitch, *Puritan Origins* p. 103; see also p. 120.

47. Zuckerman, "Fabrication," p. 198.

48. John Downame, *The Christian Warfare* (London: Felix Kyngston, 1612), in the "epistle dedicatory."

49. See the references in endnote 13, as well as *Judaism in Transition* (New York: Behrman, 1941), pp. 102, 123, 159; and Kaplan, *Meaning of God*, pp. 94–103. For Kallen's similar arguments, see "Universal Judaism," pp. 21–2; *Zionism and World Politics* (Garden City: Doubleday Page, 1921), p. vii.

50. Bercovitch, *Puritan Origins*, p. 94.

51. For a discussion of these dynamics in nineteenth-century England, see Alan Mintz, *George Eliot and the Novel of Vocation* (Cambridge, MA: Harvard University Press, 1978).

52. Franklin H. Littell, "Thoughts About the Future of Christianity and Judaism: A Christian View of Reconstructionism," *Reconstructionist* April 4, 1947, pp. 10–6; April 18, 19XX, pp. 16–22; and Kaplan's reply, "We Still Think We Are Right," May 2, 1947, pp. 14–9.

53. This discussion is indebted to Rivka Scharf Kluger, *Psyche and Bible: Three Old Testament Themes* (New York: Spring Publications, 1974), pp. 1–42.

54. See, for example, II Kings 23:27; Psalm 78:67–68; Isaiah 7:15, 41:18.

5

Is the Cup Half-Full or Half-Empty?: Perspectives on the Future of the American Jewish Community

Chaim I. Waxman

From the early 1960s until several years ago, there was more or less of a consensus among social scientists of American Jewry that a steady decline was occurring in both the quality and quantity of American Jewish life and the American Jewish community. In the spring of 1964, for example, a very gloomy prognosis for the future of American Jewry was provided in two widely read and discussed articles. One was a cover story for *Look Magazine* entitled, "The Vanishing American Jew," which focused on the declining American Jewish birth rate, and the other was Marshall Sklare's article in *Commentary* entitled, "Intermarriage and the Jewish Future," in which he warned that intermarriage is "a matter more crucial to Jewish survival than any other," and projected a bleak outlook for the Jewish future.[1] Empirical studies of American Jewish communities throughout the 1960s and 1970s confirmed the continuing decline of the birth rate and rise of the intermarriage rate and, in 1977, a *Midstream* article argued the possibility of a drop of the American Jewish population to less than a million by the year 2076.[2] Although most social scientists argued that that was an exaggeration, virtually no one questioned the trend of decline. In fact, the evidence of decline, both in proportion to the total American population and in absolute numbers, was dramatically evident. While in 1937, according to demographer Sidney Goldstein, Jews comprised 3.7 percent of the total American population, by the onset of the 1980s they were between 2.4 and 2.5 percent.[3] Nor was it anticipated that there would be any growth from one of the other major sources of population growth, immigration. Jewish immigration to the United States was very low and was expected to remain so, because the prospects for substantial Jewish immigration from the Soviet Union appeared, and continue to appear, bleak, and any other Jewish immigration to the United States was deemed negligible.

During the 1980s, however, there was a distinct change in the prognoses offered by social scientists of American Jewry. In 1983, I argued that there had been a definite shift in the assimilatory trends of American Jews, from what they had been during the first three generations of Eastern European American Jewry to that of the fourth generation. A series of developments during the mid-1960s to mid-1970s, I argued, have resulted in a much more survivalist-oriented American Jewish community, and it now seems much less appropriate to apply "straight-line assimilation" theory to the case of America's Jews.[4]

In 1984–86, there emerged a group of sociologists and journalists of American Jewry who have presented what might be called "the new Jewish sociology." Sociologists Calvin Goldscheider and Steven M. Cohen and journalists Charles E. Silberman and Leonard Fein are among the central figures within this group. Taken as a whole, they present a new revisionist perspective that sharply challenges a number of basic assumptions and, indeed, the outlook of the earlier students of American Jewry. In place of the earlier gloomy prognosis, the new Jewish sociology presents a rather optimistic, even rosy, picture of the current state and future prospects of American Jewry. One popular book, based heavily on the research of the new Jewish sociology, said that American Jews are "a certain people," with the emphasis on the certainty of this special people.[5]

This article analyzes the issues in the current debate between "the new Jewish sociology" and those who still adhere to the more traditional perspective, and evaluates the merits of each based on the available empirical evidence. At the outset, it should be stressed that there are a number of inherent weaknesses in the extent of our scientific knowledge of the national sociological patterns of America's Jews, not the least being that we have very little national data. Almost all of the available data come from local community studies that were conducted and analyzed by different researchers. Thus, in addition to the possibility of local distinctiveness, some of the conflicting national projections may derive from differences in the ways the variables were defined and the data collected in the local studies on which the national projections are based.

Above and beyond these technical issues, however, it is shown that much of the debate hinges on the question of what standards of reference are used for comparison and evaluation. Moreover, it is shown that there are several interrelated metasociologic issues that have given rise to a sharp difference between most sociologists of American Jewry and a group of religiously traditional rabbis and other Jewish communal workers over the issue of the future of the American Jewish community, and that these, too, are rooted in the different standards of evaluation used by each.

It would be a distortion simply to characterize the debate as one between optimists and pessimists. Rather, it is a debate between those who foresee the ultimate inability of the American Jewish community to survive, because they foresee the total assimilation and disappearance of large segments of the American Jewish population into the larger American society and culture; and those who provide reinterpretations of some of the older trends and evidence of newer ones, which they foresee as impeding and, perhaps, even reversing the decline. Essentially, it is a debate between empiric—but not necessarily ideological—assimilationists and survivalists.[6] It is in this sense, and solely for the sake of brevity, that the two perspectives are herein designated as optimist and pessimist.

As indicated, the two main areas of contention, insofar as the question is whether the forecast for the future of American Jewry is rosy or gloomy, are intermarriage and the birth rate. Of these two, the issue of intermarriage is probably the more complex, because it involves a variety of subsets of questions, many of which are ideologically laden. But the issue of the birth rate is also very complex, because the multiplicity of variables that determine birth rates makes them so difficult to predict.

Those who express concern over the Jewish birth rate base their anxieties both on the demographic evidence indicating that American Jews have always had a lower-than-average birth rate; that the national American birth rate has declined during the past two decades and, therefore, there is every reason to believe that the Jewish birth rate will continue to decline, as well; and, that intermarried couples tend to have fewer children than couples in endogamous Jewish marriages and, as will be discussed below, the intermarriage rate is climbing. In addition, studies of the fertility expectations of women in their childbearing years, conducted in the 1970s, indicated that although there was a decline in the gap between the expectations of Jewish and non-Jewish women, Jewish women still expected to have few children. Accordingly, Goldstein projected that, "in the absence of a drastic reversal in ongoing patterns, a decline seems probable."[7] While rejecting as exaggerated Bergman's predictions of an American Jewish population of, at best, less than one million by the year 2076, Goldstein suggests that it would probably be accurate to predict a population of between 3 to 4 million American Jews by the end of the 21st century.

Two years later, demographers Uziel Schmelz and Sergio DellaPergola wrote a more detailed demographic analysis, in which their projections were not quite as pessimistic. They presented eight different possible scenarios, none of which spelled imminent doom for the American Jewish community.

However, even they did see a population decline, ranging from about 5.2 million in the worst case, to about 5.6 million in the best.[8]

The issue of the birth rate does not only have relevance in terms of the size of the American Jewish population. It also has implications for its median age, and this is a related concern for those who see declining birth rates. American Jews have a higher median age level than does the total American population. They have a greater proportion of elderly—that is 65 years and older—and of those in later middle age. These trends are likely to continue as long as the birth rate remains low, it is argued, with severe economic and social implications for both the American Jewish population and for the resources and policies of its organized communal structure. To many, these trends place a large question mark on the future of the organized community's ability to maintain the levels and quality of activities and services it has provided until now.

Until recently, the only response offered by those who were not particularly distressed by the evidence of a declining American Jewish population was that what counts is quality, not quantity. The nonpessimists argued that Jews were always a numerically small people, relatively, and that the quality of Jewish life is more important than its quantity. Jewish couples may be having fewer children, but, in doing so, they are able to provide a higher quality to the lives of these children than they could if they had more. The leaders of the organized American Jewish community, they argued, should pay more attention to the quality of Jewish communal life and cease worrying—as if they were, indeed, worried—about its quantity. To claims such as this, some, such as Milton Himmelfarb, responded that without quantity there will be no quality to talk about.

A very different and, indeed, revisionist response was sketched out in 1984, and presented more systematically in 1986, in the work of two of the major proponents of the new sociology. According to Cohen and Goldscheider, there is no question of either quality or quantity. They argue that even in quantitative terms there is no reason to believe that there will be any significant decline in the American Jewish population. In contrast to the analyses of previous data that indicated there would be a decline in the rate of marriage among Jews, especially among Jewish women, and that they would have fewer children, Cohen and Goldscheider argue that their work indicates that Jewish women are simply marrying later and delaying childbearing, but finally have an average of 2.1 children, which is replacement level. So, even in quantitative terms, the future seems relatively stable.[9]

Since birth rates are notoriously difficult to predict, most of the pessimists remain unconvinced. The problem for them is, however, that they are also unable to present any convincing viable policy recommendations to encourage American Jewish couples to have more children. There is no evidence that warnings by religious and other communal leaders have any impact because, apparently, most couples do not make their childbearing decisions based on what is deemed to be good for the community. Rather, they seem to make those decisions based on what they see as appropriate for themselves and their own children.

Nor do community-sponsored economic incentives, such as tuition fee reductions in Jewish schools for those with a higher-than-average number of children, seem to have any impact. In fact, the evidence from cross-national studies on birth rates indicates an almost universal inverse relationship between gross national product level and birth rate; also, within societies there is an inverse relationship between socioeconomic status and birth rate. Nor have the pronatalist social policies of various Western European countries, Canada, and Israel, been able to reduce that inverse relationship. It would thus appear that all the pessimists can do is hope that the revisionists are proven correct, and the American Jewish birth rate will actually remain stable.

With respect to intermarriage, one empirical matter on which there is consensus is that the rate of intermarriage has risen sharply during the past quarter of a century. Until the early 1960s, American Jews were characterized as an endogamous group; that is, the majority of Jews married Jews. Since then, while precise data are difficult to obtain, for a variety of reasons, the available evidence suggests that, nationally, approximately 30 percent of all Jews who marry marry non-Jews.[10] However, this figure is deceptive, because it obscures wide regional variations. For example, the intermarriage rate is lower in the Greater New York City area than it is in Los Angeles, and it is highest in Denver, where it reaches well over 50 percent.[11] Even with this in mind, what the increase in the intermarriage rate means, both quantitatively and qualitatively, is the crux of the disagreement.

There are two basically different types of intermarriage, namely, mixed marriage and conversionary marriage, that have very different consequences. In the former, the non-Jewish spouse remains non-Jewish; whereas in the latter, the non-Jewish spouse converts to Judaism. The available evidence strongly suggests that the levels of Jewish ritual practice are substantially higher in conversionary Jewish households than in mixed-marriage households.[12] However, we do not have the longitudinal studies necessary to determine the future Jewish identification of the children of even conversionary intermarried couples.[13] Nor do we have in-depth qualitative studies to determine the impact of having both Jewish and non-Jewish relatives on children of even conversionary intermarried couples. We do not know how having non-Jewish close relatives affect their own sense of Jewish identity, nor do we know whether, in the future, they will continue to identify as Jews.

From a strictly demographic perspective, the impact of intermarriage is largely dependent on the proportion of conversionary marriages among all intermarriages. This is so because the available data indicate that it is extremely rare for American Jews to leave the Jewish group overtly. Apostasy, in which case the Jew converts to another religion, appears to be virtually non-existent, and even cases of defection from the Jewish population without joining another religion are statistically insignificant. However, as demographers Schmelz and DellaPergola point out, the data may be biased because they inherently omit those ex-Jewish men and, probably even more commonly, women who live in non-Jewish neighborhoods, behave in non-Jewish ways, or, in other ways, manage to evade the researchers conducting population studies for Jewish communal organizations.[14]

Assuming that, in any case, the rate of defection from the Jewish population is low, intermarriage need not spell decline if there is a high rate of conversion to Judaism. If a large proportion of the formerly non-Jewish spouses convert to Judaism, not only is there no inevitable demographic loss; there may well be a gain. The optimists, such as Calvin Goldscheider, convey the general impression "that the level of conversion to Judaism has increased and significant numbers of intermarried couples, usually over 50 percent, raise their children as Jews."[15] Silberman argues even more strongly that intermarriage does not pose a threat to Jewish continuity in America. He strongly argues that "if half the children of intermarriages are raised as Jews, there will be no net reduction in the number of Jews, no matter how high the intermarriage rate is,"[16] and he, too, argues that evidence indicates an increasing tendency for intermarried couples to raise their children as Jews.

With respect to Goldscheider's assertion of an increasing level of conversion, however, a number of recent studies paint a rather different picture. Their data indicate that not only is the conversion rate not increasing, it is decreasing. For example, in Greater Los Angeles, the second-largest Jewish population center, not only in the United States but in the world, Neil Sandberg found that mixed marriages outnumber conversionary marriages among all Jewish intermarriages by three to one.[17] The rate of mixed marriage increases by generation, from 11.6 percent among first generation American Jews, to 43.5 percent among those in the fourth generation.[18] Both types of intermarriage are related to religious affiliation, with the rates varying from 8.3 percent for the Orthodox, 20 percent for the Conservative, 37.7 percent for Reform, to a high of 66.7 percent for the unaffiliated of the fourth generation.[19] In addition, Sandberg found a higher rate of intermarriage in remarriages.[20] Given the rising divorce and remarriage rates of America's Jews, it is likely that the intermarriage rates will rise even higher.

Sandberg's is not the only recent study to find such patterns. Bruce Phillips's studies of Jewish communities on the West Coast also found that the proportion of mixed marriages among all intermarriages is rising rather than declining, as Goldscheider suggests.[21] In Denver, for example, the percentage of intermarried households rises from 53 percent among those aged 30 to 39 to 72 percent among those aged 18 to 29, and the percentage of conversionary households among the intermarried households decreases from 25 percent among those aged 30 to 39 to 9 percent among those aged 18 to 29. Similar patterns were also found in Phoenix, with the percentage of intermarried households increasing from 43 percent to 72 percent, and the percentage of conversionary households among intermarried households decreasing from 40 percent to 16.6 percent between the 30 to 39 and 18 to 29 age cohorts.[22]

Nor are such patterns limited to the West Coast. Although the percentages are definitely smaller, similar patterns manifest themselves in the East as well. For example, in Philadelphia, the percentage of intermarried households increases from 27 percent among those aged 30 to 39 to 38 percent among those aged 18 to 29, and the percentage of conversionary households among intermarried households decreases from 16 percent among the 30 to 39-year-olds to 12 percent among those in the 18 to 29-year-old cohort.[23] Even in New York, which has one of the lowest intermarriage rates in the country, less than 25 percent of the non-Jewish spouses in those intermarriages converted to Judaism. More than 75 percent of those intermarriages are mixed marriages.[24] If these patterns are characteristic of the national American Jewish trends, there is a sound basis for questioning the optimism of the "new Jewish sociology."

On the other hand, as the optimists point out, intermarriage is not an isolated variable. The extent to which intermarriage is indicative of the decline the community is also related to the response of the community to intermarriage. Until recently, it was accepted as axiomatic that Jews who intermarry have rejected the Jewish community, and their intermarriage is their final step in leaving that community. The new Jewish sociology argues that this most frequently is not the case. Conditions have changed, they emphasize, and many, if not most, of those who intermarry do so for reasons unrelated to their feelings about being Jewish or the Jewish community. They marry for love or other reasons and, at the time of their marriage, they do not consider their Jewishness to be a problem. It is only later, usually when they have children, that the Jewish issue arises. When it does arise, frequently they find that the Jewish community is unwilling to accept them. Their subsequent alienation from the Jewish community, so the argument goes, was not of their own doing. As Goldscheider notes, on the basis of his analysis of studies of the Boston Jewish community, "No ideological basis for intermarriage was uncovered which favors out-marriages among Jews, nor is there any evidence that intermarriage reflects values emphasizing assimilation. Younger Jews in their late teens and early twenties see little connection between intermarriage and total assimilation."[25] If alienation from the Jewish community does occur, it is a consequence of the Jewish community's unwillingness to accept them.

Both the reality of the sharp rise in intermarriage and this new perspective on the social psychology of intermarriage have sparked major policy changes within the organized American Jewish community. Today it is extremely rare to find the traditional Jewish rites of mourning being practiced by the families of those who intermarry. The only organized communal refusal to accept inter-marriage is that of the relatively small Syrian Jewish community, which has a firm policy prohibiting any conversion, no matter how sincere the particular individual involved might be, so that no member of that community even thinks that his or her intermarriage might ever be accepted. Aside from this rare exception, no similar explicit organized communal action exists. All of the religious branches of American Judaism have, to one degree or another, adopted a stance which David Singer has characterized as "living with inter-marriage."[26]

Reform Judaism has taken the most explicit and dramatic steps. It first adopted as policy a proposal to embark on a major outreach campaign to encourage the conversion of the non-Jewish spouses among intermarried couples. While no such *de jure* formal policy has been adopted by either Conservative or Orthodox Judaism, several Conservative and Modern Ortho-dox rabbis have recently written articles urging that traditional Judaism change its stance from one that discourages toward one that encourages conversion. Increasingly, however, it is de facto policy of most Conservative and Orthodox rabbis to encourage conversion among mixed-marriage couples.

The second major step of Reform Judaism in this regard was the adoption of a new criterion, at least in terms of the last two thousand years, of determining Jewish status. Whereas traditional Judaism historically has defined a Jew as one born of a Jewish mother or one who converted to Judaism, Reform Judaism's policy of patrilineal descent now recognizes as a Jew the child of either a Jewish mother or a Jewish father, providing the child wishes to so be recognized. The objective of this new policy is to keep the children of intermar-ried parents within the community.

Although there has been staunch criticism of this policy of patrilineal descent from both the Conservative and Orthodox rabbinic bodies, in addition to some dissent from within the Central Conference of American Rabbis (Reform) itself, there has been no major joint effort to rescind it, and the whole issue has largely vanished from the organizational agendas of those rabbinic organiza-tions. But it has not been ignored entirely.

There is a small group of traditionalist rabbis and communal workers who see the issues of intermarriage and patrilineal descent as relevant not only to the size of the American Jewish community but, at least as important, to the basic corporate unity of American Jewry as well. Among this group are such notables as Rabbis Norman Lamm, president of Yeshiva University; Irving Greenberg, founder of the National Jewish Center for Learning and Leader-ship (CLAL); Haskell Lookstein; David Novak; and Walter Wurzburger. In contrast to the perspectives of the social scientists, both old and new, this group views the condition of American Jewry to be of crisis proportions. Reuven Bulka, for example, defines this issue as contributing to what he perceives as "the coming cataclysm."[27] While not all in this group have expressed explicitly their concerns in cataclysmic terms, their expressions of imminent crisis justify labeling them cataclysmists.

To understand the concerns of the cataclysmists, it must be recognized that any evaluation is, at least implicitly, based on some comparative perspective. Good and bad, healthy and sick, strong and weak are all relative terms, and the social scientists use different standards and bases of comparison to evaluate the condition of American Jewry from those of the cataclysmists. Most frequently, the social scientists compare American Jews with other ethnic groups in the United States. From that perspective, the new sociology is, indeed, correct in being optimistic about the future of American Jewry.

American Jews are among the most highly successful groups socioeconomically; there has been a decline in anti-Semitism and, thus, they are more socially accepted; and they have been able to maintain a stronger sense of group identity than most other ethnic groups in America. Despite the ideology of cultural pluralism, the melting pot appears to be the reality for most ethnic groups in the United States. For Jews, it is much less so, and not because American Jews are oppressed; they are not. Thus, even the pessimistic sociologists are only concerned about the long-range prospects for Jewish survival in America. For the immediate future, neither group of sociologists sees any threats.

The cataclysmists, however, use a different standard of measurement. As was indicated previously, most of them are traditionalist rabbis. For them, the standard of measurement is neither other ethnic groups in America nor the American Jewish community of a generation or two ago. Rather, it is the historical standards of the traditional Jewish community. Thus, this group finds no comfort in the facts that American Jews still have a high marriage rate and lower divorce and intermarriage rates than others. They are deeply concerned that the rates are so different from what they have been traditionally in the Jewish community.

In addition, and perhaps even more worrisome for this group, are a number of issues of *halakhah* (traditional Jewish religious law) that threaten the corporate life of American Jewry, and to which most social scientists are oblivious. In brief, there are two issues related to the trends noted earlier that are of serious concern to the religiously traditional (Orthodox and traditional Conservative) rabbinic leadership. Both have to do with standards for which the patterns of other American ethnic groups are irrelevant, namely, *halakhah*. The first involves the issue of divorce and the fact that the traditionalists will not recognize the validity of Jewish divorces that do not conform with *halakhah*. This entails not only a religiopolitical struggle between rabbis of different persuasions; it has the potential for very grave consequences for Jewish communal life, because it means that members of one segment of the community, the religiously traditionalist, will not be able to marry an increasing number (given the rising rates of divorce and remarriage of American Jews) of those from the nontraditionalist segment of the community. Thus, in 1986, a number of concerned traditionalist rabbis put forth novel proposals for joint rabbinic courts to which Orthodox, Conservative, and Reform would adhere but which none would dominate.[28] Thus far, these proposals have not been warmly received in either the traditional or the nontraditional communities, and their chances of being operationalized seem remote.

The other issue also derives from the fact that *halakhah* is the standard for the religiously traditional, while it is not so for others, and it manifests itself with respect to intermarriage. For the religiously traditional, a Jew is someone who was born of a Jewish mother or has undergone a religious conversion in accordance with dictates of *halakhah*. Most Reform rabbis do not convert according to *halakhah* and, as was discussed earlier, they also accept patrilineal descent as a criterion for determining status as a Jew. This means that religiously traditional Jews will not recognize the Jewish status of an increasing number of those who are part of the religiously nontraditionalist community. To the traditionalists, these unprecedented schisms in the Jewish community are indeed cataclysmic. Nor should it be assumed that it is only for a small group of traditionalists that these are problems. On the substance of the issues there is no disagreement between the Modern, Sectarian, and Hasidic Orthodox, and Traditional Conservative. Rather, the only difference is in approach. Whereas most of the Sectarian and Hasidic Orthodox are fatalistic and have, more or less, signed off those who are not Orthodox, the Modern Orthodox and Traditional Conservative see an impending cataclysm and are attempting to prevent it. In either case, these are issues that have major consequences for the future of the American Jewish community. One of the reasons many social scientists of American Jewry fail to investigate matters such as these is that they rely on demographic data and have little grounding in either the sociology of religion or traditional Judaism, and, therefore, are oblivious to them.

Above and beyond all of the issues discussed thus far lies a fundamental disagreement between those who are confident about the future of the American Jewish community and those who have expressed varying degrees of concern for its future. Implicitly or explicitly, the two groups divide over the question of the nature of the corporate unity of the Jewish community. Those who express concern about the future of American Jewry maintain that what keeps the community together is what historically has kept all Jewish communities together; namely, a firm belief and commitment to the principles of Judaism manifested in the observance of its laws and traditions. Throughout history, this group argues, the Jewish people have maintained themselves as a people because they adhered to a religion that defined them explicitly as separate and distinct from the non-Jews around them. In sociological parlance, a basic function of the religion (although not necessarily its ultimate purpose) has been, and continues to be, to maintain the distinctiveness of the Jewish people. This was the view of the tenth-century Jewish philosopher, Saadia Gaon, who stated that "our nation of the children of Israel is a nation only by virtue of its laws,"[29] and this was the meaning of Ahad Ha-am's famous dictum, "More than the Jews kept the Sabbath, the Sabbath kept them."[30] In one way or another, they both expressed the inherent integrating function of religion, a belief that was most elaborately formulated in the literature of modern sociology by the nineteenth-century French sociologist, Emile Durkheim.[31]

Implicitly agreeing with this classical perspective, the pessimists view the changes taking place within the American Jewish community as the consequences of modernization and, concomitantly, secularization, which inevitably lead to the decline of the Jewish community. Living in an open, modern, non-Jewish society in which Jews aspire to and achieve almost complete integration, they argue, leads to the decline of Jewish culture; that is, Jewish practices and values and, ultimately, the Jewish community.

To one degree or another, the new Jewish sociology challenges the premises of the culturalist perspective. Some argue that secularization, in the sense of the decline of religion, is not necessarily the concomitant variable of modernization and change, and that there are clear indications of the persistence of Jewish values and practices in contemporary American Jewish society. For example, the lighting of Hanukkah candles and partaking of a Passover Seder continue to be widespread within the American Jewish community.[32] Moreover, some contend there are manifestations within American Jewry of a strengthening in some aspects of intrinsic Jewish culture.

The most theoretically sophisticated and explicit challenge to the fundamental premise of the classical perspective is that of Calvin Goldscheider and Alan Zuckerman.[33] They explicitly reject the premise that Jewish cohesion was maintained by Jewish values. Rather, they contend, Jewish cohesion is maintained by social structural forces. Through an analysis of modernization and its development in a wide range of Jewish communities they argue that it has not nor must it lead to a decline in Jewish group cohesion. Nor was that cohesion maintained by either ties to tradition or anti-Semitism. Rather, Jewish cohesion was maintained by the structural forces of both occupational and residential concentration; that is, Jews lived together in urban areas and Jews worked in occupations in which there were large numbers of other Jews. Since those same structural conditions persist in American society—Jews continue to be concentrated residentially in the urban centers of American society and they continue to be concentrated occupationally—those structural forces, rather than any traditional Jewish culture, will continue to ensure their group survival. "For most Jews most of the time," they argue, "the constraints of economic position and opportunity, place of residence, political limitations and rights, and tugs of family and friends have outweighed personal convictions. Where Jews share similar residences, schools, occupations, organizations, and friends their community has the highest level of cohesion, whether the individual Jews value or desire this interaction, whether they think each other apostates or reactionaries."[34] A year or so later, in his own work on the American Jew, based on his analysis of several studies of Bostonian community, Goldscheider made the same strong argument. "The Jewish community in America has changed; indeed has been transformed. But in that process, it has emerged as a dynamic source of networks and resources binding together family, friends, and neighbors, ethnically and religiously. As a community, Jews are surviving in America, even as some individuals enter and leave the community. Indeed, in every way the American Jewish community represents for Jews and other ethnic minorities a paradigm of continuity and change in modern pluralist society."[35]

Whether the optimists or the pessimists are correct is still too early to tell. The fact that both are able to support their arguments with empirical data only reconfirms the limitations of the predictive ability of the social sciences. We may have to wait and see what the future holds in store to determine who is correct. But the situation might turn out in ways that would be inconclusive, and both groups would be happy to see. The predictions of both the optimists and the pessimists are based on a continuation of the patterns that have been evident for the past several years. The optimists and the pessimists differ in their interpretation of those patterns. However, neither seems to have anticipated a pattern that has only recently come to light; namely, a resurgence of traditional religious beliefs among those who are now young adults and among parents of young children. And yet, if two recent studies concerning the religious patterns of Americans are indeed correct, that is precisely what is happening. In one, it was found that there recently has been a dramatic rise in attendance and involvement in religious organizations and services on college campuses in the New York area.[36] If substantiated and more than just a brief fad, this might signal a return of young adults to more religiously traditional patterns of behavior and, among Jews, may reverse some of the behaviors that the pessimists see as evidence of a declining American Jewish community. In an even more recent empirical study, it was found that there has been a dramatic rise in the religious involvement of Americans between the ages of 31 to 42, the so-called "baby boomers" who were the rebellious generation of the 1960s. They are now seeking more stable and long-lasting values, they find traditional religious institutions churches and synagogues supportive in this respect, and they look to them to provide their children with religious training. For this age cohort, there has been a decline in the percentage of never-married and an increase in the percentage with children.[37] If these reported patterns are, in fact, taking place in American society, there may yet be grounds for Silberman's optimism, though such a development would not necessarily prove the validity of the theory of the social structuralists.

In the final analysis, those involved in communal activity would be advised both to eschew complacency and to belie the predictions of the pessimists by strengthening the quality of Jewish life in the community and creating the institutional environment that would make it attractive to remain within the community. As the late Simon Rawidowicz suggested, Jews historically have been "the ever-dying people;"[38] that is, the leaders of each generation since ancient times foresaw impending doom for the Jewish people. While there is the implicit danger that this might lead to fatalism, it also had, and continues to have, a fundamental protective element. In addition to serving as a kind of shock absorber when tragedies did occur, the fear of doom can spur the people to action to prevent that doom from becoming reality. Given the state of our knowledge of current trends and the limitations on our ability to accurately predict the future, both optimism and pessimism seem uncalled for. Rather than speculating on the future, it would appear more appropriate to concentrate on the present and deal with it as realistically as possible.

Notes

A somewhat different version of this article appeared, under a different title, in William Frankel, Ed., *Survey of Jewish Affairs, 1987* (Associated University Presses, 1988).

1. T. B. Morgan, "The Vanishing American Jew," *Look* (May 5, 1964) pp. 42 ff.; Marshall Sklare, "Intermarriage and the Jewish Future," *Commentary* (April 1964), pp. 46–52.

2. Elihu Bergman, "The American Jewish Population Erosion," *Midstream* (October 1977), pp. 9–19.

3. Sidney Goldstein, "Jews in the United States: Perspectives from Demography," *American Jewish Year Book* 81 (1981), pp. 3–59.

4. Chaim I. Waxman, *America's Jews in Transition* (Philadelphia: Temple University Press, 1983).

5. Charles E. Silberman, *A Certain People: American Jews and Their Lives Today* (New York: Summit Books, 1985).

6. It must be emphasized that the empirical assimilationist is one who, regardless of his own personal ideology and hopes, foresees, on the basis of his interpretation of the empirical evidence, the ultimate assimilation of large segments of the American Jewish population. It may be suggested that, perhaps not so coincidentally, there is often an inverse relationship between the degree to which one is ideologically committed to Jewish survival and one's view of the empirical possibilities for that survival. This is a matter that cannot be further explored here, but may not be unrelated to the subsequent discussion of a number of the metasociological issues below.

7. Goldstein, "Jews in the United States," op. cit., p. 9.

8. U. O. Schmeltz and Sergio DellaPergola, "The Demographic Consequences of U.S. Jewish Population Trends," *American Jewish Year Book* 83 (1983), pp. 141-87.

9. "Jews, More or Less: An Interview with Steven M. Cohen and Calvin Goldscheider," *Moment* (September 1984), pp. 41-6.

10. It is important to note that this is the more acceptable way of calculating the intermarriage rate. Obviously, if one calculates the intermarriage rate based on the total number of marriages in which Jews participate as spouses, the rate would be much higher. Some of the confusion deriving from the reporting of conflicting rates may be due to differences in the manner in which the various rates are calculated.

11. Bruce A. Phillips, "Factors Associated with Intermarriage in the Western United States." Paper presented at the ninth World Congress of Jewish Studies, Jerusalem (July 1985).

12. Steven Huberman, *New Jews: The Dynamics of Religious Conversion* (New York: Union of American Hebrew Congregations, 1979).

13. For some preliminary exploration of this issue, see Egon Mayer, *Children of Intermarriage: A Study in Patterns of Identification and Family Life* (New York: American Jewish Committee, Institute of Human Relations, 1983); and Egon Mayer, *Love & Tradition: Marriage Between Jews and Christians* (New York: Plenum Press, 1985).

14. U.O. Schmelz and Sergio DellaPergola, *Basic Trends in the American Jewish Demography* (New York: American Jewish Committee, Institute of Human Relations, 1988), p. 18.

15. Calvin Goldscheider, *Jewish Continuity and Change* (Bloomington: Indiana University Press, 1986) p. 11.

16. Silberman, *A Certain People,* op. cit., p. 303.

17. Neil C. Sandberg, *Jewish Life in Los Angeles* (Lanham Md.: University Press of America, 1986), p. 53.

18. Ibid.

19. Ibid., p. 56. Significantly, 55.1 percent of the Jews in Los Angeles report that they neither belong to any Jewish religious nor any Jewish communal institution.

20. Ibid., p. 53.

21. Bruce A. Phillips, *Border Cities,* forthcoming.

22. Ibid.; Bruce A. Phillips and William S. Aron, *The Greater Phoenix Jewish Population Study, 1983-84.* (Jewish Federation of Greater Phoenix, 1984).

23. William L. Yancey and Ira Goldstein, *The Jewish Population of the Greater Philadelphia Area* (Federation of Jewish Agencies of Greater Philadelphia, 1984).

24. Steven M. Cohen and Paul Ritterband, "Intermarriage: Rates, Background, and Consequences for Jewish Identification," mimeographed, 1985. (Department of Sociology, Queens College, 1985).

25. Goldscheider, *Jewish Continuity and Change,* op. cit., p. 172.

26. David Singer, "Living with Intermarriage," *Commentary* (July 1979), pp. 48-53.

27. Reuven P. Bulka, *The Coming Cataclysm* (Oakville, Ontario: Mosaic Press, 1984).

28. For example, Normal Lamm, "Seventy Faces," *Moment* (June 1986), pp. 23-70.

29. Saadia Goan, *The Book of Beliefs and Opinions* (New Haven, CT: Yale University Press, 1948), p. 158.

30. Ahad Ha-am, *Al Parashat Derakhim* (Hebrew) (Tel Aviv: Dvir and Hotzaah Ivrit, 1964), Vol. II, p. 139.

31. Emile Durkheim, *The Elementary Forms of Religious Life.* (New York: Free Press, 1965).

32. For the most recent version of this argument see Steven M. Cohen, *American Assimilation or Jewish Revival?* (Bloomington: Indiana University Press, 1988). The pessimists are not persuaded by manifestations such as these. In their study of the suburban community of "Lakeville" in the late 1950s, Marshall Sklare and Joseph Greenblum also found that these same two rituals were practiced, and were the only ones practiced, by the majority of those interviewed. On the basis of their analysis of the rates of Jewish ritual observances of parents and their adult children, Sklare and Greenblum suggested that there are five criteria that determine the level of observance of Jewish rituals. The rate of retention in ritual observance is highest, they averred, when a ritual "(1) is capable of effective redefinition in modern terms, (2) does not demand social isolation or the adoption of a unique life style, (3) accords with the religious culture of the larger community and provides a Jewish alternative when such is felt to be needed, (4) is centered on the child, and (5) is performed annually or infrequently." *Jewish Identity on the Suburban Frontier* (New York: Basic Books, 1967), p. 57.

33. Calvin Goldscheider and Alan Zuckerman, *The Transformation of the Jews* (Chicago: University of Chicago Press, 1984).

34. Ibid., p. 241.

35. Goldscheider, *Jewish Continuity and Change,* op. cit., p. 184.

36. Dirk Johnson, "Students Turning to Spiritual Life at Campuses in New York Area," *New York Times* (December 25, 1985), pp. 1 ff.

37. David A. Roozen, William McKinney, and Wayne Thompson, "The Big Chill Warms Up to Worship." (Paper presented at the Annual Meetings of the Society for the Scientific Study of Religion and the Religious Research Association, Washington, D.C., Nov. 16, 1986).

38. Simon Rawidowicz, *Studies in Jewish Thought* (Philadelphia: Jewish Publication Society, 1974), pp. 210–24.

6

Canadian Jews and Canadian Pluralism

Morton Weinfeld

Introduction: Canadian-American Comparisons

Does Canadian Jewry differ significantly? In the context of the Diaspora of modern Western democracies, there are several important features of Canadian Jewry which distinguish it from the much larger and better-known Jewish community of the United States.

First, Canadian Jewry is a smaller segment of the population in both absolute and relative terms. The American Jewish population is seventeen times the Canadian, and comprises almost 2 percent of the U.S. population to 1.2 percent for Canadian Jewry.[1]

Second, Canadian Jews are more geographically concentrated than their American counterparts; over two-thirds live in Montreal or Toronto, and to date there has been comparatively little diffusion to the West. In the United States, by contrast, the geographic shift from the Northeast to the Sun Belt is well underway. One of the fastest growing Jewish communities is in Florida, while Los Angeles, another growth area, has more Jews than all of Canada.

Third, Canadian Jews, to put it most simply, are more "Jewish" than American Jews. They speak more Yiddish, provide their children with more intensive Jewish education, make higher per-capita contributions and more visits to Israel, are more likely to be Orthodox and less likely to be Reform, and have lower rates of intermarriage. On the other hand, Canadian Jews have only recently begun to attempt to emulate the political sophistication of their American counterparts, who have had much experience (and considerable success) in defending Jewish interests within the domestic political arena. Other differences are more subtle, yet meaningful nonetheless.

That differences exist is clear, but the reason for this pattern is less clear. Some might claim that the basic cause of the difference is the immigration sequence of the two communities. The foundations of the Canadian community were cast more that fifty years after those of the United States.[2] Most of the Canadian Jews immigrated in the mass movements at the turn of the century. Although Eastern Europeans came to both North American countries, in Canada they were free to develop their own institutions and character without the fundamental influence of the large German-Jewish population that already existed in the United States.

A much higher proportion of Canadian Jews today are themselves immigrants. In the 1980s, at least one-third of Canadian Jews were foreign born.[3] Canadian Jewry has benefitted from a proportionately larger influx of immigrants since World War II. A large number of survivors of the Holocaust came during the immediate postwar period, and more escaped from Hungary in 1956. Many of these immigrants were experienced in Jewish tradition (though not all practiced), knew Yiddish, and had participated in the various Jewish ideological and political debates of the Old World. Their experience infused the Canadian Jewish community with new life, reinforcing its ties to the past.

A second distinguishing trait of Canadian Jewry, especially its second largest community, Montreal, is the French-speaking North African group that arrived after 1957. These Sephardic immigrants brought with them, and are determined to keep, a distinctive form of Jewish identity forged in a crucible of tangible anti–Semitism and stamped with the dual cultural influences of France and the world of Islam. More recently, large numbers of Jews from the Soviet Union and other Eastern Bloc countries, as well as from Israel, have added to the high proportion of foreign–born individuals among Canadian Jews.

Each group has had an impact on Canadian Jewry. However, if it is the differences in the timing and patterns of immigration that are the chief causes of distinctions between the Canadian and the American Jewish communities, then reason dictates that these differences will prove ephemeral. As immigration to Canada slows down and generations pass, Canadian Jews will become increasingly assimilated into the general North American culture, and eventually any variations will disappear.

Another explanation for the American–Canadian contrast focuses not on the characteristics of the immigrants, but on the nature of the receiving society. If Canadian Jews are different from American Jews, according to this theory, it is because Canada differs from the United States.[4] Social scientists and other commentators have labeled Canada an ethnic mosaic in contrast to the American melting pot. The United States, they say, urges immigrants to exchange their old identities for a new—American—persona, awarded all citizens. Canada, on the other hand, encourages ethnic groups to retain at least part of their ancestral identity and heritage. If this is the true context of Canadian Jewry, it augurs well for the perpetuation of a distinctive Canadian Jewish culture.

Are the labels accurate? The answer is extremely difficult because each of the two contrasting concepts—the mosaic and the melting pot—applies at both the level of ideology and the level of social reality. The former certainly offers ample evidence to support and the idea that Canada has generally been encouraging of ethnic diversity. The British North America Act of 1867 did not declare the absolute equality of all citizens. Rather, by recognizing certain rights for religious groups (Catholics and Protestants) and linguistic groups (English and French speakers), it legitimated a collectivistic approach to the notion of rights, in contrast to the American emphasis on individual liberties. The binational origin of the Canadian state paved the way for full acceptance of the plural nature of Canadian society and acknowledgement of the contributions, values, and rights of all Canadian minority groups. With the passage of the Multicultural Act of 1971, the country adopted an official designation as a nation that is "multicultural in a bilingual framework." Public pronouncements by government leaders have periodically reinforced the image of a multicultural polity whose whole is defined as the sum of its parts. Words are backed with money in that substantial government grants are now available to assist organizations that work to perpetuate ethnic cultures. This has continued to the present day, reinforced by the provisions of the new Canadian Constitution and the Charter of Rights and Freedoms, which came into effect in 1985.

This Canadian concern with ethnicity is undoubtedly the result of the dilemma of trying to forge national unity from an originally binational society. Even religious diversity in Canada has been historically associated with, and in recent times submerged by, French–English dualism. Thus, ethnicity, language, and national origin have long been the natural dividing lines of Canadian pluralism, while in the United States they have been race and religion (the latter perhaps because dissenters played such a large role in founding the country). The French concern for *la survivance*—survival—in the midst of an Anglophone continent has brought concerns of language and culture to the national consciousness, and led to a strengthening of the ethnic or cultural dimension of modern Jewish identity. In the United States, however, Judaism is usually defined as part of the American triumvirate of religions. The 1981 census has compounded the problem in that Jews, like all Canadians, can now claim single or multiple ethnic origins. The vibrancy of Canadian Jewish life reflects the fact that Canadian Jews know that they are more than "Canadians of the Jewish faith."

Canada's commitment to pluralism is exemplified in the Canadian census, which has included questions on religion, ethnic origin, and language since its inception. (In the United States, the constitutional separation of church and state has prevented census questions on religion and limited queries to information on race, not ethnic origin). The Canadian census discourages the claiming of "Canadian" or "American" as an ethnic identity. Thus, Canadians are of English, French, Italian, Greek descent, or some other origin, even if their ancestors have lived in Canada for four or five generations.

The Canadian census defines Jews as both an ethnic and a religious group, a procedure that can lead to confusion for anyone trying to derive an accurate estimate of the Jewish population. The category of Jew-by-ethnicity includes many persons of Jewish paternal descent who have since converted out of the faith. For example, the 1971 census enumerated 276,000 Jews-by-religion, but 296,000 Jews-by-ethnic-origin; many of the extra 20,000 in the latter group, in fact, claimed various Christian denominations as their religion. The 1981 census has compounded the problem in that Jews, like all Canadians, can now claim a multiple ethnic origin. These confusions are, however, of concern mostly to statisticians and scholars. The fact is that the census' use of *both* ethnicity and religion to classify Jews reflects the realities of Canadian Jewish-ness and of Canada's ideological approach towards its ethnic groups.

When it comes to the realities of life for ethnic groups, however, some analysts have argued that the two countries are rather similar.[5] For example, the majority society in both countries has often displayed racist attitudes and practices toward Jews as well as towards nonwhite minority groups. The European and North American public often associates racism more with the United States because of its history of slavery and because the inequalities of some of its large black population, living in inner-city ghettos, are so visible. But for other minorities, little distinguishes Canada from the United States. Both countries have dismal records on native rights. Both shut their doors firmly on Jewish refugees during the late 1930s; both discriminated against persons of Japanese descent, even their own native-born citizens, during World War II; and so on, through a long, sad history. As Canada's proportion of nonwhite immigrants has increased since 1945, the incidence of overt racism towards them has also increased, as demonstrated in acts of racially motivated violence as well as in public opinion polls that reveal significantly high levels of negative attitudes towards immigrants.

If racism is one dimension in which Canadian and American societies may be rather similar, another may be the rate of assimilation—defined as the loss of ethnic culture in daily life. If we isolated comparable groups of second- or third-generation Jews in Canada and the United States, would the Canadians be less assimilated than the Americans? No binational studies have been reported using this sort of detailed comparison. However, looking at Canada alone, we do know that later generations of Jews demonstrate lower levels of Jewish identification than do foreign-born Jews (though the gap is not as large as for other ethnic groups). Certainly, too, the lay and spiritual leaders of Canadian

Jewry have expressed as much concern over the dangers of assimilation and intermarriage as have their American counterparts.

Canadian Jewry: Profile of a Community

Jewish immigration to Canada, as to the United States, occurred in waves. The first wave (more like several ripples), stretched from the mid-eighteenth century to the mid-nineteenth century. It comprised Jews of Sephardic origin, emigrating via England. They laid the foundations for Canada's oldest synagogue, the Spanish and Portuguese Synagogue of Montreal. A second small ripple in the mid-nineteenth century consisted of German and central European or Ashkenazi Jews, who also settled primarily in Montreal. A much smaller community organized in Toronto as well. Compared to later Jewish arrivals, these earlier settlers were a relatively educated, urban, affluent group, involved in commerce. They laid the foundations for a network of Jewish communal and self-help organizations. In numbers and legacy, however, their impact was weaker than that of their American counterparts.

The first major wave of Jewish mass migration began in the 1880s and consisted primarily of Jews from Eastern Europe. These Jews were motivated to move by crippling poverty in their homelands, brought about by overpopulation and increased competition in certain economic sectors from recently enfranchised serfs and other Eastern Europeans. But what turned a large economic migration into a population upheaval was the onset of pogroms, in 1881, and again in the 1890s and in 1903.

The vast majority of the Jewish emigrants joined existing Jews in major cities of Quebec, and later of Ontario. A small number moved to the West, primarily to Winnipeg. Peak years of this immigration were from 1905 to 1915. But immigration, often of first-degree relatives of those already in Canada, continued at a steady (if reduced) rate of 3,000 to 4,000 until the Great Depression. In 1901, there were about 17,000 Jews, in all of Canada, increasing to 75,000 by 1911, and 126,000 by 1921. In 1921, 76 percent of Jews lived in urban Quebec and Ontario, a percentage that increased over the years.

These Jewish immigrants were largely skilled or semiskilled working-class people. Few had been farmers or farm laborers: most had worked either in urban factories or as artisans, petty traders, and merchants in rural small towns in Eastern Europe. Almost all (of the men) were literate in Yiddish, and some in Hebrew. Most spoke and many were literate in one or more of Polish, German, Russian, or Ukrainian. Many were ideologically committed. The first two decades of the twentieth century were turbulent years of ideological debate as Europe's Jews struggled to discover answers to the perplexing "Jewish question." Nor was this debate reserved for an elite. Just the opposite—it affected Jews of all classes and backgrounds. Thus, Zionists of every political stripe, socialists, Bundists, Yiddishists, territorialists, anarchists, assimilationists, and others could be found among the Canadian Jewish immigrants.

Here we have an important difference in the immigration sequences as it may have affected American and Canadian Jewry. The foundations of the American mass migration were laid in the last two decades of the nineteenth century, before the full flowering of the national and ideological renaissance in Eastern Europe. Jewish immigration to Canada was centered more on the following two decades, beginning with the turn of the century. Their ideological formations were stronger, notably regarding nationalism of the Bundist or Zionist type. The earlier American mass migration brought with it more of the assimilationist and socialist ethos, fertile soil in which rapid Americanization, with its dilution of Jewish identity, could take root.[6]

Contrary to popular impression, the great wave of Jewish immigration to Canada was neither strongly devout nor religiously observant. Rabbinic leadership in Eastern Europe generally stayed behind, fearing the much discussed materialism and secularism of North America. Many counseled their followers to do the same. As a result, the communal leaders of the Jewish masses in Canada were resolutely secular. Ironically, many leaders of secular political groups also remained in Europe. They saw solutions to Jewish issues in domestic European reform or revolution, not in overseas migration. Canadian Jewish leaders kept one eye cocked on events in the old world even as they focused the other on the possibilities of the new. The Jewish masses brought with them, and, to a certain extent, found in the Canadian Jewish community, a deep tradition of elaborate communal organization, voluntarism, philanthropy, and self-help.

The Jewish communities of Canada absorbed substantial numbers of immigrants in the post–World War II period. Many of these were Displaced Persons, refugees from the horrors and uncertainties of postwar Europe. An estimated 44,000 Jews arrived in Canada from 1945 to 1954, the vast majority of these uprooted from Eastern Europe, survivors of the Holocaust. Hungarian survivors followed in 1956-57. The proportional impact of survivor immigrants was greater in Canada than in the United States.

These survivors had to cope with a dual burden. One was the struggle facing any poor immigrant, unfamiliar with English or French, in adapting to a new society. The other was the special trauma associated with the Holocaust—the destruction of family and friends, the disruption of career or educational aspirations, and, understandably enough, related psychological or physical problems.[7] Many joined or formed "Landsmanschaften," the Jewish fraternal or mutual aid organization of members from specific locations in Eastern Europe. Today, many of these associations are de facto groups of survivors, since most of their members are survivors or those who lost many family members during the war.

Survivors, and survivor organizations, have been seen and have seen themselves as a kind of conscience of the Canadian Jewish community on matters relating to the Holocaust and anti-Semitism. It was not always thus. When they arrived they were "DPs" dependent on the existing Jewish comunity. With the passage of time and the new importance accorded the Holocaust in Jewish self-understanding, the survivors emerged from the shadows. Now, not as "DPs" but as survivors, they speak with moral force in the community—and they are heard.

The demographic contours of the Canadian Jewish community of 300,000 are clear. The Jews of Canada can be considered an "old" group, in that 66 percent of them are Canadian-born. This figure is low in comparison to American Jewry, but it is higher than the percentages of Canadian-born for some other ethnic groups; 54 percent for Italians, 27 percent for Chinese, and 26 percent for Portuguese.

Canadian ethnic groups today cluster around two poles. The white, European groups are deeply rooted. They are more affluent and have begun to penetrate into the elite bastions of WASP privilege. They are less concerned with issues associated with poverty and immigrant adjustment, or with overt discrimination or racism. Rather, they tend to be preoccupied with questions of status, legitimacy, and cultural survival. Group political interests lie in areas like immigration policy or foreign affairs.

On the other hand, the non white, non-European groups, some from nonwestern, non–Judeo-Christian background, have larger immigrant proportions. These groups have arrived in larger numbers in the postwar period, as Canadian immigration laws were liberalized. While much of this immigration has been selective, and some of these groups face ongoing problems of racism and poverty. They are comprised mainly of Caribbean blacks, Chinese and Indo-Chinese, and Indo-Pakistanis.

By every demographic measure, and by every economic or cultural interest, Jews belong in the first category. Yet Canadian Jewish leaders, conscious of the Jewish role as historical victim, retain a visceral tie to the less fortunate visible minority groups.

Canadian Jews are also an aged group, with 15 percent over 65 years and only 34 percent who are 24 years and under. Jews also have perhaps the lowest fertility rate of comparable minority groups in Canada. Low fertility and immigration levels will reduce the relative numerical weight of Jews in Canada's population. American Jewish fertility is estimated at *below* what is necessary for population maintenance. In 1981, the average number of births per ever-married American Jewish woman was 2.24, compared to the Canadian average of 3.30. In the 25- to 29-year bracket, the rates were 0.90 and 1.29, respectively.[8]

Canadian intermarriage rates have been increasing steadily over time, as seen in the annual reports of the Vital Statistics Division of Statistics Canada, which collates provincial (excluding Quebec) data on marriages by religions of the bride and groom. By the mid-1980s the annual rate reached 26 to 27 percent, denoting the annual proportion of Jewish individuals who marry someone whose religion was not Jewish at the time of marriage. (Inclusion of Quebec data, where intermarriage rates are lower, would lower the national rate by a few points.) These rates are somewhat lower than the estimates for the United States, which rely on national surveys or community studies.

Among Jews, 13 percent claim Yiddish or Hebrew as their mother tongue and 4 percent use these languages at home. But it is important to note that both these measures may tend to understate the degree of ethnic language knowledge and use. Many Jews, for example, have a passive second knowledge of Yiddish—some words, phrases or songs—that are of symbolic importance. They may be used on festivals, religious occasions, and the like. In other words, language loyalty is stronger than would be indicated by census data alone.

Over time and over generations, Yiddish is declining in knowledge and use. Yet as Yiddish has declined, Hebrew has increased its prominence, both because of its role as the language of religious prayers and holidays and because of the impact of Israel on modern Jewish culture. Roughly half of Canadian Jewish children today are receiving some form of intensive instruction in Hebrew, whether at full-time day schools or afternoon schools. This is a much higher proportion than can be estimated among American Jews.

About 99 percent of Canadian Jews live in urban areas, and 92 percent live in the largest cities with populations of over 500,000. Indeed 77 percent of Canadian Jews live in Montreal, Toronto, and Vancouver, with a pronounced shift from Montreal to Toronto. By 1986, Toronto's Jewish population reached 141,000, or 4.1 percent of the Toronto metropolitan total, compared to 96,000 or 3.3 percent for Montreal.

Economically, Jews have "made it" in Canada. They are highly represented in those top occupational categories called by Statistics Canada, "managerial and administrative, technical and scientific." This is due, in large part, to their educational achievement. Fully 41 percent of Jews report at least some university education, compared to only 7 percent for all Canadians. These educational and occupational variations, along with the regional and urban–rural differences explain why, according to 1981 census data, Jewish average income ($26,400 for males and $12,000 for females), are by far the highest of any ethnic group, including the "British" group.

Jews, more so than other minority groups, have begun to penetrate the top ranks of the Canadian and social-economic elite. Families such as the Bronfmans, the Reichmanns, and the Belzbergs are not only personally wealthy, but have control over large pools of capital. Interestingly, these three families, and others like them, have retained their ties and commitments to Jewish life, although they are expressed in markedly different ways. A recent edition of *Toronto Life Magazine* identified what it considered the fifty most influential people in Toronto. Approximately twelve were, or appeared to be, Jewish.[9]

Studies of ethnic incomes cannot explain all the variance in group earnings. According to a 1981 study, Jews earned roughly $6,200 above the Canadian average.[10] For most people income can be explained by factors like age, sex, amount of time worked, educational level, and occupation. As a class, middle-aged men work more, have higher education, and have higher-status jobs, and thus tend to earn more. Ethnic groups whose workers have more of these traits will average higher incomes. But for Jews, 53 percent of their income advantage above the national average is due to these factors. The remaining 47 percent is somehow simply a structural "bonus" for belonging to the group. This does not mean that anti-Semitism has disappeared, or that in the past Jews were not clearly victimized; rather, this suggests that if there are negative feelings about Jews, they have few real consequences for income.

Money tells only part of the story of social acceptance. Another way to measure ethnic status is through a group's perception of how the majority sees them. Still another is by evaluating members' accounts of their own experiences of discrimination. Here a Toronto study of 1978–79 reveals an interesting story. The survey sampled eight ethnic groups, including 344 Jews chosen more or less randomly.[11]

The study finds only 78 percent of Jews see themselves accepted as neighbors "very or somewhat easily." For acceptance as would-be family members the figures show 42 percent for Jews, reflecting the complications felt about interfaith marriage among Jews, as well as perceived anti-Semitism. Moreover, for a group with such objectively high occupational levels and income, 17 percent of Jews still claim that discrimination against them is a "very or somewhat serious" problem, and 12 percent claim having experienced anti-Semitism when trying to get a job. Thus, for a minority of Canadian Jews, the old adage applies: "If things are so good, why are they so bad?"

The Jewish Polity in Canada

Even before the rise of multiculturalism as official Canadian government policy in the early 1970s, many Canadian ethnic groups had assumed the traits of a polity and were, in a certain sense, self-governing. Daniel Elazar has fleshed out the idea of the ethnic polity, using American Jews as an example.

As Elazar describes it, the Jewish polity represents the set of institutions, supported mainly by voluntary charitable contributions and fees raised within the Jewish community. Together, this structure defines organized Jewish life.[12]

The Jewish polity flourishes in both Canada and the United States. Indeed, Jews have always been comfortable with the idea of a polity, since Jewish life has a long tradition of self-regulation and autonomy in the Diaspora. Jewish communities had developed a network of communal organizations, such as burial societies, orphanages and poorhouses, and rabbinic courts and schools, to look after the internal needs of the community, including the less fortunate. This tradition, rooted both in biblical injunctions and Old Country realities, was quickly adapted and entrenched in the New World.

Today, the Jewish community is the most "institutionally complete" in Canada. It boasts a myriad of ethnic organizations and institutions of different types and objectives. Ethnic schools, newspapers, and community festivals punctuate life's rhythms. Jews can be born and can die in Jewish hospitals and old-age homes.

But institutional completeness does not mean communal uniformity. The Jewish community has been marked with intra-communal tensions and conflict. Some of this has been ideological. Organizations have split on standard left–right social issues, on Zionism and the degree of support for Israeli policy, and on religious issues. Jews also disagree about how much emphasis to devote to narrowly defined Jewish concerns.

Thus, at the 1986 Canadian Jewish Congress triennial plenary session, Rabbi Gunther Plaut called for greater external involvement on the part of Canadian Jews in the affairs and needs of other groups. It was time, he argued, to move beyond an almost exclusive focus on Jewish concerns and Jewish victimization. In fact, Jewish organizations in Canada have, at various times, played coalition politics with other ethnic groups. In Alberta, Jews fell in behind Ukrainians in lobbying the government to secure government funding for private schools. Jewish organizations have supported the Japanese-Canadian claim for redress for lost properties and damages from their forced relocation in World War II. But at times, such cooperation has been uneasy. Consider the overlapping issues of Soviet Jewry and the struggle for cultural and religious freedoms in Ukraine. Jews have tended to emphasize the right, and option, of emigration for Soviet Jews. Ukrainians have tended to stress enhanced freedom in the Ukraine through decentralization, lessening of communist ideology, and freer exercise of religion.

The Jewish polity has another source of internal tension stemming from regionalism and the size of the country. The Jewish polity has, for some time, been marked by the rivalry between Montreal and Toronto as centers of power. In recent years the action has shifted steadily from the former to the latter. But the Montreal–Toronto rivalry has only exacerbated resentful claims from the smaller Jewish communities in the Maritimes, Western Canada, and even small-town Ontario that they have been neglected systematically by the two dominant metropolitan centers.

In Canada today, Jews are enthusiastic celebrants of the multicultural ideal. The commitment to the ethnic polity is seen from the popularity of the Jewish press. Comparisons with Ukrainian Canadians, a large survivalist, and powerful group, are illustrative. Only 2 percent of the third-generation Ukrainians in Toronto read the ethnic press, as compared to over 50 percent of third generation Jews. Within the Jewish community, one publication, the English-language weekly *Canadian Jewish News,* which is sent automatically to every donor of $25.00 to the Combined Jewish Appeal, has emerged as the dominant newspaper for Ontario and Quebec, with a circulation of 48,000. Single newspapers also dominate in most Jewish centers in Western Canada.

The Canadian Jewish polity is also typified by internal turf struggles. In the organized Jewish community, the three dominant organizational groups are the Canadian Jewish Congress, the B'nai B'rith, and the local welfare federations.

The Canadian Jewish Congress (CJC), founded in 1919, and revived in 1934, has been called the "parliament of Canadian Jewry." Modeled on the British Board of Jewish Deputies, it is an umbrella "organization of other organizations," each with a voting voice in the CJC in proportion to its membership strength. There is no directly comparable unifying organization within the American Jewish community. Triennial conventions of the CJC are held in which contestants run for the various leadership positions. Some races are won by acclamation, but at times campaigning for delegate votes has been quite intense. The CJC sees itself, and is seen by others, as the main interlocutor of Jewish interests before the federal, and through regional arms, provincial governments. It takes an active role in preparation of briefs and lobbying. The CJC has elaborate offices in Montreal and Toronto and boasts a large professional staff, as well as lay members serving on committees and the executive.

Over the past decades the power and authority of the Congress has eroded somewhat. This has been due largely to the rise of the Jewish welfare federations, which administer the local welfare, social, educational, and cultural agencies of the Jewish community.

The CJC has also been criticized by some as being "too establishment" in its orientation, or, in other words, not militant enough in pursuing Jewish interests. This charge is retrospectively leveled against the CJC for its policies before and during World War II.[13] Communal leaders past and present, have been accused of toadying to the state power, selling out the community in the process. "Quiet diplomacy" has had a bad press in the post-Holocaust era. Some Canadian Jews feel today that this same timidity has marked action on matters such as the emigration of Soviet Jewry, the plight of Ethiopian Jewry, the prosecution of Nazi war criminals, and the fight against anti-Semitism.

Thus, splinter groups have sprung up occasionally with more militant postures on some of these issues. In one example, the Student Struggle for Soviet Jewry, the Congress eventually succeeded in integrating the group into the formal CJC structure. But others, such as the Canadian Association for Ethiopian Jewry, the Jewish Defense League, the Holocaust Remembrance Association, and the Simon Wiesenthal Centre, have resisted. Some have used establishment-bashing as a useful tool for fund-raising.

The B'nai B'rith is Canadian Jewry's largest membership organization. Set up as a fraternal organization, it is active in both local good works and issues of broader policy importance. Once closely linked to the Congress, the B'nai B'rith now charts its own course and openly competes for prestige in the Jewish organizations world. Its Anti-Defamation League in the United States and League for Human Rights in Canada are active lobbyists for civil rights and justice for all minority groups.

Oddly, little is known of the strength or importance of ethnic politics. Most political scientists who have studied the processes of government in Canada with particular emphasis on lobbies, pressure groups, or interest groups, have to date ignored the role of ethnic or religious groups. Others have tended to rate them as relatively unimportant or ineffective compared to the usual gamut of other interest groups, such as business organizations, unions, consumer groups, or women's groups, that historically lobby federal and provincial governments. To political analysts, and perhaps to politicians themselves, these ethnic lobbyists seem little more than a side show in the Canadian political game.[14]

Yet as the Canadian nation, politicians, and senior civil servants change in composition to reflect more adequately the ethnic make-up of the Canadian population, this too may change. As minorities become more entrenched in the middle class, they will find financial means and competent personnel to promote their interests. Perhaps the ideologic stamp of multiculturalism will also help elevate ethnic leaders from bit players to major actors. In Canada, Jews are seen as perhaps a model of a well-organized and effective ethnic lobby. But, ironically, their actual record is a mixture of victories, partial gains, and defeats. When it mattered most, on the eve of the Holocaust, Jews were unable to pry open the doors that Canada had shut tight in the face of German Jewish refugees in the 1930s. The Clark government's Jerusalem fiasco of 1979, in which the Tories backtracked on the promise to move the Canadian Embassy in Israel from Tel Aviv to Jerusalem, brought on a backlash against the Jewish lobby. Moreover, throughout the postwar period the same vaunted Jewish lobby was effective neither in barring Canadian entry to Nazis and possible war criminals nor in persuading the government to adopt a systematic effort to root them out. The strength of the Jewish lobby has been exaggerated in the past as it is today.

A high level of organizational development is only one factor that can contribute to the political clout of an ethnic group pursuing its collective interest. Large voting blocs concentrated in major electoral districts are obviously important. Urban Jewish voters in key ridings of Toronto and Montreal are important politically. Jewish leaders with ties to political parties, as well as elected politicians representing Jewish ridings, are well-placed brokers in the give-and-take of ethnic politics.

To what degree are Canadian Jews aware of this type of political activity by their leaders or "machers?" In Toronto in 1979, 89 percent knew of the ethnic organizations, and 67 percent indicated they were now or had been members. Forty-nine percent said they knew their leaders personally, and 31 percent claimed frequent or occasional contact with them. Jews also tend to feel that politicians do take Jewish leaders seriously, and that their leaders do have enough contacts. The Jewish numbers by far eclipse those of the other minority groups.

There have been very few studies of Jewish voting in Canada. The evidence suggests that in Canada, as in the United States, Jews have usually voted "left." In postwar Canada this has meant greater support for the Liberals and, to a lesser extent, the New Democratic Party, and weaker support for the Progressive Conservatives. Yet over the past two decades, there is also evidence that Jewish support for the Conservatives has increased along with that of the rest of the population. One study of young Jewish leaders (aged 25 to 40 years) in Montreal and Toronto found that more voted for the Conservatives than for the Liberals in the 1984 federal elections. It is premature to consider this a fundamental realignment.[15]

Jewish participation in electoral politics is enhanced by the overall internal organization of the Jewish polity. A cornerstone of the Canadian Jewish community is fund-raising. Like the idea of communal responsibility, the imperative of philanthropy—of voluntary taxation—was nurtured by Jews through the ages. To the uninitiated, the scope of Canadian Jewish giving can seem superhuman, and well exceeds the per-capita figures for American Jews. For example, the Jewish community of Montreal in 1986 raised $29 million for the Combined Jewish Appeal; this from a community of just over 90,000.

The story is told of an emergency meeting of wealthy givers in Montreal convened by Sam Bronfman on the eve of the 1967 Arab–Israeli War. One of the donors wrote a check for a quarter of a million dollars. "Mr. Sam" tore it up disdainfully. Whether the story is true is unimportant. What matters is that anyone familiar with Canadian Jewish fundraising has no trouble believing it. The national office of the CJC in Montreal, including the Quebec region, employs thirteen professionals and twenty support staff in the modern, four-story office building named after—who else—the late Sam Bronfman.

Canadian Pluralism: Legal and Social Dimensions

Cultural pluralism in Canada can be represented by sets of policies oriented to the achievement of two goals: (1) the survival of ethnic–cultural groups and their cultures (multiculturalism); and (2) the guarantee of full equality of opportunity (nondiscrimination) for all citizens, regardless of cultural background. Both of these goals can be found explicitly articulated as law and government policy, reflected in ministerial duties and budgets, at both the federal and provincial levels of government.

Both of these goals reflect the third stage in the evolution of government policy regarding minority groups in liberal democracies. The three stages of this evolution have been: (1) government repression of minorities; (2) tolerance or neutrality towards minorities; and (3) active governmental support for these minorities, in their realization of both the objectives listed above.

Ethnic life in Canada has become increasingly politicized in two senses. First, ethnic polities—organizations and leaders—define the nature of group life and identity, often ordering internal priorities. Second, the ethnic polity is energized externally, defining relations to other groups and the state.

Thus, the Canadian Jewish community, like other ethnic groups, finds itself today in a particularly nurturant political environment. The state has become an ally of the community in both the struggle against anti-Semitism and in the struggle to prevent cultural assimilation. A politicized ethnicity also means that Jews will behave, and will be perceived as, an interest group active in the political process rather than as a victimized minority group. As other groups adopt comparable postures in the future, the political environment may, ironically, become less supportive.

The Canadian constitution, specifically the Charter of Rights and Freedoms, contains several sections that illustrate the state's commitments to the two goals of cultural pluralism, and have specific salience for Jewish interests. However, in outlining these provisions, the reader must bear in mind the following caveat. In terms of constitutional defense of individual and group rights, the Canadian historical clock is set at about 1795. In other words, while the United States has been struggling for close to two centuries to modify or interpret the relevant constitutional provisions, Canadians—courts, legal scholars, politicians, advocacy groups—have been at it for less than a decade. Nothing is even remotely settled.[16]

Section 2 of the Charter identifies the fundamental freedoms:

Freedom of conscience and religion;
Freedom of thought, belief, opinion and expression including freedom of press and other media of communication;

Freedom of peaceful assembly;
Freedom of association.

These four freedoms provide the basis in law for the guaranteed existence of the voluntary organizations that constitute the Jewish polity, and are similar in context and consequence to American freedoms.

Section 15 establishes the principal of equal treatment under the law for individuals without discrimination based on national or ethnic origin, or religion, among other criteria, and even permit affirmative action programs— explicitly—for disadvantaged groups. In effect, the section outlaws any type of anti-Semitic discrimination (though not, of course, prejudice or ill will). Section 15.2 legalizes affirmative action programs. However, there have been relatively few concrete initiatives taken by government or the private sector. Canadian Jewish organizations, notably the CJC, have vigorously endorsed affirmative action programs. Push has yet to come to shove on the thorny issue of quotas.

Canadian affirmative action programs and the debate generally are focused overwhelmingly on women as a disadvantaged group. Native peoples and the disabled are next, with visible minorities last. There is no analog to the emotional pattern of American black–Jewish relations in Canada. As a result, confrontations on affirmative action programs—which, in the United States are focused largely on blacks and Hispanics—have not occurred.

Section 27 is a rather ambiguous provision that introduces the principle of multiculturalism; i.e., the value of ethnic cultures, as a guidepost for subsequent judicial interpretation of the Charter. It reads: "This Charter shall be interpreted in a manner consistent with the preservation and enhancement of the multicultural heritage of Canadians." Its purpose is probably hortatory. Legal scholars are unsure of its ramifications.

Apart from these constitutional sections, there are the hate literature laws in the Criminal Code of Canada (sections 281.1 and 281.2) that prohibit anyone from engaging in speech that advocates genocide or provokes hatred of groups.

This legislation was passed originally because of pressure from the Canadian Jewish Congress over the opposition of civil libertarians. Some analysts have argued that the statute is, in fact, too weak; the text of the law requires that the promotion of hatred be done "willfully," which is difficult to establish in a court of law. The law was used in the 1984–85 prosecution of Alberta school teacher Jim Keegstra, who preached the theory of the international Jewish conspiracy to his students.[17] The court in the Keegstra case ruled, inter alia, that the hate literature laws in the Criminal Code *were* constitutional, and did not abridge the rights of free speech (section 2b). It is expected that the Supreme Court would uphold this ruling. Also in 1985, philo-Nazi Toronto publisher

Ernst Zundel was prosecuted and convicted under a similar law which prohibited the deliberate spreading of "false news." (His case is under appeal.)

But Canadian Jews have found these protections against the proliferation of anti-Semitic hate to be a dual-edged sword. Both Keegstra and Zundel were tried in court proceedings that received saturated media publicity. Zundel, a Holocaust denial advocate, trotted out his band of "experts" who claimed that Dachau was a resort with swimming pools, all of which was dutifully reported day-by-day by the press. Indeed, fears of contempt-of-court citations (perhaps exaggerated) made many media outlets scrupulous in keeping their reports strictly to the trial proceedings, with no editorial comment.

Many in the organized Jewish community questioned the wisdom of the whole exercise, which gave national, uncontradicted media exposure to minor, marginal figures with no constituency to speak of. The old debates surfaced: do nothing, and risk having the poison spread; or use the law to stop the hate mongering, and risk having the exposure win new adherents. A scientific survey helped put some of the latter fears to rest. No evidence was found that Canadians who followed the Zundel trial in the media were in any way moved to anti-Semitic sentiments; quite the opposite.[18] However, the trial coverage did cause anguish among many Holocaust survivors.

Additional environmental support for Canadian Jewish life comes from ministries of multiculturalism at the provincial and federal levels. These encourage minority groups with grants and other support, to maintain their organizations and cultures. They date back to recommendations of Book IV of the Royal Commission on Bilingualism and Biculturalism, *The Contribution of the Other Ethnic Groups,* and to the Multicultural Act of 1971.

Some critics have labeled the multiculturalism programs a great boondoggle, aimed at buying ethnic votes. Visible minorities have argued that the programs are aimed more at the cultural needs of the older, European groups who have "made it," and not to the bread-and-butter needs of the nonwhite groups.

Canada does not have the strict separation of Church and State found in the United States. Thus, in certain provinces, Jewish, as well as ethnic and Catholic, (day) schools receive significant amounts of public funds, provided these schools meet certain criteria and are deemed in the public interest. (Education is a provincial, not federal, responsibility.)

This also represents a major Canadian-American difference in promoting Jewish survival, as it makes private Jewish day schools more affordable. There are also no parallels to the perennial American disputes concerning nativity scenes, or menorahs, displayed on public property. Both are on display on government property. Montreal municipal courtrooms still have crucifixes on the walls.

Constraints of space do not permit detailed elaboration of how the laws or Constitutional provisions are observed in practice and whether they have any real effect on the quality of Jewish life—they do. Jewish groups and schools do receive government grants from multiple sources. Jewish economic success and entry into major positions or sectors of Canadian society indicate that anti-Semitism has been rendered relatively impotent in limiting Jewish achievements. Individuals who commit anti-Semitic acts are dealt with by courts or Human Rights Commissions.

Yet, this environment does pose challenges. The historic approach to the analysis of anti-Semitism made assumptions concerning the motives of the anti-Semite. In other words, people committed anti-Semitic acts because of explicit or implicit animus towards Jews. However, as Jews enter the political arena as an interest group, more and more the old understanding of anti-Semitism is replaced by a newer form.

The new form focuses on actions that are deemed harmful to Jewish interests, regardless of motivation. Acts are judged by their consequences for Jews and Jewish interests. On a variety of policy issues, Jews in Canada (and the United States) will find themselves advocating positions that are opposed by other groups in Canada, or even by government. The usual examples of such cases have to do with Israel and the Middle East, and are well known. In March 1988, External Affairs Minister Joe Clark publicly criticized Israeli policy in the occupied territories at a Jewish gathering of the Canada–Israel Committee, evoking an angry Jewish response and media discussion of the dual-loyalty issue. Other examples can be found. Thus, the Jewish and Ukrainian groups in Canada find themselves at loggerheads over whether the Deschenes Commission, investigating the illegal presence of Nazi war criminals in Canada, should admit evidence from the Soviet Bloc.[19] Are the Ukrainians aiming to protect guilty parties, or to prevent a tarnishing of the group's name? And is such opposition a form of anti-Semitism?

Suppose Ontario Jews massively favor provincial financial aid to private (Jewish) schools. Are those opposed to such aid motivated by anti-Semitism? Should future Canadian grain sales to the Soviet Union be linked to progress on human rights and Jewish emigration? If policy positions are seen as harmful to Jewish interests what ought the Jewish response be? These are new waters in which the Jewish community must navigate.

The politicization of ethnicity within Canadian cultural pluralism means that Canadian Jews must move to a model of interest groups and bargaining, rather than a model of victimized minority groups claiming rights. Interest groups that compete in the political arena cannot expect to win all their disputes. Among classic decisions or outcomes are the results of coalitions, bargains, and compromises, often economic in nature, in which one can "split the difference." Jews, like all Canadian minority groups, have been used to the idiom of rights and justice, which is relatively more absolute, less amenable to bargaining. The two models of political conduct should not be confused.

The Canadian state not only acknowledges the diversity within Canadian society, but actively serves to promote that diversity, seeing in multiculturalism a strength of Canadian society. Yet, what multicultural advocates have not faced squarely is that there are obvious limits to the degree to which Canadian society can permit minority groups to live out the dictates of their cultures. When those dictates cross the boundary norms of western liberal democratic society reflected in our legal codes, or threaten the national security or unity, the right to multiculturalism would be constrained. For example, it is most unlikely that a Canadian court could excuse a criminal act based on a defense resting on section 27 of the Constitution, the multiculturalism section.

But there is an underbelly to multiculturalism, which resurrects or engenders conflict among groups. Sikh extremists in Canada allegedly blowing up an Air India flight, murdering hundreds of Canadian citizens, is but one extreme manifestation. Jews need to strike delicate balances in the game of coalition politics. Attempted alliances with older European groups such as Ukrainians (or Poles) may stoke still burning embers of older feuds, waiting to burst into flame. And alliances with the newer forces of the visible minority groups are difficult because of the enormous socioeconomic gaps between the affluent Jews and many of the others.

Canadian Jews have been visible and active in support of visible minorities, whether in terms of a more open and humane refugee policy, liberal immigration quotas, or in support of affirmative action. Yet there may also be a growing disjuncture between Jewish communal leadership, where the ideologies of liberalism hold sway, and the lifestyle of the typical middle- and upper-middle-class Jews, where the culture of materialism predominates. Income figures alone understate this affluence—the cars, the maids, the homes, the vacations, the clothes tell a fuller story.

Multiculturalism both legitimates and actively supports ethnic politics. Many ethnic groups, particularly native peoples and visible minorities, receive government grants which, in fact, help them organize, and serve in lieu of voluntary charitable donations. This contrasts with the largely self-made, and self-financed, Jewish polity. Thus, more ethnic groups take their places in the ranks of Canadian interest group sustained by large memberships, and the patina of human rights adds moral force to their claims. As more Canadian ethnic groups strive to emulate the model of the Jewish polity, it remains to be seen whether Jewish interests will be served along with that of other groups, or whether a more Hobbesian, zero-sum game will ensue.

Notes

1. A social scientific overview of the Canadian Jewish community today is found in Morton Weinfeld, William Shaffir, and Irwin Cotler, *The Canadian Jewish Mosaic*

Rexdale, Ontario: John Wiley of Canada, 1979). Other sources of data are the *Annual Yearbooks of the American Jewish Committee,* which generally include a chapter on Canada. A systematic comparison of all demographic and sociological measures of Jewish life in Canada and the United States is beyond the scope of this essay. The aim is rather to highlight a few themes, by way of introducing the Canadian case. Data on American Jewish patterns are available elsewhere in this volume.

2. For a discussion of Jewish immigration to Canada, see Joseph Kage, *With Faith and Thanksgiving* (Montreal: Eagle Publishing, 1962).

3. Unless otherwise stated, national data for Canadian Jewry in 1981 are taken from *Socio-economic Profiles of Selected Ethnic/Visible Minority Groups* (Multicultural-ism Canada, March 1986) based on the census of 1981.

4. For a general discussion of U.S.-Canadian cultural differences, see S. M. Lipset "Canada and the United States: The Cultural Dimension" in C. F. Doran and J. H. Sigler (eds.) *Canada and the United States.* (Englewood Cliffs: Prentice-Hall, Inc., 1985), pp. 108–160. The idea that comparative Jewish studies must focus on comparisons of the respective host societies was developed in S. M. Lipset, "The Study of Jewish Communities in a Comparative Context," *Jewish Journal of Sociology* 5 (1963), pp. 157–66.

5. See John Porter, "Melting Pot or Mosaic: Revolution or Reversion," in John Porter, *The Measure of Canadian Society: Education, Equality and Opportunity* (Toronto: Gage, 1979), pp. 139–62.

6. See Eugene Orenstein, "Yiddish Culture in Canada: Yesterday and Today," in Weinfeld, Shaffir, and Cotler, *The Canadian Jewish Mosaic*, pp. 293–314.

7. While the problems were real, so too were the coping strengths of the survivors. See Morton Weinfeld, John J. Sigal, and William W. Eaton, "Long Term Effects of the Holocaust on Selected Social Attitudes & Behaviors of Survivors," *Social Forces* 60 (1981) pp. 1–19.

8. See Leo Davids, "Canadian Jewry: Some Recent Census Findings," in *American Jewish Yearbook* 85 (New York: American Jewish Committee, 1985), pp. 191–201.

9. "The Fifty Most Influential People in the City," *Toronto Life,* May 1986, pp. 40–6, 66–8.

10. See Peter S. Li, "Race and Ethnic Relations," in Lorne Tepperman and R. Jack Richardson, eds., *The Social World: An Introduction to Sociology* (Toronto: Mc-Graw-Hill, 1986), pp. 35–60.

11. Raymond Breton, "The Ethnic Community as a Resource in Relation to Group Problems: Perceptions and Attitudes" (Toronto: University of Toronto, Centre for Urban and Community Studies. Research Paper No. 122); and Wsevoled W. Isajiw, "Ethnic Identity Retention" (Toronto: University of Toronto, Centre for Urban and Community Studies, Research Paper No. 125).

12. See Daniel Elazar, *Community and Polity: The Organizational Dynamics of American Jewry* (Philadelphia: Jewish Publication Society, 1976).

13. See Irving Abella and Harold Troper, *None Is Too Many* (Toronto: Lester, Orpen, Dennys, 1983).

14. See Paul Pross, *Pressure Group Behaviour in Canadian Politics* (Toronto: McGraw Hill Ryerson, 1975) and Robert Presthus, *Elite Accommodation in Canadian Politics* (Cambridge: Cambridge University Press, 1973).

15. Breton, *The Ethnic Community, On Jewish Voting,* See J. A. Laponce, "Left or Center: the Canadian Jewish Electorate, 1958-1983." Department of Political

Science, University of British Columbia, n.d. (unpublished paper) Laponce studied Canadian poll data on voting preferences from 1958–83 and Harold Waller and Morton Weinfeld "A Viewpoints Survey of Canadian Jewish Leadership Opinion," *Viewpoints* 15 (1987). Supplement to the *Canadian Jewish News*, October 8, 1987.

16. This section draws from my article "Canadian Cultural Pluralism and Its Implications for the Jewish Community." *Shofar*, 5 (Winter 1987), pp. 1-7.

17. See David Bercuson and Douglas Wertheimer, *A Trust Betrayed: The Keegstra Affair* (Toronto: Doubleday Canada, 1985).

18. Gabriel Weimann and Conrad Winn, *Hate on Trial: The Zundel Affair, The Media, and the Public Opinion in Canada* (Oakville, Ontario: Mosaic Press, 1986).

19. See Harold Troper and Morton Weinfeld, *Old Wounds* (Markham, Ont: Penguin Books Canada, 1988).

II

Politics

7

The Liberal Tradition of American Jews

Irving Kristol

American Jews, in their overwhelming majority, are politically rooted in a liberal tradition. That, presumably is, why, as Milton Himmelfarb has noted, these Jews have the economic status of Episcopalian WASPS but vote more like low-income Hispanics. How can this anomaly be explained, which is unique in the American experience? The Irish and the Italians, as they move up the economic ladder, are far more likely to shed the urban-immigrant liberalism of their parents and grandparents, shifting rather predictably to one version or another of suburban conservatism of which "interest-group liberalism" is a subspecies. They perceive their interests in a new way, and vote these interests. Such a shift is what students of sociology would expect. Why has it not happened to America's Jews? Why are they so different? Is there a single answer that can serve as an explanation?

I think there is, although it is a single answer that is not a simple answer. It incorporates the meaning of that "liberalism" to which American Jews seem so stubbornly attached, a meaning which itself is a special compound of Jewish political and religious history spanning the past two centuries. So powerful is this meaning that it has become for many Jews an integral aspect of their self-definition. There are now some signs that this self-definition is eroding finally in the face of a circumstantial reality that repels its solicitation. But it is interesting to note that Jews who move away from their familiar (and familial) liberalism will describe themselves as "disillusioned," whereas their Irish and Italian counterparts find such a movement to be natural, not at all traumatic, and not calling for any self-conscious reflection.

To be disillusioned, one must have had illusions. The liberalism of the modern Jew is one that has been especially rich in such illusions. Obviously, they were not merely illusions—to retain the loyalty of Jews for so long a time,

109

they had to be nourished by the real, outside world. "Jewish liberalism"—the term is neither invidious nor inappropriate—was connected organically to a larger non-Jewish belief that has tended to dominate the intellectual (even spiritual) life of Western Europe ever since the French Revolution. It is the intensity and obstinacy of the Jewish commitment to this liberalism that is so special.

We discuss here Continental "radical" politics that gave rise to the French Revolution and that stubbornly (if not altogether successfully) resisted opportunities for disillusionment, and have remained loyal to the ideals of that revolution ever since. What was liberal about this ideology was its opposition to monarchy and aristocracy, the *ancien régime* that was seen as oppressive, corrupt, and decadent. What was radical about this liberalism was the belief that a new order could be constructed, to be governed by a new "enlightened" state that would be representative of man's finer instincts, his most elevated thoughts. By the early decades of the nineteenth century, this belief began to incorporate a fundamental distrust and detestation of the market economy, which was perceived as incarnating self-interest as the guiding principle of the new social order. Such a focus on self-interest was thought to be inimical to "enlightened" government, which should be the master, not the servant, of social and economic realities. It is this polarity between "enlightened," powerful, intrusive government and the principle of self-interest as the bedrock of our economic system that is the driving force behind all modern socialism, whether in its social-democratic or Leninist versions.

There is, of course, another liberal tradition with a quite different conception of "liberalism." This is the Anglo-Scottish tradition represented by such thinkers as John Locke, David Hume, and Adam Smith. Although this tradition had a certain popularity in Continental Europe prior to the French Revolution, it has always been viewed by Continental liberalism as a mere preface to the more "authentic" (and more radical) liberal ideals emerging from the French Revolution.

In Anglo-American liberalism, it is an enlightened, civil society that is prized, while government is regarded as a continuing threat to individual liberty—including the liberty to pursue, within a large sphere of action, one's self-interest. Such individual liberty is the root principle of this new order. In the end, it is whether one regards a "bourgeois" civil society more favorably than an "enlightened" state, or vice versa, that determines whether one leans to Anglo-American liberalism or the radical-liberalism of the Continental political tradition.

The difference between the two ideologies can be described in quasi-Marxist terms as the difference between a "bourgeois" and "post-bourgeois" society, exemplified in the American and French Revolutions, respectively. The ideals of the American Revolution were (and are) individual liberty, social and political equality, and representative government. Those of the French Revolution stressed economic equality, political community, and a government elected freely or not that claimed to represent a sovereign popular will. It is understandable, therefore, that socialist thinkers and socialist movements of the nineteenth and twentieth centuries all looked back to the French Revolution as the appropriate paradigm of what a "real" revolution should be, while the American Revolution was regarded as a marginal event. Leon Trotsky's magisterial *History of the Russian Revolution,* for instance, takes the French precedent (or the Jacobin version thereof) as authoritative in explaining the "natural" history of revolutions in general, and specifically of the Russian one in which he played so notable a part. This explains why the drama he reconstructs is so coherent and plausible, although more fictional than real.

That European Jews should have been legatees of the political ideology of the French Revolution was inevitable under the circumstances that prevailed. They had no political philosophy or traditions of their own. Even today, and even in the state of Israel, there is no identifiable "Jewish" political thought. They knew nothing of Anglo-American political theory and not much more about the far-off American Revolution. The individualism of Anglo-American politics, in any case, evoked (and still evokes) few echoes in a communally oriented Judaism. In addition, and most important, the ideology of the French Revolution, throughout the nineteenth century, offered European Jewry tangible benefits of the utmost significance, while the opponents of this ideology were likely to be adherents of an established Christian church and social-political order that discriminated against Jews.

It was the ideology of the French Revolution, incarnated in Napoleon, that liberated European Jewry from confinement in the ghetto. Just how much this meant at the time may be grasped from a reading of Martin Buber's fascinating novel, *For the Sake of Heaven,* in which Orthodox Jews in a central European ghetto conclude ecstatically that Napoleon is their long-awaited Messiah. This same ideology, expressed in the liberal, socialist, and social-democratic movements of the nineteenth century, succeeded in extending the suffrage to Jews, and in removing legal restrictions on their freedom of movement as well as their economic opportunities. In Eastern Europe, where liberalism of any kind made only a modest impression on anti-Semitic regimes, the commitment of Jews to this ideology was correspondingly intense. While not all European Jews situated themselves somewhere on the left of the political spectrum, a disproportionate number did so. In France, Germany and Italy, there was a thin stratum of conservative and centrist Jewry, assimilated into the national cultures, but many of these Jews eventually converted or simply cast off any religious identity.

It was from Continental Europe, and mainly from Central and Eastern Europe, that Jews emigrated to the United States. They naturally brought with them their political beliefs. Those political beliefs still dominate the thinking of most American Jews. A recent *Los Angeles Times* poll revealed that when Jews are asked about the qualities most important to their Jewish identity—a commitment to social equality, religious observance, or support for Israel—the first, a commitment to social equality, was the most important. This is odd since an objective observer would see little reason today in the American Jewish condition why social equality should evoke such a passionate commitment. One might think that intermarriage, rather than discrimination or exclusion be regarded as having a greater bearing on "Jewish survival." But ideas have a life of their own, and Jewish political attitudes in the 1980s have a more direct connection with Jewish political thinking in the 1880s than with current social, economic, or even political realities in the United States.

It also must be pointed out that Jewish immigrants, congregating in the major urban centers, found there a Democratic party—usually dominated by the Irish, themselves earlier immigrants—that was hospitable to their personal and ideological aspirations. Although the Democratic party was, by no means, left-wing, its liberalism on issues of social reform, and its commitment to "balanced tickets" on which Jews were actually (although not frequently) elected to office, were sufficient to engender Jewish loyalties and establish a Jewish commitment. This was even the case for The Orthodox, who were largely apolitical and indifferent to contemporary ideologies (including Zionism).

In those urban milieus, the Republican party was seen correctly as dominated by WASPS (as we now call them) who were either outright anti-Semitites or inclined to discriminate against Jews. Until World War II, major corporations hired few Jews, and the more affluent suburbs were "restricted" to non-Jews (and, it goes without saying, to whites only). The struggle for equality of "civil rights," led by the liberal wing of the Democratic party, only reinforced the commitment of American Jews to an agenda of liberal reform.

What is puzzling, however, is the way in which the force of this commitment survived, the enactment of the agenda in the postwar years. Even while social and economic discrimination against Jews has declined with a quite unforeseen rapidity, Jews are still haunted by the specter of anti-Semitism among traditional conservative sectors of the society. And although Jews became one of the most affluent and upwardly mobile of ethnic-religious groups, their political ideology remained largely unaffected. To some degree, this can be explained by the fact that American blacks did not experience anything like the same success, leading Jews to wonder about the security of their own achievement. To some degree, too, it resulted from a justifiable skepticism regarding the Republican party's willingness to accept as permanent the "civil rights revolution"—a willingness diluted or subverted by the conservative dislike of governmental action in this field. But mainly the ideological loyalty of so many

American Jews was sustained and nourished by a change in their religious outlook—a change that reshaped the very conception of what it meant to be a "good Jew."

This change goes back to the early decades of the nineteenth century and gathered momentum with time. To simplify considerably, it was a sharp shift in emphasis from the "rabbinic" elements in the Jewish tradition to the "prophetic" elements.

One should not exaggerate the tension that traditionally prevailed between these two currents of Jewish religiosity. What today is called "normative Judaism" managed to strike a cautious and generally acceptable balance between them. After all, the high moralism of the Prophets—compassion for the poor and unfortunate, the emphasis on universal peace as a specifically Jewish aspiration—was incorporated into its rabbinical teachings, while the Prophets themselves insisted on the importance of observing traditional Jewish law. Prophetic moralism usually stopped well short of antinomianism and messianic enthusiasm, while rabbinic legalism was merely always deferential to moral sensibilities. Jews prided themselves as being "more moral" than Christians, Moslems, or pagans, and—regardless of individual behavior—the Jewish religious tradition unquestionably put a greater stress on "good deeds" and "righteous living" than on faith or dogma.

Nevertheless, the tension was there, and steps were taken to cope with it. Undoubtedly, there were incendiary possibilities in the declamations of the Prophets, and prudence required that these be minimized. Even today, a student in the yeshiva, in his early years, never studies the Prophets in isolation from a study of the Pentateuch or the Talmud. In the synagogue, the Prophets are read on the Sabbath only in the form of a commentary on the non-prophetic books of the Torah. Especially after the advent of Christianity, which can be seen as an antinomian and millenarian outburst within the Jewish prophetic tradition, it was a constant matter of concern to the rabbis that such "enthusiasm" be held in check by a more rigorous focus on lawful and orderly behavior.

After the French Revolution, however, what we call today "prophetic Judaism" acquired an ever-greater vitality and autonomy. This was part and parcel of the emerging messianic sensibility—in matters political, social, and economic—that the Revolution established throughout European society. An era of grand aspirations began. The Israeli historian, the late J. L. Talmon, opens his book, *Political Messianism: The Romantic Phase,* with the following sentences:

"The present inquiry is concerned with the expectation of universal regeneration which animated men and movements in the first half of the nineteenth century.

"No period before or after has experienced so luxurious a flowering of Utopian schemes purporting to offer a coherent, complete and final solution to the problem of social evil."

Expectations of universal regeneration—and in the foreseeable future, achieved through political and social action! In this way, and in this period, a secular version of Judeo-Christian messianism entered Western political thought and established itself there as a rational option for reasonable persons. What made it appear both rational and reasonable was its seeming continuity with the theme of social, political, economic, and, most important, technological progress that had emerged so powerfully in the previous two centuries. Indeed, it seemed not only continuous with, but a plausible extension of, the idea of progress. Why should progress be so gradual, so intermittent, so painfully slow? Why not deliberately hasten the progressive movement toward its predestined end—the universal regeneration of mankind? Now, hastening the end had always been regarded by Jewish and Christian orthodoxy as a dangerous, heretical temptation, one that its indigenous messianism made a permanent temptation, and, therefore, to be guarded against all the more vigilantly. But in a secular version, rooted not in religion but in science and the newly invented social sciences, it escaped such vigilance. Traditional religious orthodoxy was neither confronted nor refuted by the spirit of this new age, but it was ignored and left to wither away.

In such a heightened, progressive perspective, capitalism—i.e., a society centered around a market economy—posed a problem for Jews. On the matter of the relation between Jews and capitalism there has been a vast amount of intellectual confusion.

Judaism, as is generally and correctly recognized, is much more a this-worldly religion than Christianity. As a result, Jews have never been opposed to or contemptuous of business as a human activity. Making a living was always regarded as central to Jewish family life and, while Jewish law imposed some relatively mild inhibitions and prohibitions on commercial activity, there was never any sense of a conflict between the two. Becoming wealthy was similarly regarded as a legitimate, even admirable goal—so long as this wealth was used for benign (usually communal) purposes.

But business, in specific commercial markets, is not capitalism. Business is an activity; commerce is an activity; capitalism is an idea invented in the eighteenth century. Business proceeds, in one way or another, in all socioeconomic systems above the most primitive level. Capitalism is a prescription whereby business activity is incorporated into a market economy that is the major institution of civil society, an institution that is the source and guarantor of individual liberty. It is the failure to distinguish between business activity by Jews and the capitalist idea that muddles the thinking and writing of Max Weber and Werner Sombart as well as some of our own contemporaries, who are perplexed by the fact that Jews do so well under capitalism while showing so little gratitude to the system. The fact that Jews, for various historical reasons, are adept at business, and the further fact that Judaism does little to frustrate business incentives, means that Jews always manage to do very well in a capitalist society. But it does not follow that Jewish affluence or Jewish prosperity brings with it Jewish peace of mind and soul. In all existing capitalist societies Jews have done and do extremely well for themselves. In all these societies Jews—especially younger Jews—are profoundly uneasy about the legitimacy of their own success. The anti-Semitic fantasy in which Jews manage to be simultaneously wealthy capitalists and subversive radicals is but a paranoid inflation of a reality.

The only exceptions to this generalization are the strictly Orthodox Jews, who isolate themselves from modernity as a whole, and who continue to practice business in a capitalist society while being utterly indifferent to, even willfully ignorant of, the capitalist idea. For them, their religious community is the only authentic sociological reality. This makes them conservative by temperament and inclination, while remaining unaffected by modern conservative, liberal, or radical ideologies.

Jews who are not strictly Orthodox, however, are fully implicated in modernity and its ideologies. For reasons already given, they are most likely to be attracted to that version of liberal ideology spawned by Continental radical liberalism. This is most obviously the case for secularized Jews, who have been "liberated" from any formal attachment to the Jewish community, and who feel that adherence to such an ideology is an appropriate Jewish response to modernity. They find in the "secular humanism" of this ideology an adequate approximation to the ideals of the "prophetic Judaism" which emerged in the 19th century and has infused itself into all non-Orthodox versions of contemporary Judaism.

Secular humanism really exists, as does prophetic Judaism, and the connection between the two is deep and strong. Secular humanism born of the Renaissance is a form of atheism—one less interested in denying the existence of a divinity than in affirming the possibility of humanity's realizing its full human potential through the energetic application of moralistic intelligence. Prophetic Judaism is a distinctly modern form of Jewish religiosity less interested in God's word or Jewish law than in realizing a universalist version of the preaching of the Prophets here on earth.

Social and social-democratic movements are all inspired, officially or unofficially, by one version or another of secular humanism. Similarly, non-Orthodox Judaism today is, in varying degrees, inspired or infused by the teaching of the Prophets rather than of the rabbis. In the case of Reform Judaism, such an inspiration is its original raison d'être. In the case of Conservative Judaism, the prophetic teachings are allowed to dominate its secular involvements, even where there is substantial attachment to the law. And in the case of secular Jews, Prophetic Judaism merges into secular humanism to create what can fairly be described as a peculiarly intense, Jewish, secular humanism.

It is this combination of secular historical experience and the religious mutation it provoked that accounts for the political predispositions of contemporary American Jews. And not only American Jews—wherever European Jews, especially East European Jews have settled, whether it be in Canada, Australia, South Africa, or Latin America, they have located themselves left-of-center of the political spectrum. This has most strikingly been the case in Israel, where remnants of the socialist tradition still evoke a pious loyalty, despite the facts that the prevalence of socialist ideas obstructs the growth of the economy and that such ideas have no relevance to the realities confronting Israeli foreign policy.

Having said all this, however, one must add that this situation cannot endure much longer. After two centuries, the socialist idea is becoming meaningless and incomprehensible even to its advocates. In practically every country with self-styled socialist regimes, the movement is away from traditional socialism. The economic direction of this movement is toward a system in which self-interested activity in a freer market plays a greater role. Politically, it is toward a system that is either left-wing authoritarian, right-wing authoritarian, or an unstable combination of the two. The promise of a humanistic, democratic socialism, whether as an ideal to be realized or a goal to be approached, is dissolving into the mists.

This leaves American Jews in a condition of what social psychologists call "cognitive dissonance." Their political loyalties become more desperate in proclamation, more unbelievable in fact. This especially is the case as the Third World, where socialism is still a much-respected and often official doctrine, evolves toward socioeconomic–political systems that fall outside of any Western category, and have in common mainly a hostility to Western liberal civilization and religious and secular humanism. It is this hostility that shapes their attitude toward Israel, perceived as an outpost of Western civilization. More and more, a socialist, quasi-socialist, or left-liberal political outlook sympathetic to social democracy is becoming inconsistent with a concern that American Jews overwhelmingly feel for the survival of Israel.

How long this condition of "cognitive dissonance" will continue, and where it will end, is now unforeseeable. Everything will depend on how the Western democracies themselves adapt to this new situation. It is certain, however, that American Jews, even as they feel more and more "at home" in America, are going to find themselves among a much larger population of liberal Americans: the ideologically uprooted and dispossessed.

8

Towards a Politics of Paradox: The Jewish Confrontation with Power

Carl A. Sheingold

Jews are in the midst of profound changes in their relationship to politics and power. The establishment of the State of Israel obviously introduced new Jewish questions. For example, can Jews exercise state power? Can the imperatives of statecraft be reconciled with Jewish culture and values?

Equally, if on different terms, Jews in the Diaspora have become powerful. Particularly in the United States, Jewish lobbying on behalf of Israel is a powerful force being exercised in the most powerful country in the world, with the most serious consequences for the Jewish state. Internally, Jews have become an affluent group, exercising influence far beyond their numbers on the life and culture of the society.

Millennia of Jewish powerlessness preceded this period. This most intense and tragic experience immediately preceded it. It is our premise that this new situation calls for finding new ways to define authentic Jewish approaches to politics. As is often the case, the search for the new will involve rediscovery of the old. In this essay we identify some roadsigns for seeking Jewish authenticity in the kind of political environment Jews inhabit today.

A Loss of Innocence

The meaning of Jewish authenticity is a complex matter that will be addressed as we proceed. For Jews whose lives revolve around their Jewishness, the importance, if not the meaning, of Jewish authenticity is self-evident. For many others, its importance has a more indirect root: the connection between Jewish values and idealism. In political terms this connection presumes that authentic Jewish politics will respond to broader ideals than narrow self-interest.

Given such a presumption, this period of adapting to power—and the historical background to which we can only briefly allude—has revolved around a loss of Jewish innocence. This has been most obvious in regard to Israel and issues surrounding the occupation of the West Bank and Gaza, now entering its third decade. In the United States, there has been a more subtle, but nonetheless real, loss of innocence. For several decades—starting with the election of Franklin Roosevelt in 1932 and ending with the election of Richard Nixon in 1968—the political party and ideology supported by most Jews was dominant. During this period, Jews saw many of their ideas and ideals more or less acted on, with mixed results.

This can best be illustrated by the Civil Rights Movement, with which, in its early years, Jews were deeply involved. Without going into the details of events and issues, it can be said that many policies that Jews supported because of the presumption that their adoption would lead to a more just society were adopted. The results were mixed. Many now argue that policies that were supposed to increase justice have instead increased dependency.

Whatever the merits of either side of the debate, it illustrates the way in which an easy association of specific political positions and policies with broader values presumes a consensus as to the consequences and efficacy of those policies. Such a consensus is always hard to maintain when those supporting the policies achieve power.

From a purely political point of view, adapting to mixed results is a common experience. But to the extent that many Jews equated their idealism with their liberalism, and their liberalism with their Jewishness, they created a double bind. It became more difficult to make a simple equation between liberalism and idealism (for example, to equate liberal recommendations for dealing with racial problems with the value of justice). To that extent alone, the simple equation of liberalism and Jewishness became less satisfying.

Other changes were also affecting the dynamics of the latter equation. The late 1960s marked the end of a particular period of Jewish assimilation. Three events were critical. The 1967 War made many Jews aware of how much they cared as Jews about Israel's survival. The Black Power movement, and the strengthening of ethnic pride and assertiveness that accompanied it, also had profound effects upon Jews.

Finally, and perhaps most importantly, this was the period in which the first truly native generation of American Jews came of age—a generation for whom the connection to tradition was no longer automatic, but also not something that had to be severed for them to feel modern. As a result of all of these events, many Jews began to look more seriously at the content of the Jewish tradition and became more serious about their own and other's claims to Jewish authenticity.

In the decades before this, most statements in the form of "my politics reflect my Jewishness" were more biographical than philosophical. They were a way of identifying one's politics with a life experience which, for historical reasons, was common to Jews. In fact, they were statements often made by people who evidenced little interest in the issue of Jewish authenticity in other parts of their lives. Indeed, for many Jews making such statements, a flight from tradition was at the center of their lives.

In recent decades, most such people have insufficient Jewish connection to care to make such declarations, and those who do seem to care more than their predecessors did about the Jewish depth behind such statements. For this reason as well, the equation of liberalism and Jewishness began to take on a rather shallow quality. It is important to add, however, that precisely because for most, though by no means all, the return to tradition was not to a traditional life governed strictly by Jewish law, the issue of authenticity has become a subject of greater importance as well as of more heated internal and external debate.

This debate suggests another and more subtle meaning of the loss of political innocence. One meaning of innocence is to be in an unchallenged state—unchallenged by facts or contrary opinions. For many years many Jews lived politically in such a state of innocence. They had homogeneous political views. They lived in a society in which variations on those views were dominant. In Israel, similar views were dominant enough so that, from the perspective of the Diaspora, political forces and ideologies opposed to the labor/socialist movement could easily be ignored. In the last two decades, all such hegemonies have been broken. As an increasing proportion of Jews who care have become more serious about their Jewishness, the depth, complexity, and pluralism of Jewish history, life, and meaning have become more salient.

Pluralism and Authenticity

We have described a situation in which the need for guidelines for assessing Jewish authenticity in politics has intensified. But we have also seen that it is a situation in which there is no standard of authenticity about which all Jews can agree, in the political realm or any other. Jews are experiencing a kind of pluralistic crisis of meaning. At the same time, most parties to intra-Jewish politics seek, to some degree, validation by the tradition, rather than either living totally within it or seeing themselves as superceding it. Indeed, if this were not the case, there would be no crisis of pluralism—there would simply be different, ostensibly Jewish, groups, living in different worlds and in a state of mutual indifference. The heightened conflict within the Jewish community is itself a measure of the closeness and interpenetrability of the diverse worlds in which Jews now live.

In such a pluralistic environment, the claim of authenticity, particularly when applied to specific positions on specific political issues, has a built-in potential to be self-serving and inauthentic. Given the richness and diversity of the Jewish tradition and history, most political positions can claim plausibly supportive "proof-texts," historical theological backing, even if the positions around which the claims are addressed seem contradictory.

This last point may suggest both a useful approach to this subject and an appropriate audience. It is easy to find elements of a Jewish tradition and history whose importance and political significance are beyond dispute. But the terms of contemporary political debate often make them seem contradictory; hence, they are rarely cited at the same time or by the same people. Thus, it may prove useful to seek some commonly accepted benchmarks of Jewish authenticity that are typically cited in isolation from each other and consider their joint implications. To do so may lead us to the elements of Jewish political paradigm rather than a Jewish gloss on modern political paradigms.

Can the Center Hold?

The condition of pluralism also suggests something about the audience for such a venture. If there is a crisis of pluralism, it is experienced as such in "the center," both in a Jewish fashion and politically; this is true by definition. Those on the extremes do not experience a crisis, but rather a battle to be won. Moreover, those on the extremes are clear about the sources of authenticity, whether those sources be Talmud or Marx.

In this context, the center can be defined in many ways. It is the place in which an overriding goal is to hold together the whole—i.e., holding the community (however defined) together is seen as having value in and of itself. It is a place in which the desire to root one's Jewish life in text and tradition is strong, but in which, as Kaplan put it, the tradition, and particularly Jewish law (in relation to Jews collectively, if not the individual), has a "voice, but not a veto." It is a place in which secular political stances are fluid ideologically; hence, there is not only a desire for Jewish authenticity, but the potential for a more dynamic, if not deeper, relationship between the Jewish tradition and the political commitment.

For those occupying these centers (and some, obviously, occupy some but not all; for example, Orthodox Jews who have a pluralistic view of Jewish politics and communal life) there is a crisis of pluralism; indeed, the crisis is often defined by the question, "can the center hold?" It is a tactical crisis over the efficacy of moderate, consensual political tactics in a polarized environment; an idealogical crisis marked by what sometimes seems to be an absence of centrist goals other than compromise and consensus; and a crisis of authenticity, which has already been defined in general terms, but marked in the center by greater inherent ambiguity and vulnerability, and often also by the absence of usable language and concepts for ideological, political discourse resulting from the ceding of ideological/theological claims to others.

What follows is an attempt to find in Jewish tradition and Jewish history some insights with regard to Jewish authenticity in politics. We will be looking not for universally relevant insights, but, rather, insights relevant to giving Jewish definition (beyond the claims of Jewish biography) to centrist Jewish politics in a pluralistic age. We will not seek to establish a direct line from such insights to possible stances on contemporary political issues. Rather we will be seeking generic, politically relevant Jewish concerns and Jewish ways of thinking about the task of reaching political judgments.

Do Justice

There is little doubt that if we were to seek standards of Jewish political authenticity in a public-opinion poll of Jews, the first candidate would be justice as a goal, value, and commandment. It would not be a poor choice, but, as we have already implied, different meanings of justice are at the center of many contemporary ideologies, and justice (or some closely related value) provides the base for many contradictory policies and programs. An example of this is provided in a recent work of Jerold Auerbach, who notes the irony attached to the familiar effort of nonobservant Jews to root their calls for the remedy of contemporary ills in the prophetic (as compared to halakic) tradition, specifically in the constant call of the ancient Jewish prophets for justice. But the prophetic meaning of justice is linked inextricably to doing God's will, as reflected in obedience to God's laws.

It is thus important, in the context of this essay, to find a meaning of justice that is both general and clearly connected to the Jewish tradition. In other words, we must start with Jewish tradition and history, rather than contemporary ills that need fixing (whether poverty, inequality, or whatever), to find the Jewish meaning of justice.

I would suggest that the root of the Jewish value of justice is the idea that man is made in the image of God. As a consequence, a certain dignity inheres in all people, collectively and individually, the violation of which is an injustice to God. Connected to this is the idea that man was created to do God's will; the Jews, as a people, are covenanted to be "a nation of priests, a holy people"— i.e., we are here, in part, to try to make the world a more just place.

To go very much beyond this—to ask what exactly violates human dignity in a way that could be called an "injustice"—is to risk entering a world of political discourse defined by contemporary ideological sensibilities. But if we focus on conditions, rather than the means to alleviate them, some examples can be given. There are kinds of material suffering that we see on the streets of our cities, which represent and grow out of conditions that clearly violate human dignity, and which can hardly be pleasing to God. We may disagree about why those conditions exist and how best to alleviate them. But few would disagree that their alleviation would increase the amount of justice in the world. The common abhorrence of physical torture would be another example, not to mention mass murder and genocide.

Suffice it to say that while the Jewish value of justice can easily be distorted and used for ulterior, ideological ends, it remains a core Jewish value because it gets to the heart of the purpose of creation, the meaning of man as God's partner in creation, and the meaning of the covenant between God and the Jewish people. Any political approach that is indifferent to the value of justice (or, to use somewhat different but equally traditional language, indifferent to the goal of "healing the world") would have scant claim to Jewish authenticity. Precisely because so much of contemporary political action is mounted in the name of justice (however defined), this value lies at the heart of the challenge of defining authentic Jewish politics today.

Do Not Worship Idols

If there is another piece of the Jewish tradition that is an unavoidable element of Jewish political values, it is the prohibition against idol worship. The mandate to do justice reminds us that man is made in the image of God. The prohibition against idol worship reminds us that man is not meant to act as if he is God, or to treat other men or human creations as godlike.

No commandment has more direct political relevance, because this commandment is talking directly about power: To what and to whom should we grant power? In our time, as powers unimaginable to earlier generations have been granted to states and to secular ideologies (leading, among other things, to the slaughter of six million Jews), no commandment is of greater contemporary relevance.

Here, too, it is important to be clear about the core meaning. To prohibit idol worship is not to prohibit the granting of power to ideas, people, or states. It is specifically to prohibit granting or claiming godlike power or status. This commandment can be abused, just as the ideal of justice can be abused, to justify opposition to a myriad of things that have nothing to do with idol worship.

Unfortunately, our contemporary experience with totalitarian states and ideologies has provided us with many examples of idol worship that are unambiguous, of leaders who have been treated like gods and ideologies which have been treated as revelation. It is no accident that such societies have been antireligious, and, to say the least, inhospitable homes for Jews, and that such ideologies have been characterized as substitute religions.

Contradictions

If the Jewish obligations to do justice and to not worship idols stand at the heart of a Jewish approach to politics, the conflicts and contradictions between these obligations (which have been highlighted particularly in the modern era) stand at the heart of the inner tension of Jewish politics. This tension arises in part because of the tendency in the modern era to see the state—and increased state power over individual lives—as the principal vehicle for advancing justice. While granting power to the state is not in and of itself idol worship, it contains the seeds.

There is also a more subtle and pervasive source of this tension. The power that modern science and technology have placed in human hands has far outpaced progress in discovering how to use that power effectively to advance social ideals and values, from wherever they may be derived. From this gap comes a natural tendency to grant exalted status to the theories and programs we adopt to achieve our goals; indeed, to treat those means (e.g., Marxism or constitutionalism) as if they themselves were our ultimate goals. In this process lies another seed of idol worship: a tendency, if you will, to treat a provisional theory regarding how to achieve God's will as if it were itself God's will.

Put in these terms, idol worship can be seen as the most general and important form of a common risk we run in all aspects of our lives—family lives, running an organization, even writing an article; it is what the sociologist Robert Merton once dubbed "the displacement of goals." We do this when we treat means as goals, or goals as values, or the secular as divine. And put this way, it may seem as if any effort to achieve any goal, justice included, contains the seeds of idol worship, and that in obeying the prohibition against idol worship, we run the risk of adopting a stance of total passivity, which is hardly consistent with any notion of the Jewish tradition or Jewish purpose.

A Holistic Approach; The Politics of Paradox

But the inner tension between doing justice and not worshipping idols is real. The fact that the Jewish tradition calls for adherence to seemingly contradictory mandates is not unique to the political realm. It is a central (and even distinctive) characteristic of monotheistic traditions generally, and the Jewish tradition in particular, to insist that we strive for wholeness, which inevitably involves seeking to achieve, or at least to retain loyalty to, contradictory values and goals. This is true in regard to faith and action, mercy and justice, the individual and community, i.e., just as it is true in regard to justice and the avoidance of idol worship. For the purposes of this essay, it is no accident that the attempt to transcend rather than evade contradictions is also the most salient characteristic of the most serious kind of centrist politics, which does not simply seek compromise for the sake of compromise.

This suggests that the tension between the first two elements of a Jewish political paradigm should be the starting point rather than an obstacle, to further discussion. We need to assess the political implications of a more general Jewish refusal to water down the holistic implications of monotheism, which, in turn, requires the acknowledgment of contradictions and the transcendence of contradictions as a goal. We also need to find other themes to help us navigate from this position.

A Vision of Jewish History

Let us begin at the beginning. The Bible begins with the fall from innocence, less in the Christian sense of original sin, but more in the Jewish sense of a description of the human condition. After the Garden of Eden, man cannot be regarded as innocent, either as actor or as the object of action. In a sense, the political message of the story of the Tower of Babel is that human politics is not and cannot be innocent, for social homogeneity is the primary condition for innocent politics.

After Eden and Babel, we should understand the remainder of Genesis and Exodus—the stories of Noah, the Patriarchs, and the journey from slavery in Egypt to the revelation of Sinai—as a search for the social means to achieve God's purpose in creation in a complex world. The overriding theme is a narrowing of purpose and its vehicle for achievement.

This theme is realized most vividly in the shift in the narrative from the story of humankind to the story of a particular people, the Jews. Within the Jewish saga, the focus is on the inner life of the people and the legal basis for insuring that that it will be a holy life. Holiness, or at least the covenanted Jewish mission, becomes more a matter of the redemptive potential inherent in the details of the daily life of a particular people than the goal of the immediate redemption of mankind.

The biblical narratives can be seen as revelation, history, myth, or any combination of the three. But as the narrative moves across the banks of the Jordan, and we move into what is unambiguously the concrete history and historical tradition of the Jewish people, these themes remain. The focus remains on the inner life of a particular people, and the idea of holiness is understood primarily in terms of the details of that life, and the detailed implications of a legal system set up to govern it.

This becomes even more intensely and, sometimes, tragically, the case after the destruction of the second temple. Jews now ceased to have a national/

territorial unit through which to act in history. And the societies within which they lived came to be dominated by world religions with a very different view of the relationship between messianic goals and historical time. For many, Jewish loyalty to a more particularistic mission and patient view of history was, at best, a rebuke to this vision, and, at worst, an obstacle to universal redemption.

Messianism within the Details and Moments

This is not to suggest that the Jewish tradition that we inherit is without messianic elements or universalistic implications. As Gershom Scholem demonstrated, messianism is a continuing theme in Jewish history. Put more accurately, the theme of Jewish history is neither messianism nor its absence or rejection, but rather the tension between messianism and other, more quietistic tendencies. This tension has been a primary creative force in Jewish history. It has been when one or the other side of the tension has broken through in seeming "triumph" (as, for example, in the case of Shabbatai Svi, a false messiah of the seventeenth century), that tragedy has resulted.

In the end, however, Jews have consistently returned to and held onto their particular mission which, in most periods, has meant holding onto their devotion to Jewish law and their patience, with some exceptions, and often at great cost. The messianic theme, rather than triumphing over the others, has taken on meaning within them. In the case of the Jewish mystic tradition (including Hasidism), this has meant the creation of an elaborate and paradoxic system of kabelistically rooted symbols and myths, which ascribes ultimate meaning to the mundane actions of everyday life.

We also see this in the Jewish tradition of law and text. Critics and enemies of the Jews have often used the term "talmudic" to refer to an allegedly petty and ungenerous concern with the minute details of the law. But it can also be used to refer to an extraordinary intellectual and moral tradition in which scholars and jurists seek to pay attention to a holistic set of concerns within the borders of seemingly minor and mundane actions or legal issues. Even more dramatically, the Jewish tradition of textual study and exegesis provides a way to find holistic worlds of meaning by turning a single text, paragraph, sentence, or even word, "over and over and over again."

The Jewish Mission

The focus of Jewish idealism lies in holding onto, rather than evading, the details of the present moment in the life of a particular people. Traditionally, Jews have sought to invest that life and those details with holistic meaning. This is fundamentally how the Jews have conceived of and lived out their mission.

Within the details of these moments in history, they seek to do justice. But to seek to evade the details of actions and their consequences as if "the end of days" had already arrived is, for Jews, heresy or idol worship. Paradoxically, this has meant that the deep involvement of the Jews with the present is itself historical. Jews, of necessity, have rooted their vision of the meaning of the present in what preceded and what might follow it, and, indeed, in the mystery of the whole.

In doing this, Jews have conceived of themselves as partners of God in working out the ultimate meaning and purpose of creation. But it is idol worship for Jews to imagine that they can replace God and transform the current moment into the end of history by their own power. A single, distant, unimaginable God is more whole and vital, than are the tangible and accessible idols whose defining quality is partialness. Similarly, a nonmessianic view of the present permits the kind of historical understanding of the present that can infuse it with a wholeness that is real.

The Politics of Paradox

What, then, is a framework for an authentic Jewish "politics of paradox." It would be built on the following elements:

(1) It is a politics that is relentlessly non-innocent. It insists on confronting the paradox of contradictory goals and values head on. It expects and anticipates unintended consequences rather than ignoring or rationalizing them, for they will be the focus of the next stage of action. In this sense, it is holistic and dialectic.
(2) It is a politics in which attention to the details—particularly to the anticipation and assumption of responsibility for the real, likely consequences of action—is a primary responsibility. It is, to use the terms from Max Weber's classic essay "Politics as a Vocation," a "politics of responsibility" (where responsibility is taken for the actual consequences of actions taken or supported), rather than a "politics of ultimate ends" (where responsibility is taken for the apparent and immediate, if not real, connection between action and ultimate objectives).
(3) It is a politics that is deeply historical: Seeing the present as a moment in history, and understanding that contradictions (such as that between doing justice and not worshiping idols) can be transcended only through the dialectic process of history.
(4) It is a politics that is intrinsically religious; not necessarily in the sense of being built on religious observance (legal or ritual) or any particular set of beliefs, but, in the sense, to use Scholem's phrase, of "[having] . . . the feeling that there is mystery—a secret—in the world," and having respect for the necessity and power of symbols to express that mystery, as well to express the desire for meaning and solace in ways that technology cannot.

Indeed, it is precisely when centrist politics severs its ties, particularly its intellectual ties, to religion that it is also severing its ties to the symbol systems and modes of discourse that convey the larger purpose and ultimate meaning of such politics. It is then that theological and ideological ground seemingly is ceded to others.

In this context, the work of two of the most important, paradoxical, modern Jewish thinkers, Franz Rosenzweig (particularly his ability to articulate the presence of eternity in the flow of present moments) and Gershom Scholem (his counterbalancing focus on the dialectic flow and change that is Jewish history, and, more importantly, his ability to convey the Jewish meaning embedded in the process of history itself) are of particular importance.

(5) It is a centrist politics in the sense that it is concerned with the whole, and will inevitably find itself sitting in the center of competing goals and values. Perhaps more importantly, it is centrist in the sense of respecting the importance of process, which is nothing more than respecting that which permits holistic goals to work themselves out through history (and which often seems irrelevant or a hindrance to the goal of bringing the "end of days" right now).

(6) It is *not* centrist in regard to an attribute that is frequently associated with that term. It is not necessarily moderate in regard to specific positions espoused, nor is it necessarily preoccupied with compromise for its own sake. There are times when, from the perspective of the politics of paradox, it is necessary to work for a radical shift because a denigrated value or goal is in danger of extinction.

Implications

There is obviously not enough space in this essay to elaborate on the implications of the framework outlined above. As we have already suggested, the implications will not be found in the details of political debate. Put differently, what we have termed "the politics of paradox" is not likely to be the only framework from which Jews approach politics. Most of the time Jews will be Democrats or Republicans, Labor or Likud, conservatives or liberals— joining movements, taking political positions, voting for political parties or movements; in general, trying to influence the political system through the normal means available and with the limits of vision those means require.

In so doing, they will be acting in ways which, among other things, are good for the Jews and advance the interest of Jews, in a narrow sense. Often that will, appropriately, be their primary goal, and will be the subject of legitimate debate. In such circumstances, to claim Jewish authenticity for the positions being argued will generally be inappropriate.

But the issue of Jewish authenticity arises directly with regard to the way by which political positions are developed and argued, and in the standards used to assess them. Here "the politics of paradox" has some direct and important implications that can only be hinted at through some brief examples.

A. "Moral" Issues

Jews, as Jews, cannot be indifferent to issues that have a clear moral dimension, such as the threat of nuclear war or injustice in South Africa, not to mention the fate of the West Bank and Gaza. Political debate on such matters tends to revolve around strategic issues; for example, the desirability of a nuclear freeze or a particular arms control agreement, the appropriateness of divestment in South Africa, various options regarding the Arab/Palestinian/Israeli conflict in the Middle East. In the context of such debates, the Jewish tradition calls for attention to and taking responsibility for the actual or predictable consequences of the strategies adopted.

It is almost inconceivable that a particular strategy can or should be labeled the correct Jewish position, because the likely consequences of the competing strategies are the subject of debate. For example, would a nuclear freeze make nuclear war more or less likely. Would divestment enhance or detract from the justice of South African society. These are the subjects of debate.

Contradictory positions on such issues can have equal claims on Jewish authenticity. What does not have such a claim is, on the one hand, a position of indifference to such issues, or, on the other hand, an approach to such issues which amounts to the making of self-justifying moral gestures. From a Jewish perspective, there is nothing intrinsically moral in being "against the arms race." The moral issue, from the Jewish point of view, has to do with the seriousness with which the complex connection between, for example, the arms race and the likelihood of nuclear war is being addressed.

To take another example, it is hard to imagine a standard by which any from among the opposing points of view in regard to the disposition of the occupied territories on the West Bank and Gaza could be called the authentic Jewish stance. Even if the sole standard used is the physical security of Israel, plausible cases can be made for a wide range of strategies and ultimate objectives. To argue that Israeli control of these lands should be maintained indefinitely, or should be unilaterally abandoned, or somewhere in between, can all be defended plausibly. What cannot be defended, from the point of view of Jewish authenticity, is to argue that Israel should leave the West Bank because the consequences of staying "don't feel good."

Jews must insist on taking a long-term historical view on such issues. For example, for Jews to insist on providing an historical context to the current debate on the West Bank may be polemically necessary, but it is also necessary.

Because authentic Jewish politics is historical in nature, as is a historically rooted patience in interpreting the meaning of the present.

B. Jews and Totalitarianism

Much of twentieth-century politics has revolved around the emergence of totalitarian forms of government. Jews cannot be neutral on this issue. Jews must resist totalitarian approaches to politics, not just because Jews inevitably suffer in such regimes, but also because totalitarianism intrinsically is a form of idol worship—directly, by inviting the worship of the state, its ideology, and its leaders, and also as an attempt to end the processes of history.

This may seem self-evident. Few Jews would support totalitarian regimes openly. But in the post–World War II period, as totalitarianism has become more a phenomenon of the left than the right, Jews of the left have often given lip service to their opposition to totalitarianism, as they have devoted much more energy to supporting reform and revolution in the name of social justice. Sometimes Jews have been apologists for totalitarian regimes. This stance may be tenable on many grounds, but none are authentically Jewish.

C. Power and Powerlessness

Finally, in the background of much of this chapter has been the historical change in the relationship of Jews to power. I would conclude by stating that the most important general challenge confronting Jewish politics today is that of taking responsibility for power. Conversely, Jews cannot and should not take pride in feeling or acting as if they are outsiders to power (for example, by engaging in a politics of ultimate ends, built around moral gestures) when they are not.

The "politics of responsibility" is authentically Jewish politics, and has always been the norm in the internal politics of the Jewish community. The challenge today is to find ways to make it the norm—and to develop comfort and skill in acting it out—in our relationship to the larger society and world community in which we are so actively engaged and to the State of Israel.

The author wishes to acknowledge Professor Janet Burstein of Drew University, who read an early draft of this manuscript and, as always, provided insightful comments and encouragement.

9

The Jewish Electorate: California 1980-1986

Alan M. Fisher

For most of this century the study of American Jewry has been the study of New York and northeastern Jews. The American Jewish community is still overrepresented in the mid-Atlantic region but, like other Americans, Jews have also been relocating. Although the move to Florida has been well acknowledged in popular Jewish culture, it is California which has become the second most important Jewish state—numerically, economically, politically, philanthropically, and certainly in its impact on the larger American culture. Under the intellectual and communal leadership of people like Earl Raab, California has become a major force not only in American Jewry but in world Jewry as well. The larger Los Angeles–Orange County area now contains the second largest Jewish population concentration in the world. It certainly warrants more scholarly attention. This research is an attempt to provide a detailed introduction and overview to political attitudes and behavior of California Jews.

Why study California Jews? Their numbers and power alone make them noteworthy. Perhaps equally important, Californians—in the popular mind as well as demographically—represent the wave of the future. Not only do popular cultural, music, and dress styles originate there but many major sociological and political developments seem to start in California: increased divorce rates, religious cults, property tax reform. The state is a good precursor of what happens across America. Furthermore, areas of heavy Jewish concentration like Los Angeles are much more the vibrant American melting pot than are the decayed eastern rust-belt big cities. In politics, too, metropolitan Los Angeles is much closer to mainstream America than is Boston or New York. To ignore California Jewry is to ignore the immediate future of the American Jews.

California Jews

Using an ongoing survey, one study has examined demographic data on Jews in California and compared them with those in the rest of the country.[1] In broad terms they are not very different, and both tend to be differentiated similarly from the local non-Jewish populations, especially on education, vocational status, income (all higher), and size of residential area (larger, more cosmopolitan).

Nevertheless, some differences exist. Compared with other American Jews, California Jews reflect the ways in which their state differs from the rest of the country. They are somewhat better educated, of higher vocational status, and a little wealthier. Slightly fewer are married, and they are noticeably more likely to have never married. They are almost the same age as non-Hispanic Californians, whereas other American Jews, with a few exceptions in the West and Washington, D.C., are definitely older than their neighbors.[2]

Methods

In the past, it has been difficult to obtain good public-opinion data on Jews for at least one major reason. Because they are a relatively small proportion of the larger American population (about 2.5 percent of the adults), not many Jews appear in national surveys, very few of which exceed 1,500 total respondents. Even the rare survey with 2,000 people will probably contain no more than fifty to sixty-five Jews, and most national mass-media opinion polls contain a maximum of forty Jews. As a result, we cannot be very confident about their findings because the margin of error is too wide.

However, recent polling trends, especially when applied in California, help solve two major methodologic problems. Over the last decade, the pollsters increasingly survey voters as they leave the ballot box on election day; the results are appropriately termed "exit polls." Because they are less expensive to conduct than most other reputable surveys, it is possible to expand the size of the sample dramatically and, thus, also the sample of Jews. In the polls used in this research, for example, the largest Jewish subsample numbers 438 out of 6,775 total respondents (November 1986). The Jewish subsample also increases because the Jewish population of California (about 3.1 percent) is greater than across the country at large, and this is magnified because Jews constitute an even larger percentage of the actual voters (about 5 percent).[3]

Exit polls simplify a number of other methodologic complexities, but they are not without their own problems; specifically, sampling. Over the years, this sampling has improved considerably so that exit polls are more accurate instruments today than fifteen years ago.[4] Still, they are imperfect and even suffer new afflictions, especially in California; e.g., increased absentee voting, which is not tapped by exit polls. Based on the politics and region of the absentee vote, however, there is reason to suspect that it is a practice less engaged in by Jews—at least so far.

The data in this study come from six *Los Angeles Times* election-day exit polls that were administered during statewide primary (June) and general elections (November) from 1980 through 1986. The November 1980 Poll is unavailable, and the November 1984 Poll contains a national sample. The most frequently used poll is from November 1986, because it is the most recent and contains the largest Jewish subsample. Only the June 1980 Poll has fewer than 185 Jews.

There is an issue in the *Times* Poll of how Jews are identified. The question, as it appears on the survey ballot, reads; "in what religion were you raised?" This excludes those who converted to Judaism or born-Jews raised in some other religion. The latter category is minute and not a real problem; those who have actively converted to another religion are also probably few in number. But this definition does exclude converts to Judaism, who comprise a small, but significant, number of California Jews.[5] For our purposes, it would have been better to ask simply, "what is your religion?" although this also presents certain problems.

Findings

One approach to ascertaining respondents' orientations is to let them describe and label their own beliefs. The most popular dimension still runs along a continuum of liberalism and conservatism, although such general overriding concepts no longer serve as such potent indicators of a person's total political perspectives as they did thirty years ago because of growing differentiation among economics, cultural-moral issues, and civil liberties as well as between domestic and international politics and economics. Nevertheless, people's self-identification on a liberalism–conservatism dimension is still one of the best insights we have, predicting not only people's party affiliation but also their actual vote for candidates and support of specific issues.

According to the November 1986 figures in table 9.1 and concurrent CBS national data, Jews in California are slightly more liberal than Jews across the country. More obvious is that Jews still differ from non-Jews in the way they have for most of this century. California Jews are considerably more liberal than non-Jews, and decidedly less conservative. Fewer than half as many Jews define themselves as conservative or very conservative (18 percent Jews: 40 percent non-Jews). In relative percentages, this figure is not much different from what it has been nationally in the past. That is not to say, however, that no change has occurred. The predominant number of Jews (70 percent) define

TABLE 9.1. Political Ideology for California Jews and Non-Jews, 1986
(in percent)

Ideology	Jews	Non-Jews
Very Liberal	12	7
Somewhat Liberal	37	21
Middle-of-the-Road	33	31
Somewhat Conservative	15	32
Very Conservative	3	8
Total	100	100[a]
(Sample Size)	(438)	(7337)

[a]Errors in total due to rounding.
Source: *Los Angeles Times* poll (November 4, 1986).

themselves today as middle-of-the-road or somewhat liberal. The shift toward the center parallels the movement among Californians and other Americans.

Opinions and Legislative Votes

In order to understand the specific content of their ideology, we turn to the several opinion questions asked by the Poll and also to the vote on a number of ballot propositions put before the voters of California as part of the initiative and referendum. These propositions are part of a legislative process whereby citizens have the right to vote directly on whether certain proposed laws become the actual laws of the state. Thus, these questions measure real political behavior and not just abstract expressions on distant topics. These are issues that have been before the electorate, who have voted to pass or defeat this legislation just moments before they are polled.

Economics/Role of Government

Several critical questions on economic policy were asked in June 1980, when the country was still suffering from high inflation. On the general question of wage and price controls, the electorate was closely split, and among Jews it was the same split (47 percent in favor, 53 percent opposed). This is the only question in the study for which the division among Jews and among non-Jews is exactly the same. (Given subsample sizes of about 300 [Jews] and 4,000 [non-Jews], on the average we cannot be statistically confident of differences less than 5 percentage points.)

On mandatory gas rationing, a generally unpopular issue which would have increased the power of the government and limited individual usage, Jews voiced approximately the same level of opposition as other Californians (67 percent:70 percent). Two years later, a statement critical of state government for wasting tax monies also tapped generally similar levels of strong agreement; but adding up the two levels of agreement, Jews were less critical of the state (55 percent:64 percent).

In specific areas, Jews were willing to allow the government a greater role in limiting individual enterprise. There was more support to halt construction of nuclear power plants (55 percent:40 percent). There was more approval for rent control (61 percent:49 percent), even when controlling for the homeowner/renter status of the respondents. That is, both Jewish homeowners and renters were more supportive of rent control than were their non-Jewish equivalents. And Jews were more likely to vote for Proposition 11, which levied a surtax against windfall profits made by large oil corporations.

Given the publicity about the state budget surplus in the immediate post–Proposition 13 (property tax reduction) period, popular pressure grew for other forms of California state tax reduction. Proposition 9, calling for a 50 percent reduction in income tax, appeared on the November 1980 ballot. Here, Jews were even more likely than others to vote no (72 percent:61 percent). There was little question that the surplus would disappear, either by refund or by reduced ability to collect monies, as Proposition 13 enjoined.

The negative consequences of too severe a tax cut were mentioned specifically in a question asking attitudes toward a "30% tax cut even if that risks increasing inflation." Results followed along the same lines as Proposition 9; that is, strong opposition. Naturally, people with more wealth were not quite as opposed. Since the Jews have higher incomes than other Californians, that should make them somewhat more sympathetic toward the major tax cut. In spite of this demographic difference, Jews were slightly more against the tax cut (71 percent:65 percent). For each income level (e.g., less that $10,000 a year), more Jews disapproved.

During this six-year period there was one income tax proposition which would have called for a small reduction in the taxes paid by people with increasing incomes. Proposition 7 (June 1982) assured the generous indexing of tax brackets to account for inflation. Here, the Jews supported it marginally less than other Californians (58 percent:63 percent), although the Jews were more likely to benefit immediately.

The last two items, from June 1980, address government spending but deal as much with priorities as with the budget deficit. In the real world, they were two of the most important questions in determining the course of domestic politics in the Reagan years. The first asked whether voters agreed with a "federal budget cut even if that means cutting back social services." Again, wealthier people—who would be taxed more and who depend less on some of these social services—voiced greater agreement. Yet, in spite of their advantaged economic position, Jews expressed less approval than other Californians (43 percent:55 percent).

Violence

Not just symbolically, but in terms of real dollars, the most important change in the Reagan years has been the switch in spending from social services to defense. The Jews offer more opposition than do non-Jews to cutting social services. They differ even more in their opposition to substantial increases in military spending (50 percent:33 percent) at a time (1980) when there was growing support for a strong military posture.

The significant differences on defense carry over to other questions on violence or its potential. Jews are much less likely to have a handgun in the house (14 percent:34 percent), and these differences among voters probably understate the real difference out in the larger society. Moreover, according to table 9.2, Jews were dramatically more likely to vote for Proposition 15 (November 1982), requiring the registration and regulation of the sale of handguns—the proposition for which Jewish/non-Jewish differences were the greatest.

This antipathy towards violence extends to one of the most important national issues of the 1980s, the control of nuclear arms. Proposition 12 (November 1982) was a nonstatutory measure urging the President to reach an agreement with the Soviet Union to halt the production and deployment of nuclear arms. At the time, there was no consensus in California, evidenced by the bare majority the proposition received. Congruent with their position on other matters of violence, however, Jews were much more likely to approve the nuclear freeze (70 percent:51 percent).

Not only did Jews support a nuclear freeze more than other Californians as a whole; they gave greater support than any minority group. And since women are normally more antiwar, gender was also examined. For non-Jews, women were indeed more likely to favor a nuclear freeze than men (56 percent:47 percent), as almost all previous polls have shown. For Jews, however, gender was relatively unimportant, just a minor two-point difference (in the expected direction). In fact, Jewish men were noticeably more likely to vote for nuclear freeze than were non-Jewish women (67 percent:56 percent). Although gender and education are major influences on attitudes toward war, being Jewish is even more important.

Civil Rights and Civil Liberties

The domestic area which has attracted the most attention from commentators within the Jewish world has been the deteriorating relationship with blacks.

TABLE 9.2. Vote on Gun Control Legislation for California Jews and Non-Jews,
1982
(in Percent)

Proposition 15 (Gun Control)	Jews	Non-Jews
For	63	35
Against	37	65
Total	100	100
(Sample Size)	(185)	(3455)

Source: *Los Angeles Times* poll (November 2, 1982).

These data do not allow for comparison over time because the exact same question was not asked over a sufficiently long period. The *Los Angeles Times* Poll asked California voters only one specific evaluative question on racial matters, "how much attention do you think the government pays to blacks and other minorities?" Both popular and federal government vocabularies denote minorities to include primarily blacks, Hispanics, and some other ethnic groups of color. This particular question wording probably did not encourage subjective inclusion of women and certainly not Jews.

Since blacks and Hispanics fall into a special category on this question, Jews are compared only with white non-Jews. The findings from a composite average of two polls in 1982 and one in 1986 show that Jews were twice as likely as other California whites to think that the government pays too little attention to minorities (35 percent:17 percent), although a substantial number of both groups (40 percent:46 percent) think that the government is paying the right amount of attention. The remainder feel that the government pays too much attention. Clearly, the Jews are still more sympathetic than other people, but they are broadly divided among themselves.

A related dimension is civil liberties, another form of protection of the rights of unpopular minorities, here against government action; e.g., the vocational rights of sexual minorities or adherence to civil procedure to ensure the rights of people accused of crime. In response to a statement (June 1982) that "the courts have to protect the rights of the guilty as well as the innocent," 27 percent of the Jews strongly agreed, compared with 17 percent of the non-Jews. On the other side, only one-fifth of the Jews expressed any level of disagreement, compared with one-third of the others (22 percent:35 percent).

At the same time, Proposition 8 appeared on the ballot. Popularly labeled the "Victims' Bill of Rights," this measure engendered opposition in part because it relaxed certain protections granted to accused people such as the exclusion of illegally obtained evidence, and it eliminated any "diminished capacity" defense. The proposition passed 56 to 44, but the difference between Jews and other Californians parallels the previous opinion question. Jews were more likely to oppose curtailing procedural protection of the individual (54 percent: 43 percent).

A second area of civil liberties was touched by Proposition 64 (November 1986), a bill to quarantine and possibly identify people who had tested positive on the AIDS virus. Since the measure was universally rejected by the scientific community, and since it was initiated by Lyndon LaRouche supporters, it is reasonable to assume that this was little more than a frightened public chastisement and reactionary punishment of homosexuals. The measure, which was soundly defeated, evoked almost unanimous opposition from Jews, more than among others (87 percent:70 percent).

Moral Issues

For lack of a better term, the last two issues are subsumed under the Christian category of moral issues. The first, capital punishment ("for persons convicted of murder"), has been problematic in former studies in that differences between Jews and other Americans have varied over time and by individual survey, a problem with small samples. In these earlier surveys Jews have never been more supportive of capital punishment, but in some there were no differences; whereas in others, the Jews were more opposed.

Over the past decade there has been a systematic increase in support for capital punishment, reflected in these findings. In the same November 1986 poll, an unusually large Jewish sample gives very strong consent to the death penalty, although even at this high level it is still slightly lower than that of other Californians (74 percent:81 percent). Moreover, as we shall see from a major judicial confirmation (Rose Bird) vote, the Jews probably feel much less intensely about their agreement.

Abortion, the second personal moral issue, presents less of a problem to the observer of public opinion. Here, differences in the past have been sharp, and they are remarkably evident in this study. Results for the Jews strain credulity.

Two questions touch on abortion, although both are adulterated by inclusion of ancillary issues. The first (June 1980) asks about publicly financed abortions. Aforementioned data have already shown that Jews are more sympathetic to government spending for social services, so some of the difference may reflect feelings about government fiscal policy rather than purely abortion. Still, differences between Jews and others in level of approval are enormous (67 percent:37 percent), indicating much more than simply government economics.

More confidence in the lack of Jewish opposition to abortion comes from a somewhat purer measure, asking voters whether they support a constitutional amendment to prohibit abortion. This extreme form of legislation probably deflates the antiabortion numbers, although it is partially mitigated by the unusually intense feelings which abortion evokes. This is the one finding taken from a national sample (November 1984) rather than solely from California voters, although a sizable proportion of the sample comes from California. For Jews, however, this is irrelevant: 97 percent of the 184 Jews polled disagreed!

Non-Jews also voiced very strong disapproval of a constitutional amendment (75 percent). A 1986 survey by Gallup corroborates popular perceptions that Californians are more liberal on abortion (and other social/moral issues) than are other Americans.[6] Still, the Jews stand out among all Californians, and the substantial differences are minimized by the ceiling effect; viz., Jews are already so high on the scale that they cannot go any higher, hence there is a limit as to how much they can differ from others.

Political Party

In spite of major intraparty geographical and ideological differences within the two major political parties, especially the Democrats, and a few areas where bipartisanship prevails, the parties do differ from each other on a large number of critical issues. Almost invariably the Democrats take the more liberal stance. On several of these issues Jews differ from other Californians, always in the direction of the Democratic position—civil rights and civil liberties, government regulation of private morality, defense spending, and government spending for social services. Indeed, our first finding was that by self-definition, Jews were much more likely than non-Jews to identify with liberalism.

Therefore, it is no surprise that Jews also define themselves as much more Democratic. The question posed in the November 1986 Poll asked not for party of preference, as is typical, but for party of registration. There is a real benefit to register with a particular party in closed-primary states like California—the right to vote in that party's primary. Hence, few people in this survey claim party independence, as compared with about 30 percent who opt for independent on a pure opinion question tapping party preference.

Including minor parties as well as "decline to state" as part of the choices, the Jews are still strongly Democratic, much more so than other Californians (68 percent:47 percent) and they are clearly less Republican (25 percent:45 percent). The relative proportions of Jewish partisanship generally match previous national and California data, controlling for the independents.[7]

In looking at background demographic relationships underlying party attachment, three factors stand out. Two of these are expected, and probably have not changed much in direction or intensity over the last decade. As is true of the larger society, there is a gender gap: Jewish women voters are more Democratic than Jewish men (73 percent:65 percent). Second, although differences are not as strong as among non-Jews, Democratic registration generally declines with increasing income. Still, even among the wealthiest Jews, Democrats far outnumber Republicans.

The most interesting and portentous factor—although not the most consistent—is age. Just as the Republicans have done better across the country among new voters during the Reagan years, so, too, the youngest adult California Jews are strikingly more Republican than their parents and grandparents. The national-network media polls bear out this tendency, although in a less dramatic fashion; the data displayed in table 9.3 are the most exaggerated of four different polls.

For the *Los Angeles Times* data (Table 9.3), the percentage of Jews registered as Democrats declines consistently by 8 to 10 percentage points for every major age category, from 82 percent among those 65 years of age and over, to 56 percent of those ages 18 to 29. Among the oldest Jewish voters, a mere 14 percent register Republican. Only among the youngest voters do the Republicans attract more than one-quarter of the Jews. The development among California non-Jews is not parallel primarily because their senior citizens are much, much more Republican than older Jews (51 percent:14 percent). Among non-Jews under 45, however, the younger age category is more Republican.

Elections

Several important elections during this period further test ideology and party preference. The gubernatorial competition between conservative Republican George Deukmejian and moderate black Los Angeles Mayor Tom Bradley was run in 1982 and repeated four years later. Deukmejian was a generally popular governor and the California economy seemed in reasonable shape. Deukmejian had no identifiable ties with the Jewish community, although he was publicly supportive of attempts to commemorate the Holocaust. Bradley, on the other hand, had a long, solid connection with Jewish liberal Democrats and had publicly supported Israel consistently and frequently. Therefore, it was not surprising that he had done very well among Jews (75 percent) in his narrow defeat in 1982.

In 1985, however, Bradley held out against public condemnation of the anti-Semitic black Moslem Louis Farrakhan before his speech in Los Angeles. Although Bradley did speak out afterwards, the refusal became a short-lived but intense issue in the Los Angeles community, leaving some Jews bitterly disappointed with Bradley. During the election campaign the next year Bradley made many concerted public efforts to appeal to the Jewish vote.

Mostly because the state economy was relatively strong and there had been no major scandals in his administration, Deukmejian handily defeated Bradley the second time (62 to 38). As in the rest of the population, except for blacks,

TABLE 9.3. Party Registration by Age for California Jews and Non-Jews, 1986
(in Percent)

| | Age of Jews | | | | | Age of Non-Jews | | | | |
Party	18–24	30–44	45–46	65+	Average	18–24	30–44	45–46	65+	Average
Democrat	56	64	72	82	69	43	50	46	46	47
Republican	40	25	24	14	25	46	40	48	51	45
Other	3	4	2	1	2	7	6	2	2	4
Decline to State	1	7	2	3	4	4	4	4	1	4
Total	100	100	100	100	100	100	100	100	100	100
(Sample Size)			(438)					(7340)		

Source: *Los Angeles Times* poll (November 4, 1986).

Jewish support for Bradley weakened. However, given the one-sided outcome, Jewish support was still respectable. As figures in table 9.4 show, not only was the vote of Jews and Anglo non-Jews a gaping 27 percentage points apart, but there was virtually no difference between how the Jews and the much poorer Hispanics voted.

In delineating the reasons contributing to the peoples' votes, the Poll listed nine issues, ignoring the Farrakhan incident. Of those presented, Jews were generally similar to other Californians in their ranking on half the issues. They were less likely to list law and order and government spending. They were more likely to list the excessive influence of special-interest groups and Jews differed most noticeably in their greater concern about toxic wastes, an issue that benefitted Bradley.

Results from two Senate races tell a similar story. In 1982, the generally liberal, somewhat enigmatic Democrat, former governor Jerry Brown, ran against the moderate-conservative Republican mayor of San Diego, Pete Wilson. By that time Brown's star had dimmed. He had run unsuccessfully in

TABLE 9.4. California Gubernatorial Vote, 1986, by Ethnic Groups (in Percent)[a]

| | Ethnic Group | | | | | |
	Jews	All Non-Jews	White Non-Jews	Blacks	Hispanics	Total[b]
Deukmejian (Rep)	43	63	70	8	41	62
Bradley (Dem)	57	37	30	92	59	38
Total	100	100	100	100	100	100
(Sample Size)	(438)	(6299)	(4847)	(432)	(458)	(6737)

[a]Calculated only on vote for two major candidates. The official result was Deukmejian (61 percent), Bradley (37 percent), other candidates (2 percent).
[b]Includes other groups and mixed respondents.
Source: *Los Angeles Times* poll (November 4, 1986).

two presidential campaigns, he initially opposed the popular Proposition 13, and the novelty of his New Politics, high tech, and spiritualism had begun to wear off. As a result, he lost the two-candidate vote (53 to 47). However, his Democratic party affiliation, generally liberal politics, and strong support of Israel earned him a strong 71 to 29 Jewish vote—a difference of 24 percentage points compared with the non-Jewish vote, even more with the white non-Jewish vote.

A somewhat parallel set of ideological circumstances obtain in the 1986 race between senior liberal, strongly pro-Israel Democrat, Alan Cranston, and a much junior Republican Congressman, Ed Zschau, whose politics shifted irregularly to both sides of the center and who, as pro-Palestinian Paul (Pete) McCloskey's successor, was himself circumspect on Israel.

This election, in which Zschau almost pulled off a major upset, should have elicited strong Jewish support for Cranston; indeed, it did. Four out of five Jews supported Cranston, lower than the figure for blacks but considerably higher than the two out of three Hispanics. Slightly more than four out of ten non-Jewish Anglos (80 percent:43 percent) voted for Cranston. As Cranston is well aware, without the Jewish vote he definitely would have lost.

Respondents were again queried about the main reasons for their vote. For most of the ten reasons listed, Jews and other Californians did not differ significantly. Jews were less likely to list Rose Bird as one of their two main reasons, and they were less likely again to select government spending. They were more likely to be concerned abut the candidates' (read as Zschau's) reversals on positions, but primarily they differed in the importance of support for Israel. In a suprisingly high figure, 35 percent of the Jews listed this as one of the two main determinants, compared with just over 1 percent of non-Jews.

In California, the same Progressive thrust that led to the initiative and referendum also devised a system wherein state Supreme Court justices need to be reconfirmed by the electorate. One such special judicial confirmation in November 1986 stands as one of the most salient races in the decade. Supreme Court Chief Justice Rose Bird, appointed by Governor Jerry Brown, was sympathetic to the poor and disadvantaged and opposed by big business, but that seemed to be little known. What was known and publicly advertised was her rejection of capital punishment, in direct opposition to the California electorate. Bird became a focal point in the elections, an albatross from whom many Democrats sought to flee while Republican candidates never seemed to tire of mentioning her name in their campaigns. Not only was Bird unpopular but more Californians pointed to her election as being the most important one facing voters that day. And more (non-Jewish) Californians checked off Rose Bird as the most salient issue in deciding how they were going to vote for governor than any of the other nine issues listed.

Rose Bird was soundly defeated, worse than her two liberal colleagues, Joseph Grodin, a Jew, and Cruz Reynoso, a Hispanic. The Jews were one of the few groups who voted for her, much more so than all non-Jews (56 percent:32 percent) and Hispanics (47 percent), though less than blacks (64 percent). Even women, who tend to be more against capital punishment and more Democratic, voted solidly against Bird (64 to 36).

The last vote is that for Congress. The only recent poll with these California data available is from November 1982. Calculating only the two-party vote, Jews voted 77 percent Democratic compared with 51 percent for the non-Jews. These *Los Angeles Times* California figures are only slightly higher than for media polls for Jews across the country and they do not differ much from the findings of the smaller sample California Field Polls.

President Reagan

Because the presidential elections contain only a partial California sample, difficult to access, good data are not yet available. Based on party registration and voting patterns in other elections, one can safely predict that California Jews voted primarily Democratic, in numbers similar to the national data (67 to 70 percent in the network polls cited by Lipset and Raab[8] and 68 percent in the national *Los Angeles Times* survey).

A strong correlate of one's vote for President is the evaluation of the President. Citing a good deal of unpublished Gallup data, one study showed that Jews across the country regularly ranked Reagan lower than did non-Jews.[9] Is there greater Jewish sympathy in Reagan's home state where he has been very successful among voters at large?

A question in November 1986 asked for a general impression of Reagan at a time before the Iran–Contra scandal, when Reagan's popularity and evaluation were still high. Among other Californians, taking only those who expressed a definite opinion (92 percent), the favorable impressions are more than double the unfavorable ones (68 to 32), whereas among California Jews that proportion is 45 to 55, more unfavorable not only relatively but absolutely. And, again, note that recurring differential in the range of 20 to 25 percentage points (68 percent:45 percent) between the non-Jewish and Jewish vote. Perspectives on the Reagan administration complement the California Jewish attitudes toward both national and state politics. However, among Jews, the youngest (18 to 30 years of age) were the most positive about Reagan, unlike other Californians, whose evaluation is relatively homogeneous across age.

Review and Discussion

Data from *Los Angeles Times* exit polls provide a number of significant benefits. Expanding the Jewish subsample by an order of magnitude provides much more confidence in the findings. This, in turn, will facilitate the research on change over time. And polls in California are particularly helpful because they tap not only opinions but also electoral behavior, both for candidates and for statewide propositions, a form of direct democracy in which voters play the role of legislator.

Because earlier surveys rarely asked the exact same questions and because the subsamples were much smaller, it is impossible to measure precisely change over time although we can discern general patterns. A second specific restriction on these polls is the limited number of questions. As a consequence, much of this discussion must remain speculative and in need of further testing.

The overall findings suggest that California Jews differ from their non-Jewish neighbors in the same way that Jews have differed from other Americans since the mass East European immigration. There is no single political question for which Jews are more conservative and only a handful for which they are even similar. That Jews are more liberal and considerably less conservative can be found simply by asking respondents to describe themselves. If Jews feel comfortable labeling themselves as liberal in the 1980s—when liberalism has been under attack—one might expect that mentality to flourish when the pendulum shifts again in the post-Reagan years.

These ideological labels are good predictors of several attitudes and party vote. However, a better picture of the differences can be found by looking directly at the issues.

Clearly, demography sets a background for political attitudes. The biggest post–World War II change in California (and American) Jewry has been the sharp upward mobility—wealth, education, and vocation. Jews have moved very far and very fast from the semiskilled-labor status of their immigrant grandparents. As a result, Jews no longer congregate in the socialist camp, although it is unlikely that they were ever there in massive numbers.

Not unexpectedly, the smallest difference between Jews and other Californians obtain in economics. Unfortunately, we have too few questions to make a detailed diagnosis. Differences are almost nonexistent for general programs like wage and price controls and for a policy that would have a (short-run) negative personal impact like gasoline rationing. This provides some evidence of Jews defining their economic interest narrowly, like most other Americans. Thus, Jews are only slightly less likely to agree with indexing income taxes, a measure which shelters some income from taxes. Along with hard-earned wealth comes a strong desire to protect the privileges.

However, narrow economic self-interest does not explain the greater Jewish reluctance to lower overall personal income taxes. The argument on behalf of taxes is that it ultimately enables a greater redistribution of goods and services, as well as a check on excessive private accumulation of wealth. This explanation is tested more specifically in the greater Jewish refusal to reduce taxes with the specific consequence of cutting back on social services, presumably to the less fortunate. The same argument also finds support in greater empirical backing for a populist proposal to tax excessive windfall profits enjoyed by large oil companies.

This populist–socialist mentality is expressed in lesser concerns for government spending, and in the greater willingness to allow government the power to curb private evils and to help the poor and disadvantaged. Jews think that government should do more to help racial minorities. They are considerably more likely to agree with government halting the construction of nuclear power plants. And Jews are more likely than others to approve of rent control, which provides some measure of relief to people on limited incomes. The limits on government are relaxed for humanitarian reasons.

This nonideological humanism is most clearly manifested in attitudes toward violence, an issue where the link with Jewish tradition is very strong. In California, Jews consistently express much greater opposition to the use of violence—by both the state and individual—than do non-Jews. Jewish history, full of regular and often widespread violent attacks, is a good guide to contemporary Jewish anxieties and behavior.

Even in America, at a time when they have not been the frequent victims of violence (although it still occurs), Jews remain much more repulsed by it and more afraid of its potential occurrence. These attitudes and votes reinforce the popular (and correct) perception that Jews are highly overrepresented among peace activists. Raab and Lipset have explained that Jews generally are politically hyperactive.[10] Here, their prominence reflects a much greater concern and commitment to nonviolence among the masses of Jews than among the non-Jews.

Another arena in which Jews are visibly overrepresented is civil rights and liberties and, again, that reflects a real difference in popular attitudes. Parallel to their support for the poor, Jews sympathize with other neglected or oppressed groups, especially on behalf of their legal and economic rights. In spite of the rift, Jews still are much more sympathetic to the condition of blacks than are other white Californians. However, this support faces real limits; e.g., a divergence of opinion on government attention to black problems and, as is commonly known, strong opposition to quotas. Moreover, as for other whites, the plight of blacks is no longer a high priority for most Jews.

Concern for the rights of the individual against the government normally correlates with higher education, although many educated, committed, religious Christians argue that their moral beliefs take precedence over any ideology of individual rights. But Jews do not carry most of that baggage, although among Jews undoubtedly the more Orthodox show less solicitude for individual rights against the moral standards of the community, seen in extreme in Israel.

Some of that regulation of private morality is specifically Christian and hence not applicable to Jews. Some issues (e.g., abortion) have been emphasized by both Roman Catholic and Protestant Churches, although traditional Judaism maintains a kindred (though not equivalent) position. The overwhelming opposition by Jews to rigid anti–abortion measures suggests that either most Orthodox Jews have also adopted the secular Jewish position, their numbers in California are very small, they do not turn out to vote, and/or they are underrepresented in the sampling.

Some of the traditional theological positions are, in fact, both Judaic and Christian (e.g., homosexuality), yet the Jews are much less willing to infringe on the civil rights of homosexuals. Pat Robertson and Jerry Falwell, who are both pro-Israel, do not appeal to Jews because they want to impose conservative Christian morality on public and private life.

As part of this concern, Jews continue to share an identification with the oppressed minority. The historical experience of oppression has seemingly been learned and reinforced by current American politics and intermittent episodes of anti-Semitism. Jews are still less willing to take away the rights of other minorities.

Party affiliation, which initially tends to be transmitted parentally, needs to be reinforced to remain stable. California Jews have inherited a strong Democratic tradition from their immigrant grandparents. Additionally, their own attitudes place them ideologically much closer to the Democrats than to the Republicans, a factor which keeps Jews firmly entrenched in the more liberal party, as indicated by a behavioral measure of party registration.

Given the strong Democratic bias and a supporting set of opinions much closer to the Democratic platform, the Jewish vote is naturally strongly Democratic. In all the elections reviewed there was a stereotypical party ideological differentiation between Democrats and Republicans, and where the Republican was moderate (Zschau), the Democrat was very liberal (Cranston). Zschau's 20-percent vote represents the hard-core Jewish Republican constituency, economically biased toward the upper-middle class.

In one of the angriest campaigns, the drive to push out Rose Bird, the Jews resisted making a decision based solely on capital punishment, even though they clearly support it. Their vote (in favor of Rose Bird) was likely based more on behalf of civil liberties and the rights and needs of the poor and less powerful minorities; and perhaps a recognition that the forces in society hostile to Bird— both big business and the reactionary right—are also the forces traditionally opposed to Jews and to Jewish perspectives. And yet, as always, Jews were not immune to the larger developments in society, in particular, increasing violent crime. Thus, the level of Jewish (and non-Jewish) support for Bird was considerably lower than for other liberal Democrats.

The election campaign against the Bird confirmation was distorted by the emotional response to crime and capital punishment. A better, more accurate picture of deep-seated party propensity occurs in off-year congressional elections, when personalities and media images play a much less important role. There, the vote is very strongly Democratic, in numbers (about three-fourths) matching the recent nationwide vote.

Issues, party identification, and voting behavior all predicted the comparatively low vote by Jews for Reagan, especially in 1984. And it follows naturally that Jews continue to give less support to Reagan and to his policies, a finding which replicates those of a national study conducted during the first term of Reagan's administration.[11]

What is the political future for California Jews? If the immediate past is an indicator, we should expect the Jews to move in the same direction as the rest of the citizenry, certainly as other whites. Simply, Jews, no less than their neighbors, are as affected by social and economic movements as by earthquakes. Growing support for capital punishment and declining support for Bradley and Bird are just a few examples.

In matters influenced by education, such as civil rights and civil liberties, it is likely that non-Jews will continue to move in the direction of Jews; that is, more liberal and tolerant of differences except during revival periods of Christian morality. However, revivalism notwithstanding, the public today is far more tolerant than it was thirty years ago.

Similarly, in their attitude towards violence, especially war, the larger public is moving in the direction of the Jews as they are on the means to control domestic violence, although differences for each remain large. Jews are much more likely to advance humane solutions (e.g., handgun control and providing more public services), although data from a scattered group of other polls suggest that American Jews have also become increasingly supportive of more severe retribution for criminals (e.g., longer jail sentences and capital punishment).

Marx, the pamphleteer, used to say: if all the political and social factors were in one balance and economics in the other, then economics would outweigh them all. Indeed, except between 1952 and 1968, economics has been the single most dominant factor in almost every national election in this century. As Jews move from the sweatshops to the professional class there is a great pressure on them to adopt the norms of the upper-middle class.

The limited data suggest that this transformation has already begun even though Jews are not yet Babbitt Republicans. They still vote for butter, not guns. They believe that the state should spend more money for the welfare of the disadvantaged and for humane purposes. But on economic matters, even where differences with non-Jews occur, they tend to be relatively small. Insofar as economic issues put the immediate needs of the have-nots against those of the haves, there will be a pressure to move away from the "soak the rich" mentality. Middle-class Jews will become more sympathetic to the concerns of the haves.

Economic mobility should have led to a greater Republican identification and vote, it has not. But cracks are appearing in the Democratic wall, the most noticeable of which is age. The youngest Jews are much more likely than their elders to register Republican, and every age group is regularly less Democratic than its elders. Data from national polls are less exaggerated, but they all point to problems for the Democrats in the future. Certainly, the *Los Angeles Times* Poll findings presage a Jewish community much different electorally in twenty years.

Even if the data are essentially correct, however, it does not necessarily follow that young Jews must continue to stay Republican in large numbers. First, party affiliation is normally most tenuous and labile among the young, who have the least political experience. Second, some of that affiliation may be appended to a strong economy (for the middle class) and to Reagan, who seems unable to transfer his popularity to other Republicans. In support of this qualification, and contrary to the gubernatorial vote, the youngest Jews dispro-portionately rejected Zschau in favor of Cranston. Moreover, age differences do not carry over to ideology. Young Jews do not see themselves as more conservative than older Jews.

Against these qualifications stands the hope of young California Jews to continue their upward mobility, which will provide more economic impetus to stay Republican. Moreover, most people do not change their party affiliation. And this is a sample not of residents but of voters, or people who are likely to stay active in the political world. The Democrats should not expect these young adults to drop out in the future.

Last, there is one major caveat about the Jewish party vote. This discussion presupposes that the party ideological and issue differences will not change dramatically in the near future. Second, it assumes that the parties will not alter their support for direct Jewish issues like Israel, Soviet Jewry, and anti-Semitism. Given the generally balanced, competitive party system, it is un-likely that one of the parties would voluntarily relinquish a chance for the vote of Jews, especially in the absence of groups that oppose Jewish issues. That might partially change if the Arab vote continues to grow. But this would lead to a complicated economic–ethnic–political scenario whose exact course is hard to foretell.

In the meanwhile, the best insight into the future of American Jewry lies in the attitudes and behavior of the young and those who are mobile. California may be the best place to see that future.

Notes

1. Alan M. Fisher and Curtis K. Tanaka, "California Jews: Data from the Field Polls," *American Jewish Year Book* 86 (1986), pp. 196–218.
2. See Fisher and Tanaka, "California Jews"; Gary Tobin and Alvin Chenkin, "Recent Jewish Community Population Studies: A Roundup," *American Jewish Year Book* 85 (1985), pp. 154–78; Bruce A. Phillips, "Los Angeles Jewry: A Demographic Portrait," *American Jewish Year Book* 86 (1986), pp. 126–95.
3. Jewish population figures are taken from yearly reports in the *American Jewish Year Book*.
4. See Mark R. Levy, "The Methodology and Performance of Election Day Polls," *Public Opinion Quarterly* 47 (1983), pp. 54–67.
5. Phillips, "Los Angeles Jewry," pp. 177–8.
6. *Gallup Report* (January/February 1986), p. 18 for a differentiation according to four geographic regions; also Gallup Poll reviewed in *Los Angeles Times* (November 11, 1987), pp. 1, 28.
7. For recent California data, Field Institute, "A Digest of California's Political Demography" (San Francisco, January 1988), p. 5. For earlier Gallup data, Alan M. Fisher, "The National Gallup Polls and American Jewish Demography," *American Jewish Year Book* 83 (1983), pp. 116–7.
8. Seymour Martin Lipset and Earl Raab, "The American Jews, the 1984 Elections, and Beyond," William Frankel, ed., *Survey of Jewish Affairs 1985* (Rutherford NJ: Fairleigh Dickinson University Press, 1985), p. 141.
9. Alan M. Fisher, "Changing Attitudes of American Jews toward Ronald Reagan," mimeograph, Society for the Study of Social Problems, San Francisco (September 1982).
10. Earl Raab and Seymour Martin Lipset, *The Political Future of American Jews* (New York: American Jewish Congress, 1985).
11. Fisher, "Changing Attitudes."

This research was possible only with the cooperation of the *Los Angeles Times* Poll, in particular the unusual generosity of its first-rate data manager, Henrietta Martinez, to whom the author is much indebted. Access to data was also provided by Kelly Hanley of ABC News and Keating Holland of CBS News.

III

The Community

10

The Jewishness of the New York Intellectuals: Sidney Hook, a Case Study

Edward S. Shapiro

One of the more interesting aspects of recent American intellectual history has been the growing interest in the "New York intellectuals." The autobiographies of Alfred Kazin, Irving Howe, William Phillips, William Barrett, and Sidney Hook have been joined on the library shelves by monographic studies of Daniel Bell, Will Herberg, and Lionel Trilling, by several doctoral dissertations on the New York intellectuals, and by major studies of these intellectuals by Alexander Bloom, Terry A. Cooney, and Alan Wald. In these pages, many of the major intellectual developments of modern America—the growth of socialism during the 1930s, the struggle over literary modernism, the emergence of neoconservatism—appear to be little more than intramural debates within the New York intellectual community.

The mostly Jewish New York intellectuals and their magazines—*Partisan Review, Commentary, Dissent, New York Review of Books, Public Interest*—have assumed an almost mythic position among American intellectuals. Thus, Elizabeth Hardwick once noted that she had left Kentucky to become a New York Jewish intellectual (her conversion took place in the office of the *New York Review of Books*). Hardwick was not alone in assuming mistakenly that to be a New York intellectual (or any intellectual at all) one had to be Jewish. Victor Navasky, the editor of the *Nation,* jested in 1966 that "rumors to the contrary notwithstanding, you don't have to be Jewish to be an intellectual."

During the past half century or so, the only other group that has had a comparable impact on American intellectual life has been the Southern critics and writers. It would be difficult to conceive of two more different groups of intellectuals. Yet, the Southern writers and the New York intellectuals were similar in at least one major respect: both were forced to come to terms with the conflict between the parochial and traditional cultures in which they had been raised, and the cosmopolitan intellectual communities of which they sought to become a part. As Allen Tate noted, the southern writers had a "peculiarly historical consciousness" because they lived at a time when the traditional South of cotton, the Lost Cause, and rural ways was being obliterated by a new South of cities, factories, and progressive ideas.[1]

The histories of the New York intellectuals have also stressed this sense of marginality, alienation, and living at a crossroads. Bloom's *Prodigal Sons: The New York Intellectuals and Their World* (1986), Cooney's *The Rise of the New York Intellectuals:* Partisan Review *and its Circle* (1986), and Wald's *The New York Intellectuals: The Rise and Decline of the Anti-Stalinist Left from the 1930s to the 1980s* (1987) argue that the creativity of the New York intellectuals resulted in part from the rejection of the religious and ethnic insularity of American Jewish life. They were, in Bloom's words, "prodigal sons" living on the margins of American and Jewish culture. Fleeing from Jewish culture, they become part of a world of radical sectarian politics that had little relationship to or relevance for America. Cooney also noted the marginality of the New York intellectuals. They took their bearing "from the sense that they stood outside two cultures. It was Jewishness that made possible the assertion of a double exile that promised exceptional insight."[2]

The argument that Jewish intellectuality stemmed from marginality and alienation was, of course, not new. Beginning in the early nineteenth century, both supporters and opponents of Jewish emancipation in Europe noted that one of its side effects had been the emergence of cosmopolitan, secular, and often revolutionary intellectuals. The nineteenth-century German Jewish socialist J. L. Bernays rejoiced in the fact that the modern Jew had "rescued men from the narrow idea of an exclusive fatherland, from patriotism, by liberating men . . . from everything that reminded him of race, place of origin, dogma and faith." Three-quarters of a century later, in his important 1928 essay "Human Migration and the Marginal Man," the University of Chicago sociologist Robert E. Park argued that the modern Jew was the quintessential marginal man, existing "on the margin of two cultures and two societies . . . the first cosmopolite and citizen of the world." The Marxist historian Issac Deutscher used the term "the non-Jewish Jew" to describe the phenomenon of Jewish intellectuals who have "dwelt on the borderlines of various civilizations, religions, and national cultures . . . [and] lived on the margins or in the nooks and crannies of their respective nations."[3]

Some of the New York intellectuals have also emphasized their marginality and estrangement from the world of their parents. Thus, in 1944, at the height of the Holocaust, Issac Rosenfeld and Alfred Kazin stressed their indifference to their Jewish background. Being Jewish, Rosenfeld argued, "should occupy no more of a man's attention than any ordinary fact of his history." Kazin recounted that of all the forces shaping his outlook, he had been "most deeply influenced by my struggle against a merely imposed faith, and against a sentimental chauvinism." What was Jewish about the American Jew, he asked. "What does he believe, especially in these terrible years, that separates him at all from our national habits of acquisitiveness, showiness and ignorant brag? . . . What a pity that he should 'feel different', when he believes so little; what a stupendous moral pity, historically, that the Fascist cutthroats should have their eyes on him, too, when he asks for so little—only to be safe, in all the Babbit warrens." For Kazin and the other Marxist Jewish intellectuals, Jewishness was a particularistic anachronism fated to disappear in the socialist cosmopolitan future.[4]

Marginality is a major theme in Irving Howe's appropriately titled autobiography, *A Margin of Hope*. During the 1930s and early 1940s, Howe wrote that, Jewishness "was not regarded as a major component of the culture I wanted to make my own, and I felt no particular responsibility for its survival or renewal. It was simple *there*. While it would be shameful to deny its presence or seek to flee its stigma, my friends and I could hardly be said to have thought Jewishness could do much for us or we for it." They were Deutscher's non-Jewish Jews, living on the margins. "Our partial assimilation—roots loosed in Jewish soil but still not torn out, roots lowered into American soil but still not fixed— gave us a seemingly endless range of possibilities." Above all, they were excited by "the idea of breaking away, of willing a new life." One manifestation of Howe's own breaking away from Jewishness was his opposition during the early 1940s to American entry into World War II. American involvement, this youthful Trotskyite argued, would bolster British imperialism and strengthen worldwide capitalism. This was too high a price to pay for stopping the Nazis.[5]

Critics of the New York intellectuals, for their indifference to Jewish concerns, would seem to have a good case. Thus, Ruth Wisse, a professor of Yiddish literature at McGill University, has argued that the price paid by the New York intellectuals for their intellectual independence and their flight from particularistic loyalties was political irresponsibility and moral insensitivity. "One of the greatest moral and intellectual failures of the New York intellectuals," she concluded, "was their disregard of the Jewish fate, both before and during World War II and in the decades that followed." She quoted the Yiddish critic Shmuel Niger's cry of anguish during World War II. European Jewry suffered from "Jews who are too coarse, but also from Jews who are too sensitive."[6]

The problem with this picture of the New York intellectuals is that it is too pat and neat, too dependent on that sociological abstraction of the deracinated Jewish intellectual. The New York intellectuals were unable to completely withstand the ties of tradition and peoplehood. Just as the Southern intellectuals sought to salvage something of value from the culture of the rural South, so the Jewish intellectuals sought to preserve something of value from the culture of their immigrant Jewish neighborhoods. Even the seemingly most emancipated and universal of the intellectuals were reluctant to reject their Jewish background completely. The Alfred Kazin who proclaimed his revolt from Jewish sentimental chauvinism was the same person who wrote in an autobiography titled *New York Jew* how the Holocaust became the consuming event of his life. "In my private history of the world I took down every morsel of fact and rumor relating to the murder of my people . . . The line-up was always before my eyes. I could imagine my father and mother, my sister and myself . . . fuel for the flames, dying by a single flame that burned us all up at once." Kazin's book also contains a moving description of his trip to Israel after the Six-Day War.[7]

Irving Howe's relationship with Jewishness was also more important than one would assume at first glance. The recounting in his autobiography of his alienation from Jewish commitments was in the chapter "Jewish Quandries" where he noted that what the New York intellectuals felt regarding Jewish matters "was rarely quite in accord with what we wrote or thought . . . This was a kind of culture lag, recognition behind reality." The Holocaust had the same impact on Howe as it had on Kazin and other Jewish intellectuals. As Norman Podhoretz has remarked, it demonstrated "the inescapability of Jewishness." For Howe, the Holocaust was simply "the most terrible moment in human history." It was primarily a Jewish tragedy, "the culminating ordeal in the sequence of ordeals which comprises the experience of the Jewish people. One's first response—not the sole response, but the first—had to be a cry of Jewish grief." As a result of the Holocaust, Howe had begun "timid reconsiderations of what it meant to be Jewish," reconsiderations which would result in editing several volumes of Yiddish literature and writing *World of Our Fathers* (1976), a prizewinning elegy on the culture of the Jewish immigrant, working-class generation.[8]

The acrimonious debate over Hannah Arendt's *Eichmann in Jerusalem* also played a part in the growing Jewish consciousness of Howe and other New York intellectuals. Arendt's volume forced them to come to terms with their own failure to do more to rescue European Jewry. The passions aroused in the intellectuals were, as Howe wrote, "overwhelming. I cannot think of anything since then that harrassed me as much except perhaps the Vietnam War. You might say that it was a tacit recompense for our previous failure to respond."[9]

This route to Jewishness "wasn't, of course, a very forthright way of confronting my own troubled sense of Jewishness, but that was the way I took," Howe wrote. "Sometimes you have to make roundabout journeys without quite knowing where they will lead to." His final destination was to be "a partial Jew," embodying the tradition of secular Jewishness. Unsympathetic toward either Judaism and Zionism, Howe's Jewish identity had little to sustain it, existing in "a state of prolonged interregnum, between the denied authority of total faith and the sterile prospects of assimilation."[10]

Howe's friendly critic Sidney Hook has also been a secular Jewish intellectual. Although Hook has not often been thought of as Jewish intellectual, for over half a century he has wrestled with the question of American Jewish identity. Hook's initial prominence came during the 1930s when, as a philosopher at New York University, he was one of the few admitted Marxists on the faculty of a major American university. He participated in virtually all of the major internecine controversies that convulsed the Left during the Depression. His *Towards the Understanding of Karl Marx: A Revolutionary Interpretation* (1933) and *From Hegel to Marx: Studies in the Intellectual Development of Karl Marx* (1936) were among the first serious American studies of Marx and Marxism. For orthodox Marxists, Hook's attempt to synthesize Marxism with the pluralism and instrumentalism of his teacher, John Dewey, were heretical. After World War II, Hook was a consistent and fervent opponent of communist totalitarianism, and an equally strong supporter of democracy and what Arthur M. Schlesinger, Jr. has termed "the vital center." A grateful nation has accorded Hook its highest honors. In 1984 he gave the Jefferson lecture at the Library of Congress, and in 1985 he received the Medal of Freedom from President Reagan.

Hook's contribution to the debate over American Jewish identity has been shaped by his commitment to democracy and Deweyite liberalism. The problem he confronted was the same one that has faced American Jewry from the late eighteenth century—reconciling the "pluribus" and "unum" of America. Could the particularism of Jewish identity, American Jews pondered, be compatible with the universality of an American identity which transcended ethnic and religious distinctions? For intellectuals, the problem was complicated by the contrast between the parochialism of Jewish culture and the cosmopolitanism of Western culture of which they felt a part.

Hook was too much a child of the heavily Jewish Williamsburg section in Brooklyn to reject his ancestry, and too much a product of the City College of New York and Columbia University to affirm a particularistic religious or nationalistic definition of American Jewish identity. Instead, he sought to reconcile Jewish and American identities through the liberal and democratic pluralism of Dewey and Horace Kallen. For Hook, the most important element in American Jewish life was not religion or Zionism, but democratic values. There was, he contended, a symbiotic relationship between American Jewry and American democracy. Jewish identity strengthened democracy which, in turn, was strengthened by democracy.

As is true of Kazin and Howe, Hook has propagated an image of initial estrangement from Jewish concerns. In recalling the stance of the New York intellectuals toward Jewish concerns, he said, "We took ourselves for granted as Jews and were concerned with the Jewish question primarily as a political one." On another occasion, he denied any interest in Jewish affairs. "I suppose I have been in the thick of every controversy in the intellectual and political life of the nation during the last 60 years," he wrote in 1984. "But there is one area I *never* got involved in except in a civil libertarian way. That is Jewish affairs. A number of reasons account for this—the suspicion that its affairs are so tangled that if I got involved I would have no time for any other struggle, the fact that although I believe that the Jews ought to have a homeland of some kind, I have never been a *political* Zionist, etc."[11]

This stance of remoteness from Jewish affairs is difficult to reconcile with Hook's deep involvement in Jewish concerns, particularly during the 1940s. (It is revealing that Hook did not dwell on these in his 1987 autobiography *Out of Step*.) He helped raise funds for the United Jewish Appeal among the New York University faculty; he was active in New York University's Jewish Culture Foundation, and chaired the committee that planned the dedication of the Foundation's library; he was a member of the Academic Council of the Hebrew University; he solicited funds in behalf of the Jewish magazine *Menorah Journal*; he prepared a lengthy self-study for the National Council of Jewish Women; he chaired the Advisory Committee of the Palestine Project of the National Council of Jewish Women; he was an advisor to several Jewish cultural agencies, including the Federation of Jewish Student Organizations of New York; he often spoke on Jewish themes before Jewish secular organizations and synagogues; and he was under contract to the Jewish Lecture Bureau of the Jewish Welfare Board and was a member of the Bureau's Advisory Committee. While at the Hoover Institute of Stanford University, during the 1970s and 1980s, he received (and read) the *San Francisco Jewish Bulletin* and contributed regularly to the annual campaign of the San Francisco area's United Jewish Appeal. He also published two significant essays on American Jewishness: "Promise Without Dogma: A Social Philosophy for Jews" (1937) and "Reflections on the Jewish Question" (1949).

In contrast to Howe and other New York Jewish intellectuals, Hook never made a fetish of alienation. He was perfectly comfortable as an American and as a Jew. In 1952, for example, he noted that he was perplexed by the intellectuals' continual "laments about the 'alienation' of the creative artist in American culture." He never regretted being an American, and he was contemptuous toward those he termed "amateur Gentiles," self-hating Jews who denied their ancestry. His closest friends have been Jews, particularly the philosopher Ernest Nagel, the political scientist Milton Konvitz, and the sociologists Lewis Feuer and Daniel Bell; both of his wives have been Jewish; and, for a short period, he sent his son to a Hebrew school in a Brooklyn synagogue.[12]

Hook's effort to carve out a Jewish identity was complicated by his opposition, which he shared with most of the other New York intellectuals, to the two most important modern manifestations of Jewish identity—Judaism and Zionism. Even before he was thirteen, Hook proclaimed he was an atheist and threatened not to take part in the hypocrisy of a bar mitzvah ceremony. He relented only after his parents pleaded with him not to shame them in the eyes of their neighbors and relatives. Hook's rejection of Judaism was facilitated by his superficial Jewish education, and by the primitive state of the Judaism of the immigrant generation. "Judaism seemed mainly a mass of superstitions taught by tyrannical old men who brooked no contradiction or honest doubt," he recounted. "There was little familiarity with enlightened, alternative versions of Judaism."[13]

Hook's initial rejection of theism stemmed from his inability to resolve what, since the time of Leibniz in the early eighteenth century, has been termed "theodicy"—reconciling the existence of evil with the goodness and sovereignty of God. Hook had first been drawn to the problem of theodicy when he learned that one of his siblings had died at an early age. What Richard Rubinstein and other "God is Dead" theologians had concluded during the 1960s as a result of meditating on the Holocaust, Hook had concluded a half century before. The problem of theodicy would remain Hook's major defense against the appeals of the religious. "I don't expect the innocent man to be vindicated tomorrow," he said in 1987, "But I do expect him to be vindicated before he goes to the scaffold. I don't expect the tyrant to be struck by a thunderbolt. But I would expect, if there is a God, that he would not die comfortably in his bed."[14]

Hook's atheism was deepened when he became a student of John Dewey while working toward his doctorate during the 1920s at Columbia. Dewey's naturalism and faith in the method of scientific experimentation bolstered Hook's denial of a supernatural God, and his stress upon pluralism encouraged Hook to begin thinking about America as a pluralistic and culturally diverse nation. Hook was also influenced by his friend Horace Kallen, America's most prominent exponent of ethnic cultural pluralism. Dewey and Kallen convinced Hook that democracy required cultural diversity. The real issue for Kallen and Hook was the nature of the Jewish contribution to this cultural mix.

Kallen was also skeptical of traditional Judaism, and sought to base American Jewish identity on something other than theism. The atheist son of an Orthodox rabbi, Kallen preferred to call himself a Hebraist rather than a Judaist. He argued that American Jews were essentially an ethnic group rooted in Hebrew culture. Hook agreed with Kallen that ethnicity, in general, and Jewish ethnicity, in particular, had enriched American life; that religion need not be the central component of Jewish identity; and that the most valuable elements of Jewish culture were ethnic, rather than religious. In contrast to

Kallen, Howe, and many of the other New York intellectuals, Hook was unfamiliar with Yiddish and Hebrew culture and with the classic Jewish texts.

Consequently, he emphasized that the essence of American Jewish ethnic identity lay not in language, custom, literature, religion, or nationhood, but in Jewish "values," which resembled those of Dewey. This was poles apart, for example, from Howe's secular Judaism that was indebted to the culture of Yiddishkeit he so movingly described in *World of Our Fathers*. For Howe, but not for Hook, the world of his parents provided a standard of judgment against which a capitalistic and materialistic America could be judged.

For Hook, the most important of these Jewish values was democracy. "As Jews we plead guilty to the charge that we are defenders of the democratic way of life," he asserted in a lecture of the 1930s. "Our goal and our hope must be that without ceasing to be Jews, we can become its most zealous defenders." He argued that there was a mutually reinforcing relationship between Jewishness and American democracy. "As I interpret Jewish culture," he wrote in "Promise Without Dogma," "its noblest feature is the characteristic way in which its traditions have fused passion for social justice with respect for scientific method and knowledge. When Jews forsake this method, they forsake a precious part of their tradition." American Jews, he maintained, were united not only by a common history, but also by a commitment to American democracy and by traditions of science and justice. He omitted any mention of religious or national ties.[15]

According to Hook, the "democratic way" meant three things: (1) economic justice, particularly the elimination of economic insecurity; (2) the recognition of the desirability of group differences and cultural pluralism; and (3) the pragmatic, scientific method of John Dewey. As long as American democracy remained strong, he contended, anti-Semitism would have little appeal. Hook's interpretation of the sources of anti-Semitism was a product of the 1930s as well as his own affinity then for an economic interpretation of history. Since Hitler had come to power during the Depression and promptly abolished German democracy, Hook naturally concluded that economic security and democracy were antithetical to anti-Semitism.

Hook did not flinch in the 1930s from carrying his assumptions regarding Jewishness and democracy to their logical political conclusion. Besides the complete separation of church and state, cultural diversity, and the pragmatic method, democracy implied a socialist welfare state. Socialism, he declared, was the most acceptable social philosophy for Jews, since it alone wedded "the ideals of the good life in the good society to the methods of intelligent analysis and action." Hook's ideal Jew combined the best of Marx and Dewey. For Jewish survivalists, the problem with Hook's approach was the absence of any positive and distinctive Jewish content since, as he readily admitted, the social philosophy he recommended to Jews was equally applicable to Gentiles, and its model practitioner was John Dewey. Furthermore, the twentieth century's experience with socialism hardly demonstrates that Jewish survival is most likely under conditions of socialism.[16]

This ahistorical view of the Jewish past tells us more about the values of Hook and those of the editors of the *Menorah Journal* than it does about Jewish tradition. This tradition is, in fact, more theocratic than democratic, and while Jewish texts are eloquent regarding the charitable and moral responsibilities of the individual Jew, they offer little in the way of a blueprint for social justice. Furthermore, Jewish tradition is largely concerned with following God's laws and not with conforming to the dictates of the scientific method.

While both Kallen and Hook agreed as to the ethnic character of American Jewry, they differed regarding Zionism. For Kallen, Zionism was important in the development of a vibrant American Jewish identity. Hook, in contrast, became an anti-Zionist when he became a Marxist while a teenager. For Marxists, Zionism was a bourgeois nationalist ideology that distracted the Jewish proletariat from revolution. This view of Zionism was common among the New York Jewish intellectuals prior to the Holocaust and the establishment of the state of Israel. Socialism, not Zionism, was their answer to the Jewish question. "Having transcended American nationalism by our allegiance to a universalist ideal, in which all men were brothers, we were not going to settle for a more parochial national ideal," Hook recalled. "The Jewish problem— and we all knew what that was—would be solved when the economically classless society of the future was established." Hook and Howe also feared that Zionism would lead to war between Jews and the indigenous Arab population in Palestine.[17]

In his autobiography, Hook asserted that one of the greatest errors of the New York intellectuals, himself included, was their failure prior to World War II to recognize the intensity of European anti-Semitism. Anti-Semitism supposedly was an anachronism, destined to disappear with the inevitable coming to power of socialism. While sensitive to the national aspiration of persecuted peoples, the New York intellectuals lapsed into a "proud universalism" when it came to the Jews.[18]

Hook's opposition to Zionism, rooted as it was in radicalism, was strengthened when he encountered the liberal anti-Zionism of Morris Raphael Cohen, the legendary City College professor of philosophy. Hook was particularly impressed by Cohen's 1919 article "Zionism: Tribalism or Liberalism?" which appeared while the Versailles Conference was debating the nationalistic claims of various European ethnic groups, including those of the Jews. Cohen did not oppose Zionism as a philanthropy working to establish a refuge in Palestine for persecuted Jews. But he did oppose those European Zionists who argued that Zionism was the only answer to the Jewish question, that the possibility of Jewish assimilation was chimeric, that all Jews were united by indissolvable ties of ideology and blood, that Judaism and Jewishness could only prosper in a Jewish state, and that Palestine should be an exclusively Jewish state. Cohen described them as "zealous enthusiasts" propagating an antiliberal program of group autonomy and "mystic and romantic nationalism" that was "profoundly inimical to liberal or humanistic civilization."

According to Cohen, a Zionist Palestine would mean a state founded on a tribal religion, dominated by one ethnic group, and justified by a doctrine of racial supremacy. Contrary to Zionist ideology, the future for American Jews lay in the United States, not in the Middle East. "The supposition that the Jews in Palestine would be more fortunately situated to make contributions to civilization than the Jews of America is contrary to all human experience." The amelioration of the Jewish condition depended not on a Zionist tribalistic fantasy, but on the spread of the enlightenment values of toleration, individual liberty, and reason.

Zionism, Cohen claimed further, was profoundly opposed to Americanism. Whereas the essence of Zionism was immutable group loyalties and group autonomy, the essence of Americanism was freedom and individuality. In contrast to Zionism, America stood for the separation of church and state, and the fluidity of ethnic and religious identities. Cohen warned American Jews that Zionism would distract them from the need to adjust to American conditions. "The glory of Palestine is as nothing to the possible glory of America. If history has any lesson at all it is that never have men accomplished anything great by trying to revive a dead past."[19]

Hook's definition of Zionism was the same as Cohen's—Jewish nationalism—and he opposed it for the same reasons, on liberal principles. Prior to the establishment of Israel in 1948, he rejected political Zionism and sympathized with Judah Magnes' proposal for a binational state in Palestine, a plan he later admitted was "utopian" because it lacked Arab support. In a letter published in the *New York Times* of December 4, 1948, Hook, joined with Albert Einstein, Hannah Arendt, and other leading Jewish intellectuals in protesting the racism, nationalism, chauvinism, terrorism, "religious mysticism," and even facism that supposedly permeated Menachem Begin's right-wing Herut Party. (During the 1970s, Hook modified this harsh judgment of Begin, perhaps because he concluded that Begin's pessimistic view of the Arabs had merit, and perhaps because of Hook's antipathy toward Begin's critics on the Left.)[20]

Hook could not accept the Zionist argument that a Jewish state was necessary because of the inevitability of anti-Semitism. In a long career, extending over six decades, Hook has been a prolific writer, and his bibliography runs to forty pages; but it does not contain even one item on American anti-Semitism. It was simply incomprehensible to him that America would ever experience anything similar to the Dreyfus Affair, much less the Holocaust, and that American Jews would ever have to flee to Palestine.

In his 1947 analysis of the activities of the National Council of Jewish Women, written at the height of the political debate over the proposed Jewish state, Hook supported the Council's neutrality regarding Zionism. He agreed with the Council that the major concern of America's Jews must be the future of American Jewry, and that political Zionism caused legitimate questions to be raised regarding the loyalty of American Jews and their commitment to an American future. His only caveat was that the Council had been needlessly defensive because of an exaggerated fear of offending Zionist extremists. Opposition to political Zionism did not mean, however, that American Jewry should not assist the Yishuv or lobby for unrestricted immigration into Palestine. American Jews properly recognized the cultural importance of Palestine for all Jews, admired the economic accomplishments of Palestine Jewry, and welcomed the social and economic principles underlying the kibbutz. Hook's position was not far from that of mainstream American Zionism prior to the World War II Biltmore Conference when American Zionist leaders, for the first time, united in support of a Jewish state. Prior to that, American Zionism had emphasized the succoring of persecuted Jews and charitable efforts in behalf of the Yishuv rather than Jewish nationalism.[21]

After 1948, Hook's position toward Israel resembled that of most American Jews, including the New York intellectuals. He was interested in the country's welfare, and sympathized with the outlook of the Israeli Labor Party and the Histadrut. But he had no intention of settling in the Jewish state or even visiting it, despite invitations from Israeli academic circles, and he rejected the notion that, as a Jew, he had any special relationship or obligation to Israel. In 1949, he cautioned American Jews about the danger of ethnic chauvinism resulting from Israel's military victories in her war of independence. "A people that has, by and large, been rational and pacific," he warned, now sought through militarism, ultranationalism, and "the *mystique* of action . . . to prove that they are like everyone else—inconsistent, fanatical, atavistic." In the 1950s, Hook even praised the activities of the anti-Zionist American Council for Judaism. Another indication of his attitude toward Israel was the fact that he did not discuss in print the founding of Israel, the development of the country, or the Middle East wars of 1948, 1956, and 1967.[22]

The Six-Day War of 1967 was a watershed in the attitude of the New York intellectuals and other American Jews toward Israel. It took the threat of an Israeli defeat to make them realize how much Israel meant to them. But while most New York intellectuals were driven primarily by fears of a second holocaust, Hook was motivated by admiration for an Israel that defeated the clients of the Soviet Union. Israel's primary significance for Hook was its role as an ally of the West in the struggle against the Soviet bloc and its western dupes. His support for Israel was conditional on her remaining part of the western coalition.

Hook dissented from the disenchantment with Israel among New York intellectuals after Begin's election in 1977 as Prime Minister. He defended the 1982 Israeli invasion of Lebanon, which most New York intellectuals firmly opposed, and argued that the media's assault on Israel had generated "an atmosphere of pogrom-hatred against Jews." Accusations by Arthur Hertzberg, Irving Howe, and other intellectuals that Israel had "lost its soul" because of the Lebanese invasion struck Hook as nonsense. "Norman Podhoretz is closer to the truth in his order of priority of blame—the PLO first, and Israel last."[23]

Hook's attitude toward Israel was a by-product of his staunch attempt, beginning in the 1930s, to shore up western defenses against the dangers of communism and Soviet power. In contrast to most of the other New York intellectuals during the 1930s and 1940s, he was more concerned with the danger of communism than facism, and his anticommunism was deeper and more consuming. While facism was the greater military threat to the West, Hook perceived communism to be the greater threat to the "democratic way of life" within the world of the universities and intellectuals.

The Holocaust did not have the same impact on Hook as it had, for example, on Kazin or Howe. His infrequent writings on Nazism tended to downplay its unique demonic character, and he was too much the universalist to argue, as did Howe, that the significance of the Holocaust lay largely in its Jewish dimension. He implicitly rejected the argument—most forcefully presented by the historian Lucy Dawidowicz—that World War II was, for Germany, "a war against the Jews." According to Hook, Nazism was simply one manifestation of the totalitarian impulse whose purest and most malignant form was Stalinism. This interpretation of totalitarianism differed sharply from that of most other American Jewish intellectuals, and particularly from that of Jewish emigres from Germany. For them, the totalitarian paradigm was Nazism; for Hook it was Stalinism. Hook's relative lack of interest in Nazism also accounts for his uncharacteristic silence during the controversy of the early 1960s over Arendt's *Eichmann in Jerusalem*.

In a guest column in the November 26, 1938, *New Leader* entitled "The Tragedy of German Jewry," published two weeks after Crystal Night, Hook claimed that Nazi Germany had learned how to deal with unpopular and vulnerable minorities from the Soviet Union. Stalin had taught Hitler "the art of uprooting and wiping out whole groups and classes of innocent citizens . . . If, as it is rumored, Hitler intends to convert the Jews into serfs to work on canals, fortifications and roads, he will merely be tearing a leaf out of Stalin's own book." For Hook, the Nazis were evil, but their evil was hardly unique.[24]

Hook continually emphasized the importance of the communist theory of "social fascism" in facilitating Hitler's accession to office in 1933 and in solidifying his power. This theory, which declared the major danger to the German working class to be social democracy and not Nazism, supposedly prevented cooperation between the German Socialists and Communists which could have prevented the Nazis from coming to power. Hook asserted that the Nazi–Soviet Pact of August 1939 and the cordial relations between the two dictatorships until the German invasion of Russia in June 1941 were not idiosyncratic, but stemmed from the fundamental similarities between the two regimes.

One important aspect of Hook's interpretation of Nazism was its downplay of anti-Semitism. Since anti-Semitism had no place in official Soviet ideology, an emphasis on Nazi anti-Semitism would have undermined Hook's argument that Nazism derived largely from Stalinism and was not *sui generis*. "The Tragedy of German Jewry" contended that, while the condition of German Jews was "one of the darkest shadows on our Century" and could be resolved only by their mass exodus from Germany, it did not require a western response different from that toward other minorities persecuted by the Nazis and Stalin. In protesting against German anti-Semitism, he told his readers, "we are also protesting against his hounding of all other religious and political minorities. We are protesting against the murderous liquidation of all groups whose only fault has been that they have fallen foul of arbitrary, dictatorial decrees."[25]

Hook's most important analysis of National Socialism, "Hitlerism: A Non-Metaphysical View," appeared in the February 1944 issue of the *Contemporary Jewish Record*, published by the American Jewish Committee. Its readers must have been surprised by its downplaying of the popularity of anti-Semitism in accounting for the appeals of Nazism. According to Hook, anti-Semitism and other such "metaphysical" ideological factors were unimportant in the Nazi triumph in Germany. Nazi leaders had been attracted to Hitler solely by the promise of "material plunder and other prerequisites of office and prestige," and his support from the masses stemmed from economic insecurity, rather than from any widespread sympathy for his racial fantasies. "It was not Hitler's rhetoric and propaganda they believed but his promises." Hook's solution to the Nazi problem followed logically. "Immunization from another plague of Nazism is conditional upon profound social and economic changes to be carried out by a democratic revolution which will give the masses security of existence without terror."[26]

This refutation of metaphysical explanations of Nazism was a continuation of Hook's famous conflict during the early 1940s with Mortimer J. Adler, the Thomistic philosopher from the University of Chicago. Adler had claimed that democracy must be grounded in metaphysics and theology, that philosophical relativism and agnosticism were greater threats to American democracy than Hitler, and that the West needed to counter the ideologies of its enemies with an ideology of its own. Hook attributed Adler's ideas to a "failure of nerve" and a hankering for "transcendental consolation," which were incompatible with the nineteenth-century sources of liberal democracy and the methods of modern scientific inquiry. His failure of nerve was "a desperate quest for quick and all-inclusive faith that will save us from the trouble of thinking about difficult problems." His philosophical monism was dangerous because, by repudiating secularism, pluralism, and respect for the "method of free, critical intelligence," it rejected the foundations of modern democracy. It also undermined the security of American Jews, which depended on secularism, democracy, and the scientific spirit. Hook's definition of American Jewish identity stemmed from this defense of democracy against the totalitarianism of the Left and the medievalism of the Right.[27]

Hook's view of American Jewish identity struck some new notes in the post-Holocaust era. The first was the difficulty he had in determining whether Jewish identity was a matter of fate or choice. Hook now emphasized that the key to this identity was neither democracy, the scientific method, or leftist economic planning; rather, it was the common lot of Jews which, "whether they like it or not or whether they like each other or not, cancels all their other not inconsiderable differences." The hold of this fate was so strong that even the most alienated of Jews was unable to separate themselves from it.[28]

Echoing Kallen, Hook argued that it was psychologically destructive for Jews to hide their Jewishness, capitulate to irrational prejudice, and "deny kinship with their own fathers and mothers who, often against heroic odds, had courageously kept their integrity and faith whatever it was." Hook was wrong since many Jews did not feel any burden of a common fate with other Jews, nor were they afflicted with psychological traumas as a result of denying their ancestry. While rejecting the monistic definitions of Jewish identity of the Orthodox and the Zionists, Hook was close to accepting a monism of biological determinism and involuntary ethnic identity. He agreed with Kallen's famous statement that a person could change anything except his grandparents. There was, Hook said, "no dignity in denying one's origins or in living as if they were something to be apologetic about." This was a strange conclusion for a disciple of Dewey.[29]

Dewey's open and pluralistic social philosophy affirmed the right to reject as well as to affirm group loyalties. The belief that a person must remain in the same social and cultural situation in which he was born, Hook said, was "a piece of antidemocratic presumption." Whether a person chose to identify as a Jew in a democracy was a matter of voluntary choice. But Hook's commitment to Dewey's philosophy of openness and diversity was limited by his contempt for "amateur Gentiles" and his ethnic interpretation of American Jewry.[30]

Hook now sought something more substantive and distinctive than liberalism to define Jewish identity. While liberalism allowed for group identity, the nature of this identity had still to be defined in Jewish terms, and it had to involve more than opposition to anti-Semitism. "The psychology of mere defense," he wrote, "is ultimately self-defeating unless there is some positive awareness of *what* we are defending, its significance and value." The challenge to American Jewry was to provide an identity which would be attractive even to college-educated youth afflicted with self-hatred. Hook's partial answer to the problem of Jewish identity among the young was the creation of a nonsectarian university, under Jewish auspices, to be run on democratic, secular, and progressive principles. Such an institution appeared in 1948, when Brandeis opened. But Brandeis would never be able to educate more than a tiny percentage of Jewish youth.[31]

Hook's 1949 essay, "Reflections on the Jewish Question," was prompted by the publication of Jean-Paul Sartre's *Anti-Semite and Jew*. Sartre had argued that Jewish identity was largely a response to anti-Semitism. For Sartre, the quintessential Jew was the martyr—eliminate anti-Semitism and Jews would no longer have any need to remain Jewish. Hook agreed that Jews were unified by a "negative togetherness." This resulted from "a common historical condition which, whether they like it or not or whether they like each other or not, cancels out in the eyes of others their not inconsiderable differences." But Hook went beyond Sartre in affirming the possibility of a positive Jewish identity, although his distaste for ideological straitjackets and "muddy metaphysics" prevented from advancing beyond vague generalities.[32]

He argued that a secular and democratic American Jewish culture could be the basis of American Jewish identity. Such a culture would have to flow from indigenous American sources and be compatible with American social and political values. He proposed establishing a host of artistic, literary, and philosophic organizations, journals, schools, theaters, and museums to stimulate American Jewish culture "through music, through art, through literature and drama, through common celebrations, religious or secular, and especially through study." Young Jews would not be attracted to Zionism and traditional religion and a Judaism of Deweyite liberalism was too tepid in the post–World War II environment of heightened Jewish consciousness. A revived Jewish culture, in contrast, "interacting and integrated with whatever American life it can reach," would enable American Jews to avoid the extremes of acculturation and parochialism.[33]

But Hook was silent regarding the critical issue—what precisely would be the nature of this American Jewish culture of significance and value. His pluralism and suspicion of ideologies prevented him from moving from process to content, from how to what. For Hook, the son of immigrants and the product of a Jewish neighborhood, defining Jewish culture was unnecessary. One does not have to define what is in your very bones. But definition would be necessary for later generations, whose ties to the Jewish past were more fragile and whose Jewishness could not be taken for granted. Hook, himself, had been unable to provide any reason why such Jews should wish to be the cultural heirs of Moses rather than of Jesus or Marx.

Furthermore, as Will Herberg's *Protestant-Catholic-Jew: An Essay in American Religious Sociology* pointed out, Hook's view of Jewishness as "a distinctive expression or articulation of American civilization" had no place for those religious impulses which, transcending the particularities of time and place, sought to judge rather than to sanction society's values. Without a sense of the transcendent, Judaism could be used to legitimize whatever social, economic, or political orthodoxy was in fashion, just as Hook, in the 1930s, had equated Jewishness with socialism. Ironically, during the 1960s and 1970s, Hook condemned precisely the same tendency within Christianity when he attacked "liberation" theology for attempting to synthesize Christianity and Marxism.[34]

Hook explored the nature of American Jewish identity in his examination of the National Council of Jewish Women. He began the study, he told the Council, with only one major assumption—"a firm belief in the desirability of Jewish group survival in the United States." The report repeated familiar themes. It emphasized the right and duty of American Jews to create a separate collective existence since democracy involved an equality of diversity and not an equality of unanimity. The report rejected all efforts to establish a single definition of Jewishness since heterogeneity was the major characteristic of American Jews. A Jew was *anyone who for any reason calls himself such or is called such in any community which acts on the distinction.* Jewish unity was a product not of beliefs but of "a common lot and destiny." Hook did not explain how a group which was so economically, socially, and geographically diverse could share a common lot and destiny.[35]

Instead of describing the specific contributions Jews could make to the American mosaic, Hook's recommendations to the Council focused on the strengthening of cultural pluralism. These included opposing all efforts to breach the wall of separation between church and state, supporting educational programs showing the cultural and ethnic diversity of America, and attacking discrimination against any ethnic or racial group. The content of Jewish cultural activities seemed less important to Hook than the occasion they provided for Jews to interact. "Wherever Jews meet *as Jews* for a common purpose," he said, "an opportunity is at hand for the development of character-istic Jewish experiences." One of the beneficial results of Jewish education was that it lead to "ongoing activities."[36]

Certainly Hook was correct in seeing Jewish communal identity as important and not needing any justification. As Leonard Fein has noted, "the core method of Judaism is community. Ours is not a personal testament, but a collective and public commitment. . . . What defines the Jews *as Jews* is community; not values, not ideology." But a method is only a means to an end.

Hook did not discuss why heterogeneous Jews would want to be part of a community. It is doubtful whether sociability for sociability's sake, what Hook called "continuing association and common activity," could sustain a continuing Jewish commitment in a nation where the barriers to assimilation are so easy to navigate. This is particularly true among younger Jews for whom the campus provides a rival community.[37]

The surprising thing about Hook's attempt to define an American Jewish identity along liberal and secular lines is not, as he later admitted, that it failed, but that it took place in the first place. That an intellectual of Hook's stature should concern himself with the seemingly parochial question of American Jewish identity is symptomatic of the inability of the New York intellectuals to divest themselves of their Jewishness, whatever that might mean to them. If Hook failed to resolve the tension between universalism and particularism, he is in good company; no one else has, either. This tension, Fein has written, "is not, as is so generally believed, a dilemma to be resolved but an existential condition to be lived and even savored. Alone, each is precarious; together . . . they are an arch, two weaknesses leaning into a strength."[38] Hook's own effort reflected a confidence in the compatibility of American democracy and Jewish continuity. Only time will tell whether he was correct. You don't have to be Jewish to like Levy's Jewish rye, and you don't have to be Jewish to like American democracy. But, according to Sidney Hook, it sure helps.

Notes

1. C. Vann Woodward, *The Burden of Southern History* (Baton Rouge: Louisiana State University Press, 1960), pp. 31–32. I have discussed the nature of American Jewish identity in "Jewish Identity in America," a two-part essay that appeared in the *World and I*, 3 (May and June 1988).

2. Alexander Bloom, *Prodigal Sons: The New York Intellectuals and Their World* (New York: Oxford University Press, 1986), pp. 142-155; Terry A. Cooney, *The Rise of the New York Intellectuals:* Partisan Review *and Its Circle* (Madison, WI: University of Wisconsin Press, 1986), p. 242; Alan Wald, *The New York Intellectuals: The Rise and Decline of the Anti-Stalinist Left From the 1930s to the 1980s* (Chapel Hill, NC: University of North Carolina Press, 1987). See also David J. Hollinger, "Ethnic Diversity, Cosmopolitanism and the Emergence of the American Liberal Intelligentsia," *American Quarterly*, 27 (May 1975), pp. 133–51.

3. Stephen J. Whitfield, "After Strange Gods: Radical Jews in Modern America," *Forum*, #56 (Summer 1985), pp. 34–35; Cooney, *Rise of New York Intellectuals:* p. 14; Deutscher's essay "The nonJewish Jew" is in Tamara Deutscher, ed., *'The NonJewish Jew' and Other Essays* (New York: Oxford University Press, 1968), pp. 25–41.

4. Cooney, *Rise of New York Intellectuals,* pp. 14, 240; Leonard Fein, *Where Are We? The Inner Life of America's Jews* (New York: Harper and Row, 1988), p. 189.

5. Irving Howe, *A Margin of Hope* (New York: Harcourt, Brace, Jovanovich, 1982), pp. 151–61.

6. Ruth R. Wisse, "The New York (Jewish) Intellectuals," *Commentary*, 74 (November 1987), pp. 34–38.

7. Alfred Kazin, *New York Jew* (New York: Alfred A. Knopf, 1978), pp. 26–34.

8. Howe, *Margin of Hope:* pp. 247–51; Norman Podhoretz, *Making It* (New York: Random House, 1967), pp. 118–22.

9. Howe, "The Range of the New York Intellectual," in Bernard Rosenberg and Ernest Goldstein, eds., *Creators and Disturbers: Reminiscences by Jewish Intellectuals of New York* (New York: Columbia University Press, 1982), pp. 285–86.

10. Howe, *Margin of Hope:* pp. 260–80.

11. Wald, *New York Intellectuals,* p. 28; Sidney Hook to Joseph J. Jacobs, January 9, 1984; Hook Papers (Hoover Institution, Stanford University).

12. Hook, "Our Country and Our Culture," *Partisan Review*, 19 (May–June 1952), p. 570.

13. Hook, *Out of Step: An Unquiet Life in the 20th Century* (New York: Harper and Row, 1987), p. 33.

14. Hook, *Out of Step:* pp. 33–4; Tom Bethell, "A Stroll With Sidney Hook," *American Spectator*, 20 (May 1987), pp. 12–13.

15. The outline of this speech is in the Hook Papers; Hook, "Promise Without Dogma: A Social Philosophy for Jews," *Menorah Journal*, 25 (October–December 1937), pp. 273–88.

16. Hook, "Promise Without Dogma"; Hook to Edward S. Shapiro, May 11, 1988. For two different responses to Hook's essay, see Shlomo Grodzensky, "Sidney Hook Faces the Jewish Problem," *Labor Zionist News Letter*, January 15, 1938, pp. 5–9, and "Alvin Johnson, "A Social Philosophy for Jews," *Menorah Journal*, 26 (January–March, 1938), pp. 1–5. Hook's response to Johnson is in *ibid.*, pp. 103–04.

17. Hook, *Out of Step*, p. 33.

18. Hook, *Out of Step*, p. 5.

19. Morris R. Cohen, "Zionism: Tribalism or Liberalism?" *New Republic*, XVIII (March 8, 1919), pp. 182–83.

20. *New York Times*, December 4, 1948; Hook, "Israel and American Jewry," unpublished manuscript, Hook Papers.

21. A copy of Hook, "The National Council of Jewish Women on the Present-Day Jewish Scene: A Program Survey of the Organization" is in the Hook Papers.

22. Hook, "Reflections on the Jewish Question," *Partisan Review*, 16 (May 1949), p. 466; Hook to Leonard R. Sussman, March 7, 1957, Hook Papers.

23. Hook to Joseph P. Bachman, undated; Hook to Jonathan Harlen, November 24, 1982, Hook Papers.

24. Hook, "The Tragedy of German Jewry," *New Leader*, November 26, 1938.

25. Ibid. For a general discussion of the response of American intellectuals to totalitarianism, see Stephan J. Whitfield's essay "American Jewish Intellectuals and Totalitarianism," in his *Voices of Jacob, Hands of Easu: Jews in American Life and Thought* (Hamden, CT: Archon Books, 1984), pp. 9–29.

26. Hook, "Hitlerism: A Non-Metaphysical View," *Contemporary Jewish Record*, 7 (February 1944), pp. 146–55.

27. Hook, "The New Medievalism," *New Republic*, 103 (October 28, 1940), pp. 602–06; Hook, "The New Failure of Nerve," *Partisan Review*, 10 (January–February 1943), pp. 2–23.

28. Hook, "Reflections on the Jewish Question," p. 475.
29. Hook, "Reflections on the Jewish Question," p. 479; Hook, "The Plural Sources of Jewish Life in America," unpublished manuscript, Hook Papers. This is a twenty-one page paper Hook delivered at the 1947 conference of the American Jewish Committee.
30. Hook, "Reflections on the Jewish Question," p. 482.
31. Hook, "Plural Sources of Jewish Life"; Hook, "National Council of Jewish Women."
32. Hook, "Reflections on the Jewish Question," p. 476.
33. Hook, "National Council of Jewish Women"; Hook, "Plural Sources of Jewish Life."
34. Hook, *Out of Step*, p. 350.
35. Hook, "National Council of Jewish Women."
36. Ibid.
37. Fein, *Where Are We?* p. 168.
38. Fein, *Where Are We?* pp. 160–61.

11

Developments in Jewish Community Organization in the Second Postwar Generation

Daniel J. Elazar

A New Generation and a New Agenda

In 1976, I published *Community and Polity: The Organizational Dynamics of American Jewry,* a description and analysis of developments in the American Jewish community through the first postwar generation—roughly 1946 through 1976.[1] Those were the years in which the American Jewish community completed the development of its communal structure, modes of Jewish affiliation, and basic patterns for collective action. American Jewry, along with the United States and the world as a whole, has since passed into the second generation of the postwar and, indeed, postmodern epoch.

As could be expected, the new generation brought a new agenda that it is presently in the process of defining. In some cases, trends from the first generation have continued to play themselves out. In others, there have been reversals of previous trends, sometimes unanticipated. New organizations and institutions have developed along with new issues. All told, twelve years into the new generation, while we are still seeking appropriate ways to deal with the new agenda, a preliminary description and analysis of these new developments is in place. This article is, in that sense, an update of *Community and Polity* to show how both the American Jewish community and its polity have developed in the new generation.

The focus here is on the community and its polity as they are organized countrywide, locally, and increasingly on a statewide and regional basis. In particular, I discuss the transformations that take place in local community federations and in the countrywide federation movement; the decline of the

173

mass-based organizations, and the exceptions to that decline; the shift in the forms and organization of Jewish education; the changes taking place in the synagogue movements in response to a stabilization of membership at a lower level than anticipated; and the problems of Jewish unity generated by inter-movement competition, the new ambiguity in the sphere of community relations, the impact of demographic shifts on Jewish community organization, the institutionalization of new relationships between the American Jewish community and Israel, the emergence of new model organizations to mobilize and serve the Jewish community, and the emerging changes in communal leadership.

Transformations in the Jewish Community Federations

At the end of the first postwar generation, the Jewish community federations had become the framing institutions of virtually every local Jewish community of any size in the United States. As such, the local federation raised about half the money raised from Jews for Jewish purposes (excluding fees for services). Its influence extended into every sphere of Jewish activity; in most cases, with the exception of the religious congregational sphere, where the synagogue still remained fully or substantially independent. Through its powers of the purse, the federation had undertaken responsibility for community planning in such a way that it did as much as any single Jewish organization possibly could to shape organized Jewish life.

There were, of course, limitations on the newly powerful federations. Some were situational. Federations had no significant influence over Jewish demographic trends; birth rates, intermarriage, or interneighborhood, city-suburb, or interregional migrations. To these forces they could only respond and not always well. Federations had little, if any, influence on synagogues, not even in such matters as their relocation or building campaigns, which had a significant impact on the larger Jewish community. Federations did not choose to have an impact on the content of Jewish education except in peripheral ways. While federations had extended their control over the community relations sphere by bringing the local community relations councils (CRCs) under their control to the extent that they exercised a veto over CRC activities if they did not set the CRC agenda, they still had to deal with relatively independent branches of the national community relations organizations.

The federations' dominance in the communal welfare sphere was more complete. Even so, individual agencies remained a part of the framing institution, not subordinate to it. Federation domination may have been most complete in the Israel-overseas sphere, at least in the realm of fundraising, and since there were few other local community connections with Israel, that was sufficient.

The new generation has brought a number of important developments modifying the previous situation:

1. Federations have become more involved in the educational-cultural and religious-congregational spheres. As more Jewish education has become day-school education and a greater share of the day school budgets have come from federations, federation involvement has grown as part of the normal processes of Jewish communal governance. By the end of the previous generation, concern over the state of federation-synagogue relations had led to the development of coordinating committees in most communities. While these committees soon found that they had relatively little to do and synagogues still remain very much in the category of private institutions, ways have been found to provide federation aid to synagogue programs in many communities and a certain amount of intersynagogal coordination under federation auspices or with federation encouragement is emerging.

2. Within those spheres in which federations already had a strong presence, some have begun to move toward direct-control arrangements. This has been the historic pattern in the so-called "integrated federations," where each of the communal functions is handled by a department or committee rather than a separate agency. But the federated pattern is by far the more common. Recent efforts to either absorb formerly federated agencies as federation departments or to take over the budgeting process of still nominally federated agencies in such a way that their freedom of decision-making is reduced to mere housekeeping, is an increasing trend.

    Much as the growth of federations was a good thing for the American Jewish community, there are signs that this new trend is not healthy for the community. While it may seem like a logical extension of the earlier movement from fundraising to financing to community planning, it is, in fact, a break from the federated pattern toward a unitary one, and unitary government has never worked either in the United States or in the Jewish polity unless it is a result of coercion from the outside. People will simply vote with their feet and no longer volunteer. As we shall see, as the federations have become more powerful, there is every evidence that their share of the total Jewish fundraising dollar has declined, as new people who do not find the federation establishments open to them or advancement through federation sufficiently rapid or far, seek other places to put voluntary contributions of time, effort, and funds.

3. One of the characteristics of the new generation has been more direct Diaspora involvement in those aspects of Israeli development where Diaspora funds are involved. The greatest and best example of this is Project Renewal, where local communities, the larger ones alone and small ones in consortia, were twinned with Israeli neighborhoods and development towns to undertake urban revitalization projects. While some may have been reluctant at first, most of the stronger federations seized this opportunity as

it became clear that they would have more direct operating responsibilities than most have in their own communities.[2] By 1985, some forty federations had appointed their own representatives in Israel, in most cases to work with Project Renewal, but in at least four—New York, Los Angeles, Chicago, and San Francisco—to be comprehensive representatives of federation interests and local community programs in the Jewish state. From this, it was an easy step to demanding that the federations choose the community representatives to the governing bodies of the Jewish Agency, even if they are formally nominated by the United Israel Appeal.[3]

Another important element in the growth of the federations' power is the expansion of federation endowment funds. The effort of the past twenty years to increase those funds has now begun to bear fruit. The income from these funds has given the federation leadership increasing amounts of discretionary money to initiate or support programs that might not otherwise pass through the normal allocations process.

4. Already at the end of the previous generation it was becoming apparent that federations were forming alliances with a newly resurgent, if still numerically small, Orthodox Jewry in a manner similar to the alliances between the leading nonreligious parties and the religious camp in Israel. Since then these alliances have spread and deepened. There are several reasons why this became a natural development. Mainstream Orthodox Jewish institutions do not compete with federations. At the same time, they can use federation services and, indeed, are excellent clients for services that non-Orthodox Jews no longer require or seek from the Jewish community. Hence, cooperation with federations strengthens the federations' role in the community, and if the Orthodox can be persuaded to contribute as well, in return for services, that role is further strengthened.

All this is enhanced by the growing strength of Orthodoxy on the American Jewish scene. In raw percentages the differences do not seem to be important. Orthodox Jews still constitute approximately ten percent of the American Jewish population. But a more careful analysis reveals that, increasingly, the ten percent consists of real rather than nominal Orthodox Jews. Nearly all of the ten percent Orthodox are actively Jewish, something that cannot be said for the 60 percent of American Jewry who identify with one or another of the non-Orthodox movements, of whom only about half are active at best and a third is probably a more accurate figure. Those who identify with no branch of Judaism are virtually all inactive. The one-third non-Orthodox Jewish actives constitute 20 percent of American Jewry, while Orthodox Jews constitute nearly 10 percent, which gives Orthodox Jewry approximately one-third of all active Jews in America. Thus, the Orthodox community has acquired real weight on the American Jewish scene.[4]

If we add to this the minimal interest of the Reform movement in federation services, and the long-standing (although now diminishing) antagonism between many Conservative rabbis and the federations, the picture comes into even sharper focus. In the first postwar generation, the Reform movement had almost no demands on federation services. Whatever services Reform Jews used, they used as individual members of the community. This has changed somewhat in the second generation, as segments of the Reform movement have sought more intensive Jewish education and federation support for their day schools and even their supplementary schools. Also, its struggle for presence and standing in Israel has led the Reform movement to try to mobilize federation support for Jewish Agency allocations to their Israeli institutions. Still, there is nowhere near the level of utilization of local services among Reform Jews that there is in actuality or potentially among the Orthodox.

During the first postwar generation, when Conservative synagogues were expanding vigorously, they were disturbed by competition with Jewish community centers for their youth, a real antagonism developed between the Conservative rabbinate and the federations. Now that it is apparent that few, if any, Conservative congregations will become all-embracing synagogue centers and the movement's new leadership has come to perceive what it means to be in conflict with the federations, changes are in the offing, but they have just begun, and it is too soon to assess how strong the shift is likely to be.

5. All this is reflected in the new presence of observant Jews in the federation civil service. Gone are the days when most federation personnel, especially senior personnel, were secularists from socialist or communist backgrounds who had found their way back to the Jewish people through their careers in Jewish communal service. This remained true through the first postwar generation, but shifted rapidly in the 1970s, and is continuing to shift.

Today, Jewish communal service, like the rabbinate or Jewish education, attracts those who are committed to Judaism in all its facets and who find a Jewish career environment makes life richer for them as observant Jews. We do not have percentages available, but the change is palpable, especially among the younger age groups, although the fact that the executive vice-presidents of the Council of Jewish Federations, and the Conference of Presidents of Major Jewish Organizations, the World Jewish Congress, and Anti-Defamation League, and the National Foundation for Jewish Culture are Orthodox Jews speaks for itself.

One clear indication of the shift is to be found at the annual General Assembly of the Council of Jewish Federations, the major gathering of the American Jewry. Until just a few years ago, the Orthodox services had trouble attracting more than two or three minyanim even on Shabbat, as compared to the hundreds attending non-Orthodox Sabbath services. In 1987, the Orthodox service on Shabbat had approximately 250 participants, leaving it still in third place but in the same size range as the Conservative and Reform services. Moreover, it was the Orthodox service that drew the highest percentage of senior Jewish civil servants.

Nor should it be thought that all the traditional Jews in Jewish communal service are Orthodox. The non-Orthodox on the federation staffs are drawn increasingly from among the serious Conservative Jews, whose personal and family observance level is high and who are participants in havurot and Solomon Schechter day schools, as well as products of the Ramah camps.

6. The annual campaign has become more locally oriented. Federations rose to their present positions of power in great part because they became the principal fundraisers for Israel. For years, Israelis and supporters of Israel charged that the local communities were living off the back of Israel, raising large sums of money in her name and then keeping much of it at home for local purposes—that in the days when up to 70 percent of the campaign was allocated to Israel. Toward the end of the first postwar generation, the percentage of funds allocated to Israel began to decline and has continued to do so, so that the average is now more or less 50-50. This has served to intensify the claim.

At least since the Lebanon War in 1982, however, there has been a tendency to shift the emphasis in the campaign to local needs, downplaying Israel. In recent years, there have even been campaigns in some cities in which Israel is barely featured. This is partly a result of the fear of the federation leadership that Israel's bad press has made her less attractive to donors, but it is also a reflection of the increased consciousness of the donors of local Jewish needs, especially in the realm of formal and informal Jewish education.

The spread of the Jewish population around the country has moved an increasing number of federations to begin to develop new forms of statewide and regional organization to accommodate a situation in which most Jews are no longer located in clear-cut metropolitan concentrations. Statewide organization first came in an effort to find a basis for providing federation support for Jewish programs on the college campuses. Since many universities, including many that are most attractive to Jewish students, are located outside of normal federation service areas (even those within metropolitan areas draw students who do not originally come from the local community), the need to develop an equitable basis for supporting Jewish campus services led to regional or statewide consortia of federations.

These consortia were paralleled by the establishment of intrastate regional federations for small Jewish communities, such as those of southern and central Illinois. In the first, a number of very small Jewish communities created one common federation to service the Jews in the southern third of the state, while in the second, a number of separate federations, created a "federation of federations" to deal with the Jews in the central third. More recently, statewide confederations of federations have been established in Florida, Illinois, and New Jersey, in part for joint representation at the state capital, and for a wider range of joint activities designed to serve statewide populations.

This is a new departure for American Jewry, which had always been organized on a citywide or metropolitan basis. As yet it is not a major transformation, but it may be a significant one. Indeed, the Council of Jewish Federations is now discussing countrywide planning to deal with such demographic trends as the Jewish move to the Sunbelt.[5]

Declines in the Mass-Based Organizations

A second great change taking place in American Jewish community life is the decline in membership of the great mass-based Jewish organizations. B'nai B'rith has been in serious trouble since the mid-1970s, as its older members have died and fewer and fewer younger people find it attractive. New forms of leisure-time activity have replaced the traditional B'nai B'rith bowling leagues and brunches, which were the primary attractions for many otherwise marginal Jews. The insurance packages offered by the organization, once attractive benefits, especially to the self-employed, now compete with insurance and pension plans that do not require organizational membership. Nor has B'nai B'rith's Jewish content been focused enough to attract those who seek Jewish activity.

The women's organizations, including Hadassah, have also been hard hit by the changing environment. The women's movement, with its emphasis on careers for women in areas once considered the province of men, has attracted many of the younger women, occupying their time so that they no longer have the need, the energy, or the leisure for voluntary organizational activity in women's groups. Those who do find time for such activity are more likely to seek expression in what were once men's groups that now recruit leadership regardless of gender, such as the federations themselves, their agencies, synagogue and school boards, or the local chapters of AIPAC (the American–Israel Public Affairs Committee).

This has had two consequences. On one hand, the role in Jewish life of general-purpose mass-based organizations outside the synagogue in Jewish life is diminishing. B'nai B'rith has, for all intents and purposes, transferred its most important functions to other bodies. ADL has become even more independent than it was. The Hillel Foundations have become part of the federation world. The synagogues have become the only places where large numbers of Jews assemble regularly. If they cannot compete with the federations for leadership in the Jewish community, they do play a mobilizing role that federations cannot. Hence, there now is a greater incentive for both federations and synagogues to develop linkages based on the special ability of each to mobilize either funds or people.

Stabilization in the Congregations

At the end of the first postwar generation, the situation in the synagogues looked gloomy. The great religious revival of the 1950s had ended about 1962. Few new congregations were founded after that date, except where migration brought Jews to areas without synagogues. Hence, synagogue membership actually began to diminish, a decline that continued for the next thirteen years. The situation stabilized about 1975, just at the generation's end, and has since remained stable. While there has been little, if any, growth in synagogue membership, the drop in other forms of jewish association, particularly among the mass-based Jewish organizations, has actually strengthened the synagogues' overall position in the community somewhat, while improved federation–synagogue relations have reinforced those two institutions as the twin pillars of the local community.

Within the different synagogue movements, there have been apparently contradictory trends. The Reform movement has benefitted most from such growth, to the point where it now is at least equal in membership to the Conservative movement in most communities. The trend to more traditional observance in Reform congregations has continued, and the National Federation of Temple Youth, the Reform youth movement, is undoubtedly the strongest of the synagogue youth movements. On the other hand, the drift of most Reform Jews away from comprehensive Jewish experiences is equally pronounced.

The Conservative movement has suffered the greatest decline of all. By the end of the postwar generation, members of Conservative congregations fell into three categories: a very small percentage, probably no more than five percent, were seriously practicing Jews who found their Jewish expression within Conservative congregations. These were the authentic Conservative Jews who lived up to the formal requirements of Conservative Judaism. There were perhaps 50,000 members in the United States, and most were rabbis, Jewish educators, cantors and their families. For that small nucleus the havura became a major vehicle—a few separate from established congregations, and an increasing number within the congregational framework.

Between 25 and 30 percent of the movement's congregational membership could be identified as following accepted Conservative practice, concerned with the religious practice of Conservative Jews, but not fulfilling the mitzvot in the formally required manner. These people maintained kosher homes but did not observe kashrut outside of the home. The other two-thirds of the members of Conservative congregations had not found themselves a Conservative way of life beyond synagogue membership.

Many of their children began moving to Reform, leading to a serious decline in Conservative movement membership and a religiously leftward swing in most Conservative congregations.[6]

As already indicated, Orthodox synagogues were undergoing their own changes. Those congregations whose membership consisted primarily of the nominally Orthodox either declined or were transformed by the new seriously Orthodox and new congregations of the latter grew in strength. By and large, Orthodox congregations moved to the right religiously.

New Trends in Jewish Education

The early 1960s also witnessed a peaking of the number of Jewish children enrolled in Jewish schools and the beginning of a long downswing that as yet has not been arrested. This is in part due to the sharply declining Jewish birthrate. At a time when 85 percent of the Jewish population is over the age of 16, there are not that many Jewish children available. Beyond that, there is also some slackening of interest in Jewish education. In part, this is a matter of increasing geographic deconcentration of the Jewish population. Jews who have moved far away from centers of Jewish population find the cost too great in terms of travel time. In other cases, it is simply that the issue of Jewish identification is less important and the idea of Jewish education as a "inoculation" to enable Jews to live in a hostile world has diminished.

On the other hand, there have been shifts in the forms of Jewish education.[7] Day school enrollment, even thirty years ago almost negligible on the Jewish education scene, has now reached 25 percent of the total enrolled in Jewish elementary and secondary schools. The growth of day schools has come at the expense of more serious supplementary schools. Supplementary Jewish education today has been reduced from the six-hour norm of a generation ago to an average of four hours per week. The drop in number of hours is even more apparent at the secondary level.

Significantly, while day school education has become quite popular on the elementary level, there are still very few secondary day schools outside of the Orthodox community. Perhaps this is because parents are worried about their children's chances to enter college, even though the record of such secondary day schools is very good in that respect. Be that as it may, there are very few substitutes at the secondary level, so that children who graduate elementary day schools frequently do not continue. They have their Jewish education arrested at the age of 13, as their parents had theirs arrested at the same age through bar or bat mitzvah. Most supplementary high school programs are extremely weak, often involving two hours a week of courses on subjects such as medical ethics, feminism and the Jewish experience, or teenage sexuality—all important subjects in and of themselves, but hardly the substance of a Jewish education as traditionally conceived.

The day schools themselves are mixed. Some are quite serious, others less so. Many are under ultra-Orthodox sponsorship, even though they appeal to a broader population, and, hence, face a certain disharmony that effects their results. Today, however, every religious movement has its day schools, and there is a communal day school network as well.

A good part of this growth has been stimulated by the general trend to private schools among the upper middle class. Many Jewish families of limited religious commitment decide that if their children are going to go to private schools, it would be good for them to go to Jewish ones. The more these schools reach out to a cross section of the Jewish public, the more problems they have in squaring their educational goals with the Jewish behavior of the home, creating new problems, but at least good ones from the point of view of the Jewish community.

Jewish education at the college level has continued to expand quantitatively in the number of positions, chairs, and Jewish studies specialists. It is now well accepted that any university or college of full status will have some kind of Jewish studies component. Qualitatively, on the other hand, university-based Jewish studies have been a disappointment. As student interests shifted in the 1970s to become more career oriented, enrollment in Jewish studies programs dropped, along with enrollment in all courses not career relevant. Moreover, students who do enroll not only do not become majors, they do not even go beyond one or two courses, usually taken out of curiosity or to fulfill a liberal arts requirement. Third, the popular courses are those on the peripheries of the discipline, such as courses on the Holocaust or Jewish feminism. Courses in classical Jewish studies, especially those that require even basic knowledge of Hebrew, languish and, unless specially endowed, tend to be cancelled by cost-conscious universities.

One result of this, unanticipated by most, has been the revival of the Hebrew colleges. While they, too, have had to compromise their Hebrew standards, they still provide a more intensive education in Jewish studies than any other tertiary institutions. Moreover, a number of them have developed a wide range of professional programs leading to the Masters degree (often jointly with professional schools at nearby universities), in Jewish education, social work, and communal service, which have given them a new clientele and a new lease on life. In the process, they have begun to upgrade their organizational and staff facilities, moving from the old normal-school model to one more approximating the general university.

It should be noted that the oldest independent graduate school of Jewish studies, Dropsie University, ceased to exist for all intents and purposes in

1987, long after it ceased to be an effective source of Judaica scholars. It was converted into a center for advanced study in Middle East and cognate fields.

Ambiguity in the Community Relations Sphere

The Jewish community relations agenda remains ambiguous following the break up of the black–Jewish coalition in the late 1960s and the diminution of the ethnic movement in the 1970s. On one hand, the Jewish community, especially those active in the community relations field, remain as sympathetic as ever to the complete integration of blacks into American society. On the other hand, affirmative action, which often became quotas under another name, was recognized by most as a blow to the basic Jewish interest in a fully open society in which advancement was based strictly on merit, and there were increasing differences of opinion among opinion-molders in the Jewish community with regard to the new liberal agenda. The responses to this differed from community to community, depending on the voluntary and professional leadership of the community relations agencies, but in no place were the answers easy. One result of this was that the traditional community relations agencies lost much of their energy and drawing power with individual Jews seeking more specialized single-interest groups that reflected their special concerns, whether AIPAC or the New Jewish Agenda.

Small Town and Rural Jews

For approximately a hundred years, from the Civil War to the 1960s, the trend in American Jewish settlement patterns was from smaller to larger places. With the countercultural revolution and the deconcentration of economic activity of the 1960s and 1970s, a growing number of Jews began to settle in small towns and rural areas away from the major metropolitan centers. They did so not necessarily to leave their Jewishness behind, but, rather, sought to bring it with them. Thus, new Jewish organizational frameworks emerged in many parts of the country where Jews had hardly been seen before. In most cases, these fell within traditional frameworks—synagogues, local chapters of Hadassah—but they also developed some new dimensions.

Two examples of this are to be found in rural New England and the Colorado mountains. As Vermont became a center of the counterculture, many Jews settled in that state. Smaller numbers settled in rural areas of New Hampshire and Maine. Collectively, they have organized on both a local and regional basis to provide at least a minimum of organized Jewish life with regular activities up to an annual regional meeting which, in the spirit of the counterculture, is more in the form of a happening than for organizational business.

One can find a similar phenomenon in the Colorado mountains, without the regional organization. There, Jews who have settled in the ski resorts or the mountain exurbia within commuting distance to Denver have organized congregations that tend to meet sporadically but offer a framework within which to associate as Jews. A curious phenomenon has taken place in connection with these congregations. Normally, the pattern for naming synagogues is to choose some biblical phrase or Hebrew words indicating their moral purpose (Emit V'Emunah or Beth Shalom). These new mountain congregations have names such as Beth Evergreen or Beth Vail after the towns in which they are located.

Changing Relationships in the "National Agencies"

The first postwar generation marked a shifting of power away from the community relations agencies to those of the federation movement. In the second postwar generation, there has been a shift within the community relations sphere as the old-line agencies, such as the American Jewish Committee, American Jewish Congress, and Anti-Defamation League, have given ground to newer ones such as the Conference of Presidents of Major Jewish Organizations, the American–Israel Public Affairs Committee, and the Simon Wiesenthal Center. This is not to suggest that there has been an absolute decline in the old-line agencies, only a relative one, with the traditional agencies becoming more limited and specialized and less able to draw attention.

Their replacements are either identified heavily with Israel or with the Holocaust, as distinct from being identified with the fight against anti-Semitism and for such traditional liberal causes as separation of church and state that are characteristic of the old-line agencies. The latter have tried to adapt to these new issues, but the public image remains strong. Moreover, the new power brokers have found it more to their liking to build new bodies rather than try to capture the old ones.

The Conference of Presidents, founded over thirty years ago, first surfaced on the American scene when Yitzhak Rabin was Israel's Ambassador to the United States. He wanted a vehicle through which American Jewry could approach the White House without having to rely upon the president's aide for Jewish affairs. The Presidents' Conference position was further strengthened when Menachem Begin cultivated it when he was Prime Minister of Israel. These steps made the Presidents' Conference more visible, but not necessarily more influential. It is only in the second generation that its influence began to grow under the leadership of its new executive director, Malcolm Hoenlein.

AIPAC (the American-Israel Public Affairs Committee), followed a similar pattern. Originally a small organization of insiders, discretely lobbying the U.S. Congress on behalf of Israel, its name emerged as a way to be associated with insiders. In the 1970s, it began to attract federation leadership looking for a vehicle to work politically for Israel. They joined AIPAC on an individual basis, and both its power and visibility grew. With the nearly successful AIPAC fight against the sale of Phantom jets to Saudi Arabia, which brought the organization headline attention, many more people sought to join. Tom Dine, the new executive director, saw the possibility of transforming AIPAC into a mass organization with local chapters, a larger budget, and increased activities, and he moved the organization in that direction with great success. Today, AIPAC is one of the most dynamic membership organizations on the American Jewish scene, but continues to pursue its single issue.

Very different, but equally successful, is the Simon Wiesenthal Center. Founded and operating entirely outside of the establishment (except for a link with Yeshiva University), the Center's director, Rabbi Marvin Hier, adopted the latest in mass-mailing techniques and, by exploiting the Jewish fascination with the Holocaust and perennial fear of anti-Semitism, managed to build a large base of contributors who provided a very large budget in small segments. At the beginning, the Center raised money but had no visible program. When its leadership felt it was ready, it moved into Nazi hunting and, once again, mastering the public-relations aspect, made front-page news doing what other organizations have been doing for years.

The shift taking place is in part, a reflection of the new generation's desire to funnel their funds into very focused activities or single-issue organizations. Thus, multipurpose organizations, where the use of funds is left to the discretion of the senior leadership, have had a hard time reaching out to the younger generation. Beyond that, the breakdown of the liberal consensus in the community has also had its effect. While a higher percentage of Jews than of any other white ethnic group vote for Democratic candidates, it is down from the astounding totals of the New Deal years. Presently one-third of all Jews, among them a group of serious-minded intellectuals and activists who have developed their own organizations to express what has become known as the neoconservative point of view, regularly vote Republican in presidential elections. Thus, the Presidents' Conference is strictly neutral and AIPAC has avoided liberal or conservative positions, while the hard-line position of the Wiesenthal Center would have to be considered on the conservative side of the spectrum.

Changing Roles in the Communal-Welfare
and Israel–Overseas Spheres

At present, three giant organizations dominate this sphere countrywide—the Council of Jewish Federations, the United Jewish Appeal, and the United Israel Appeal. A fourth, the Joint Distribution Committee, is somewhat smaller but one of the most respected organizations in the Jewish community.

The end of the last generation found the CJF in the process of initiating a self-study in preparation for a transition to new leadership. The end result was some strengthening of its internal organization, a modest expansion of its budget (and, consequently, its organizational capacity), and a substantial increase of its role in Israel and overseas programs. The catalyst for that growth was the intrusion of UJA into the sphere of activity of the local federations, especially in leadership development. With its larger budget skimmed off the top of funds received from the federations, the UJA was able to expand its program freely, while the Council was constricted by the caution of the local federations toward expanding its role and their resultant reluctance to increase its budget. The Review Committee almost immediately recognized this issue, but decided that the way to deal with it was through quiet action rather than formal recommendations. As a result, CJF initiated a process which, in effect, brought UJA to heel, demonstrating convincingly where the power lay in the American Jewish community.

The principal vehicle used by CJF to do so was the United Israel Appeal. Once the United Palestine Appeal, the fundraising arm of the Zionist movement's Keren Hayesod in the United States, the UIA had lost its direct fundraising role with the establishment of the UJA by joint action of UIA and JDC in 1937. While it continued to be of importance for another decade, its role was further reduced in the 1950s, and it became a paper organization whose major function was to accept funds from UJA and transfer them to the Jewish Agency.

With the reconstitution of the Jewish Agency in 1970, the UIA acquired a new lease on life as the body that formally designated the American community representatives in the Agency's new governing institutions. The CJF reorganized the revived UIA and restored its governance of the UJA, and through CJF representation on the UIA was able to secure a restoration of UJA to something closer to its proper position in the constellation.

One result of this was the continued growth in importance of the UIA as a principal arm of the American Jewish community in overseeing the use of funds raised for Israel. While the three organizations continued to have substantial overlapping board memberships as well as constituencies, each developed its own functions in the ensuing years. The CJF is the coordinating body for the federations, with a primary responsibility for community planning. The UJA is the federations' fundraising arm for Israel and overseas needs, with a primary responsibility for fundraising. The UIA is the federations' arm for overseeing the use of the funds in Israel, with a growing responsibility for oversight and evaluation. This is not to suggest that competition does not continue to exist between the three. It is almost a given that there should be a certain amount of competition and tension at their points of intersection and overlap. This leads to periodic suggestions that the three should be consolidated into one organization. In fact, what has developed is a kind of system of checks and balances among the three, which may very well strengthen the community's governing processes.

A new concern with the Jewish Agency and how federation-raised funds were being spent in Israel became the dominant feature of the new generation. The reconstituted Jewish Agency soon became a major item on the agenda of the federation movement. This was manifested through a strong commitment to making the Jewish Agency Assembly, Board of Governors, and Executive more responsive to Diaspora—meaning for them American—Jewish concerns. From there it developed into programmatic concerns, particularly after Project Renewal was launched in 1977–78 and individual federations began to be involved in specific Israeli communities. At every stage it was concerned with achieving greater efficiency and accountability.

Organizational Changes in Jewish Education

The changing face of Jewish education, while particularly manifested locally, spilled over into the countrywide arena. The old American Association for Jewish Education, deemed a failure even by its friends, was subject to critical examination. This led to its restructuring as the Jewish Education Service of North America (JESNA), a body designed to play more of a service than a promotional role. However, because JESNA's principal constituency consists of the central agencies for Jewish education and the constituency of the central agencies is primarily the declining supplementary schools, JESNA has found it difficult to find an appropriate role for itself other than to represent Jewish education in the give-and-take of the national agencies.

The Coalition for Alternatives in Jewish Education (CAJE), on the other hand, is a prime example of a new phenomenon in American Jewish life, a countrywide, grassroots organization whose annual "happening" rapidly became the most exciting activity on the North American Jewish educational scene. CAJE was developed as a countercultural instrument, sparked by the young veterans of the Jewish countercultural revolution of the late

1960s who saw Jewish education as the place where they wanted to make their contribution, but refused to do so through what they perceived to be the tired institutions of the Jewish education establishment. Originally spurned by the educational establishment, CAJE demonstrated that, year after year, it could draw hundreds of teachers who came, at their own expense, to learn and socialize together for a week every year. Today, it has established itself, holding several summer conferences in different parts of the country and, in 1988, in Israel.

Religious Challenges to Jewish Unity

We have already noted the growth and strength of Orthodoxy, which became the major force in Jewish life during the second postwar generation. Israel continued to be the central concern of American Jews, but Zionism was no longer a prime source of energy. Nor could the non-Orthodox groups generate the kind of energy that Orthodoxy could. The Conservative movement, as we have noted, began to lose the children of its more casual members, fourth-generation American Jews and beyond, who drifted into the Reform movement or nothing in about equal proportions. The Reform movement was more successful than the latter in building important institutions on the American and, indeed, the world Jewish scene, as the Conservative movement had been a generation before. But as important as these were, they could not generate the same level of motivation as did Orthodoxy in either the religious or political spheres.

One result of the new ascendency of Orthodoxy was a boldness on the part of the ultra-Orthodox in challenging the legitimacy of non-Orthodox Judaism. This issue was exacerbated by the rising tide of intermarriage, the perennial problem of nonhalakic conversions conducted by Reform rabbis, and the new and even more difficult problem of the Reform movement's recognition of patrilineal descent as a means of becoming Jewish. Orthodox reluctance to recognize the religious acts of non-Orthodox rabbis was exacerbated by these new phenomena. The Orthodox refused to recognize the acts of Conservative rabbis, no matter how fully halakic, in an effort to deny them legitimacy; with regard to Reform, the denial could be on halakic grounds alone.

Israel's position was key here, since the determination by the Knesset of who is a Jew for purposes of the Law of Return, while affecting very few American Jews directly, struck at the self-esteem of virtually all those who identified with non-Orthodox movements. Thus, the issue became a cause célèbre for both sides, with the ultra-Orthodox groups pressing for more rigid definitions of who is a Jew designed to protect the Orthodox monopoly, and the non-Orthodox insisting on full recognition of their legitimacy. By the mid-1980s, people were raising the question as to whether or not there would be a split in the Jewish people. The reluctance of virtually all Jews to allow such a drastic step to happen led to an effort on the part of the various groups to find some common ground and to avoid any ruptures.

In the meantime, the Reconstructionist movement replaced the Reform as the most radical religious group on the American Jewish scene. By the end of the previous generation, the Reconstructionists had emerged as a fully articulated operation, separated from its Conservative parent, although still in the Masorti (or Conservative) camp. Led by the Reconstructionist Rabbinical College and its student body, the movement separated from the Masorti camp in the direction of far more radical positions during the 1970s.

The original Reconstructionist movement rejected the binding character of halaka, but still looked to halakic tradition for a vote, although not a veto, to paraphrase Mordecai Kaplan. The new Reconstructionists had no interest in halakah, except for historical purposes. Rather, they sought Jewish self-expression along the lines of the current liberal and radical agendas. Like the Reformers, they found a place for homosexual Jews, going beyond the Reform movement to welcome them into the rabbinate as well. Because of their radical commitment to free individual choice, they were able to tolerate individual expressions of Jewishness.

New Model Organizations

One of the features of the new generation was the emergence of new model organizations. We have already mentioned the growth of the Wiesenthal Center and the transformation of AIPAC. In addition, what was originally founded by Rabbi Irving Greenberg as the National Jewish Conference Center and which in turn, became the National Jewish Resource Center and CLAL (Center for Learning and Leadership), an organization fostering adult leadership education, has become a featured player in the Jewish arena. A communal body led by an Orthodox rabbi who has premised that the federation movement is the most significant, CLAL cultivates the federation leadership as its most important constituency. CLAL preaches a religion of what Jonathan Woocher has termed "sacred survival," in which the survivalist and communal dimensions of Jewish life were emphasized, embellished by certain key religious rituals designed to impart transcendent significance to the very act of survival, and the activities necessary to ensure it.[8]

Still another new model of Jewish organization is the Center for Jewish Community Studies/Jerusalem Center for Public Affairs. It is a worldwide Jewish policy studies center, with offices in Jerusalem, Philadelphia, and Montreal, designed to provide the Jewish people and Israel with a think tank on the model of the Brookings Institution or the American Enterprise Institute. Less a direct teaching institution than CLAL, it is an institution of the new information society in which the acquisition, organization, and analysis of information are important tools for communal growth. The Center also turned principally to the federation leadership for its support, and attracted many of the most significant figures of American Jewish life. It focuses on policy research and interpretation, ranging from questions about the political behavior of American Jews, to specific studies of the Conservative movement on the occasion of its 100th anniversary, or the proper role of the Boston Hebrew College, all anchored within the intellectual framework of the Jewish political tradition.

Yet another group of new model Jewish organizations are the large philanthropic foundations founded by wealthy Jewish families or individuals. Until recently, Jewish family foundations were vehicles for relatively modest contributions for general support of established Jewish institutions such as the UJA or the local Jewish hospital. There were a few private organizations that engaged in funding worthy projects through an open competitive process rather than a preordained one, but it is only recently that very large private foundations (with assets in the tens, if not hundreds, of millions of dollars) have been established under Jewish auspices. Among these leading foundations are the CRB Foundation, established by Charles Bronfman of Montreal, focusing on Jewish and Canadian interests; the Koret Foundation of San Francisco, focusing on Jewish and San Francisco Bay area interests; and the Wexner and Wexner Heritage Foundations, both founded by Leslie Wexner, the first group specializing in the development of better Jewish professional leadership, and the second, better Jewish voluntary leadership. These foundations have assets that make them major players on the American Jewish scene, and there will be others coming along. It is too soon to assess the implications of this new source of wealth dispensed by private individuals following the personal preferences of their founders.

The Blurring of Lay and Professional Roles

One of the unexpected developments of the new generation has been the blurring of roles of the voluntary and professional leadership in many organizations in the Jewish community. The first postwar generation was characterized by the sharpening of the distinction between the two sets of leaders. The rise of a new body of senior civil servants for the Jewish community, working full time, trained for their careers, and possessing the information needed to make decisions, led observers to speculate that professionals would dominate the communal leadership to such an extent that voluntary leaders would become no more than decorations. Quite the contrary has happened.

Despite the professionalization of the senior civil service, voluntary leaders have increasingly become involved in decision-making, to the point of interfering with legitimate professional prerogatives. This led recently to a number of resignations of top professional leaders from major Jewish organizations and institutions. Why has this change taken place? One reason is the diminution of educational differences between voluntary and professional leaders. In previous generations, many of the top voluntary leaders were self-made men who left school early out of the necessity of making a living, and had prospered. Today, both volunteers and professionals have the same level of education, similar intellectual interests, and read the same periodicals, general and Jewish, so that the difference between the two groups is one of specialization, rather than level of competence. The situation is compounded by a modest movement of volunteers into the ranks of professionals and vice versa, which has not always been successful, and an equally modest movement of Jewish academics into Jewish communal service, of which results are not clear. What this will do to the confidence of the carefully crafted Jewish communal service remains to be seen.

The Unraveling of the Progressive Solution

The American Jewish community organization as we know it developed during the Progressive era and is a product of the organization theories of the Progressives. These include reliance upon professional managers and experts functioning under the general direction of nonprofessionals, federated organizational structure, emphasis on localism, reliance on functional organizations rather than traditional patterns of communal philanthropic activity, and the treatment of those activities as civic actions to be fully insulated from politics.

This Progressive approach has remained dominant in Jewish community organization, and has contributed much to the amazing growth and vitality of Jewish organizational life. It is one of the secrets of success of the organized Jewish community. Now, however, over two generations after the end of the Progressive movement as an identifiable force, parts of this Progressive–Jewish synthesis may be unraveling.

Not only are lay and professional roles mingling, but as the American Jewish community involves itself in the larger Jewish world, the distinction between the civic and political dimensions of organized Jewish life are becoming less distinct. Other Jewish communities and, most especially, Israel, never adopted the distinction. For them, public affairs are inevitably political. This has led to clashes between the American Jews and the others in the world Jewish arena, and has influenced the American Jewish leadership, moving them more into politics.

At a time when the new organizational theories emphasize the virtues of competing units, it is not surprising that American Jews, along with other Americans, are finding their way back to a more diffuse system. Just as the organizational diffusion called for by organization theorists works only because of the existence of strong federal and state framing institutions, so too is it likely to work in the Jewish community as long as the local and countrywide institutions remain strong. Today, the trends are pulling in two directions. Within the federation family, there is a trend toward centralization, while the scope of activities of the agencies may be undergoing some reduction as people choose to give their support to other organizations. The spheres of communal activity continue to grow closer together, but the institutions within those spheres may be further dividing. As always, then, contradictory trends exist side by side.

Notes

1. Daniel J. Elazar, *Community and Polity, The Organizational Dynamics of the American Jewish Community* (Philadelphia: Jewish Publication Society, 1976).
2. Cf. Paul King, Orli HaCohen, Hillel Frisch, and Daniel J. Elazar, *Project Renewal in Israel* (Lanham, MD: University Press of American and Jerusalem Center for Public Affairs, 1987), and Charles Hoffman, *Project Renewal: Community and Change in Israel* (Jerusalem: Renewal Department, Jewish Agency for Israel, 1986).
3. Cf. Daniel J. Elazar and Alysa Dortort, eds., *Understanding the Jewish Agency* (Jerusalem and Philadelphia: Jerusalem Center for Public Affairs, 1985), revised edition.
4. I have elaborated on this in "Who is a Jew—and How?" *Jerusalem Letter/Viewpoints* VP40 (May 12, 1985).
5. Cf. Carl Schrag, "The American Jewish Community Turns to the States: The Springfield Office of the Jewish Federations of Illinois," *Jerusalem Letter* JL100 (February 21, 1988).
6. Daniel J. Elazar, Steven M. Cohen and Rela Geffen Monson, "Planning for the Future of the Conservative Movement," A Study by the Jerusalem Center for Public Affairs/Center for Jewish Community Studies (February 8, 1987).
7. Fred Massarik, "Trends in U.S. Jewish Education: National Jewish Population Study Findings" in *American Jewish Year Book* vol. 77 (1977), pp. 240–46.
8. Jonathan Woocher, *Sacred Survival* (Bloomington, Ind.: Indiana University Press, 1987).

12

The Emerging Jewish Public-Affairs Culture

Lawrence Rubin

The mission of Jewish community relations is to safeguard the civil and religious rights of individual Jews and the Jewish people as a whole, both here and around the world. A corollary to that is the commitment of the field to create, sustain, and assure a moderate, constitutional government in the United States, wedded to the rule of law, respectful of divergent points of view, and mindful of the rights of minorities.

Jewish historic experience has demonstrated amply that a stable democracy provides the climate in which the well-being of the Jewish body politic is nurtured and advanced. Economic security does not insure political security. In many countries around the world—e.g., South Africa, Iran, parts of Latin America—one finds Jewish communities that, though prosperous, are not protected. In such places, Jews live on the edge of uncertainty, although frequently in the lap of luxury. Moreover, the absence of democratic institutions and traditions—as in the case of the Jews of the Soviet Union, Ethiopia, and other Third World countries—often leads neither to prosperity nor freedom.

Earlier generations of Jewish immigrants found a political climate in the United States that allowed the community to approach the goals outlined above. Over the years, however, perspectives have changed concerning the appropriate means of realizing the mission of the community relations field. From the viewpoint of today's highly charged political atmosphere, earlier outlooks appear both quaint and quixotic. For instance, an anonymous document in the files of the Philadelphia Jewish Community Relations Council, written in the late 1950s, reflects a heady optimism about the possibility of achieving communal goals by changing individual and group behavior. It states,

> Community Relations can be defined as the science of helping members of all religious, racial and nationality groups to work together and to live together constructively by equalizing their opportunities and deepening their understanding and cooperation with each other.[1]

The very anonymity of the document highlights the author's enthusiasm for the belief that the social sciences are indeed scientific disciplines, and that the behavior and values of people can, in fact, be changed if only we understand the basic causes of human conflict. From these assumptions, it is reasonable to place upon the leadership of the community relations council the responsibility to recognize that "the most difficult thing to do is to change people—they usually change themselves, but you [as a leader] provide the stimuli for the change."[2]

The universe of community relations as expressed in the late 1950s is thus defined, circumscribed, and safeguarded by experts, scientists, and social engineers. It appears that the prime function of the field is to promote social (and individual) change. Its principal tool is the power of observation rather than that of persuasion.

A sober historic reflection was provided by Arnold Aronson who describes six stages in the evolution of the field.[3] He relates these to the principal function each sought to address:

(1) Group Welfare. During this stage, the arrival of large numbers of immigrants altered Jewish life in America. It was characterized by the development of Jewish social welfare institutions to meet the needs of the newly arrived Jews. The thrust of these activities was largely internal.

(2) Defense. The main activity in this stage, which evolved before and during World War I, was combatting anti-Semitism through investigation, exposure, and protest largely (and quietly) undertaken by influential individuals speaking on behalf of the community.

(3) Education. Extending the lessons learned in the preceding stage, the field undertook positive programs projecting the image of the Jew as a person like everyone else. Such programs reflected the "melting pot" mythology and suggested that Jews are like all other Americans. The effort peaked during the Hitler era.

(4) Intergroup Cooperation. The driving idea in this stage, which evolved in response to Nazi and fascist doctrine, was the notion that defending each group's rights is every group's responsibility. Functionally, Jewish agencies no longer conceived of their mandate as narrowly confined to protecting Jewish rights but as including opposition to the denial of the rights of others.

(5) Social Action. The field perceived that strengthening democracy was necessary to protect society from racist ideologies. Thus, the goal of the

community was to change defects in society by government reform. This was achieved frequently through demonstrations, litigation and lobbying. Agencies became more specialized and strove consciously to increase their membership base.

(6) Community Relations. In this stage (when Aronson's article was written), the field was characterized by a recognition that a pluralist society requires a setting in which respect for difference is a central principle. The stage grew out of an emerging consciousness in the Jewish community, largely influenced by World War II, of group identity and cohesion. The role of the field was now seen as building an American culture from the interplay and competitiveness of its many groups.

In a more recent article that might be seen as an extension of Aronson's, Bertram H. Gold, executive vice president emeritus of the American Jewish Committee, describes the current state of Jewish communal life as one of "Jewish Introspection." The central phenomenon of the late 1960s, Gold suggests, was the growing isolation of Israel in the international polity accompanied by a turning inward of the American Jewish community with an attendant heightening of domestic concern with matters of Jewish identity.[4]

While correct in his analysis, there are two other relatively recent changes in the Jewish community that have shaped both its internal character and the face it reveals to the broader population. At the same time as Jews became aware of the depth of their interconnection to Israel, their Soviet Jewish brothers and sisters began to articulate their own Jewish yearnings. The renascent Jewish community in the Soviet Union, therefore, place an additional claim on American Jews—to join the struggle to return this heretofore isolated commonality to the Jewish people.

Second, the emergence of a vigorously debated religious schism focused communal attention and energy on the historical context of Jewish experience. While most Jews are unaffected by the halakic inferences regarding patrilineal descent, mamzerim, conversion, or the role of women in Jewish life, many sense the implications of these largely rabbinic issues for their ability to live together as a group.

The evolving pattern described by Aronson and Gold leads to a central paradox of Jewish life: while democratic government is good for Jews and Judaism, it might not be so positive for the Jewish people. Although evidence of Jewish individual and communal success is all around us, it might be argued that these have been bought at a very high price in terms of increased rates of intermarriage, assimilation, and loss of Jewish identity.

Faced with this tension between external political needs and the requirements for internal group cohesiveness, the Jewish community is evolving a new organizational stage for achieving its goals in the public policy sphere that might be called the Public-Affairs Culture.[5] While not yet clearly evolved or defined, this new public-affairs culture has certain characteristics. First, it continues what has been defined as the "liberal" response of the Jewish community to external conditions. The community relations field remains politically intense, and committed to a far-ranging social and economic justice agenda whose principal goal is meeting the needs of the disadvantaged in the general populace. Its agenda encompasses a wide range of issues from Israel, Soviet Jewry, and church–state separation through public education, welfare reform, housing, child care, and care of the elderly. Implicit in such an agenda is the continuing commitment of the field to coalition-building as a fundamental strategy for a minority group—any minority group—in achieving its goals.

Second, the language of the field relies increasingly on the injunctions of the Judaic tradition to justify communal participation. More and more, one finds these activities justified by the Judaic principle of *tikkun olam* [repairing the world] or by reference to the so-called prophetic tradition, which commands Jews to care for the widow, the orphan, and the stranger at our gates, for we were strangers in the land of Egypt.

At the same time, the perceived internal condition of Jewish life—or, more properly, threats to it—have an impact on both the priority of the external, public-affairs issues and the manner in which these are to be approached. Many analysts have concluded that the gravest dangers to the Jewish community in the United States are internal rather than external. As noted above, the evidence of Jewish alienation, disaffiliation, and acculturation far outweighs in its ominous portent any presumed danger to Jewish survival from an unjust society.

This point of view yields two contradictory conclusions. Many of its adherents opt out of the political process altogether to focus on core issues of Jewish survival—Jewish education, intermarriage, Jewish "identity." Conversely, others continue to be involved in the political process but believe that single-issue movements and organizations provide the most effective channel for achieving their political objectives. Implicit in this is the notion that only Jews can help themselves, that ultimately *goyim* cannot be trusted, and that single political Truths should be pursued single-mindedly.

However, where concern for Jewish survival intersects with involvement in the politics of the broader community, one finds the emergence of a particularist, single-issue politics that represents a serious challenge to the accepted principles of the field. It is not too great a leap of judgment to conclude that, since American democracy has itself proven to be a threat to Jewish continuity, American pluralism and Jewish communal institutions that have thrived within the system have, ipso facto, failed to protect the interests of the Jewish community.

The principal political implication is reflected in the belief that the Jewish community cares exclusively about a mere handful of public issues. These obviously include the survival and security of the state of Israel, the principle of separation of church and state, and the Soviet Jewry advocacy movement. While each of these can be addressed strategically by coalitions and other broad-based political alliances, it is obvious that the community is addressing one or the other in increasingly particularistic ways. For example, the recent decision of the Council of Jewish Federations to increase the responsibility and funding of the National Conference on Soviet Jewry with regard to the advocacy movement was premised on the notion that the issue is of such importance as to require an umbrella structure of its own. Such a view mistakenly assumes that a public policy matter can exist in a vacuum. It is insufficiently sensitive to the role that community relations networks, relationships, and alliances play in assuring support for the core issues of coalition members.

As nowhere else in Jewish political life, the rise of Jewish political action committees (PACs) has heightened the perception of Jews as a single-issue constituency.[6] Given the high level of political interest and activity in the Jewish community, it was inevitable that a number of PACs would be established to represent communal concerns. While the first Jewish PAC was not created until 1978, today there are over eighty pro-Israel PACs in operation. They contributed only $85,000 to candidates in the 1980 elections but over $3 million to senatorial and congressional candidates in the 1984 elections. Press accounts suggest that this rate of increase continued during the 1986 off-year elections. The *Wall Street Journal* reports that pro-Israel PACs spent nearly $7 million on Congressional races, making them "the highest-spending, narrow-issue interest group."[7] By all accounts, they reached new spending heights in the 1988 presidential campaign.

In spite of the relative degree of success of Israel-related PACs and the amount of communal pride expressed in having adapted to the new political "game" so well, many Jewish leaders are deeply concerned that the growth of PACs is in the best interest neither of the American political system nor of the Jewish community.

Concern with the general proliferation, growth, and influence of PACs stems from a number of factors. Perhaps most importantly, many people believe that PACs encourage the tendency to balkanize our nation into competing self-interest groups with little taste or use for our traditional system of political parties that resolve public policy conflicts through compromise and coalition-building. Strong American parties have been centrist, and encouraged the selection of moderate candidates who were acceptable to disparate elements within the body politic. PACs tend to weaken the parties in that they provide candidates with ample opportunities to reach for campaign funds outside the structure and discipline of the party. Since almost all PACs are based on single-issue concerns, candidates can now raise large sums of money by appealing to single-issue constituencies across the country.

Furthermore, while PAC supporters claim that PACs increase participation in the political process, the opposite is, in fact, more likely the case. After individuals make their contribution, they have little say as to whom the PAC contributes. While larger contributors may in some instances, meet to parcel out the money, more often than not decisions about PAC contributions are made by a small number of people.

As noted above, the field of Jewish community relations has always believed that Jewish interests are best achieved through coalition-building and open public discourse. Jewish PACs demonstrate all too clearly—and, in the judgment of many, wrongly—that support for Israel is the single-minded interest of the Jewish community. Assuring support for Israel is thought of as a Jewish imperative. Such a viewpoint is politically dangerous; in the end it is highly unlikely that 2.5% of the population can assure America's pro-Israel policy against the growing, competing claims on our nation overseas, and the insistent voices within our own borders arguing that the pressing domestic needs of poorer Americans are of transcendent importance at this time. The alliances that have delivered the votes for foreign aid to Israel in the past have also been integral parts of the informal educational network that has reminded the American people that support for our democratic friends abroad is not in conflict with meeting pressing domestic needs.

Support for Israel has always been a reflection of the kind of coalition politics at which Jews are so adept. It would be lamentable and dangerous if pro-Israel PACs are seen as the sole political representatives of the American Jewish community, for this would create the false impression that Jews are little more than the Israel lobby and simply another single-issue constituency. The attendant political isolation would be dangerous for any minority group, and could be disastrous for the Jewish community.

As Hyman Bookbinder, the recently retired Washington representative for the American Jewish Committee, has said, "Israel's cause is best served by a multi-issue approach, and not just because it looks nicer. We need allies. You don't get allies when you're seen as only caring about one issue."[8]

Today, support for Israel exists among all groups in the United States, in all sections of the country, at all levels of the socio-economic ladder, irrespective of race, religion, or sex. This did not just happen. The political, moral, and strategic affinity that exists between our two countries has been taught and retaught to the American people for decades, by the Jewish community. Jews have made their cause the cause of others—perhaps not with the same intensity, the same history, nor same love—but to the same political end.

Speaking at the 1984 Conference of Jewish Communal Service meeting in Los Angeles, Earl Raab defined the "central mechanisms" in Jewish communal life that strive to bring some semblance of order to Jewish activity in the public affairs arena. The principal characteristics of a central mechanism, he said, are that it is (1) public affairs intensive, (2) multi-issue, and (3) represent-ative. Many organizations with some involvement in the public-affairs agenda share one or more of these characteristics. Few, however, possess all three. Zionist organizations, almost by definition, are not multi-issue, although some, like ORT and Hadassah, are working to change that perception. Federa-tions, Raab said, are multi-issue and, arguably, representative, but tend to flee the thought of being considered public-affairs intensive.

Yet, in the intervening four years, it is increasingly apparent that federations are throwing off their reluctance to become involved in the political agenda. More and more, local groups are being seen as the central voice of the Jewish community, not only on budgeting and allocation issues, but on public policy matters as well.

When community relations councils are created, they invariably are consti-tuted as committees of the federation, not independent structures. Accompany-ing this is a growing pattern of closer collaboration between the CRC and other Jewish communal agencies as, for example, in the burgeoning number of statewide Jewish coalitions working on behalf of increased funding for communal institutions.

Arnold Aronson's 1960 analysis led him to conclude that the evolution of the field points to the creation, nurturing, and ultimate primacy of the local community relations council or committee. The growth of the field following World War II, he said, "is attributable largely to the recognition that commu-nity relations . . . have their existence in the communities, where people live and are brought into contact with each other—where people are and relate." While correct in describing the direction in which communal power would flow, Aronson did not forsee that the federations themselves would reach for the mantle of supreme authority in the communities.

As federations have increased their role as principal address for the Jewish community, new questions are raised not only about the future role of the CRC but also about the role of the national agencies. The expertise developed by the national agencies in the period of "social action" in the use of law to promote social change, in intergroup relations, and in mobilizing disciplined constitu-encies to achieve political goals appears to have been outstripped by federa-tions or not to have kept up with the kinds of problems faced by today's Jewish and general communities. One observes local Jewish leaders affiliating more often with the federation as the perceived path to top leadership in the commu-nity.

National agencies are acutely aware of this problem. A number of them have developed programs that assist the Jewish community—which means, usually, the federations—to articulate social policies to enhance its viability. Since these policies are generally implemented at the local level, they suggest the growing sovereignty of the federations over Jewish affairs. Bertram H. Gold observed with alarm the growing functionalism of local federations and national coordinating organizations and spoke approvingly of a "new [Jewish] pluralism [that] is devoutly to be wished. It comes at a time when we are rethinking the relationship between public affairs and the Jewish interest, and provides a valuable counterbalance to the drive toward centralization."[9]

Most objective observers would conclude that the national agencies have failed to stem the tide of centralization. It has been observed that the agendas of the principle national agencies—American Jewish Committee, American Jewish Congress, and the Anti-Defamation League of B'nai B'rith—seem increasingly interchangeable. It is ironic that in a period publicly lauding pluralism in communal life, the inability of the national agencies to define their uniqueness is striking (with the exception of ADL's apparent hegemony regarding the issue of anti-Semitism).

Earl Raab has described a community relations agency as combining the attributes of an expert knowledge and a public will organization.[10] Where one provides the knowledge base for managing issues, the other assures that the sensibility of the community is accounted for in the development of public policy. The national agencies tend to emphasize the former while local CRCs are more likely to resemble the latter. Each, Raab stresses, plays an important role in the creation of Jewish public policy.

The public-affairs culture is a resilient one, for it enables the community to come to grips with the multiplicity of ambiguities, dilemmas, and tensions facing the Jewish public-policy agenda. Among the issues to which the community relations field must respond are: the relative significance (both substantively and instrumentally) of the domestic political agenda when measured against the international agenda; the pull of liberal vs. conservative ideologies; the instrumental value of traditional coalitions, and the utility of functional coalitions; evidence of growing Jewish consciousness in political support for Israel and Soviet Jewry vs. increasing disaffiliation by young Jews; the pull of "special interest" Jewish politics, and the strategy of working for the "common good"; and the tension between democratization vs. centralization in Jewish life.

Viewing the Jewish political structure as a public-affairs culture is significant, for it encourages and enhances the interplay of the often-competing forces suggested above. More importantly, it implies the essence of politics: achieving the possible through compromise and give-and-take so that the political structure can remain intact. For the Jewish community, there is the added responsibility of maintaining a commitment to the principles of voluntarism, which allows individuals to stay within the system, and common cause, which encourages the finding of consensus. At the same time, a political model presupposes willingness to embrace differences without destroying the system. There is certainly evidence to suggest that the Jewish community may have reached the moment where it must develop and encourage the use of mechanisms to maintain community cohesion by exploring diversity rather than insisting on unity.

Notes

1. Unpublished typescript, Jewish Community Relations Council of Greater Philadelphia, undated.
2. JCRC of Great Philadelphia, notes during training sessions held for volunteers, speakers, and staff associates, typescript, March 29, 1960, p. 4.
3. Arnold Aronson, "Organization of the Community Relations Field," *Journal of Intragroup Relations*, Spring 1960.
4. Bertram H. Gold, "The Jewish Community on the Move—From Immigration to Reaffirmation," *The Journal of Jewish Communal Service*, 59 (Fall 1982), pp. 4–11.
5. Earl Raab is perhaps the first community relations practitioner to refer to participation in community relations as working on public affairs agenda. Raab has also observed that politics is now the "main business" of the field.
6. Some material regarding PACs is based on a paper by Burton Siegel, associate executive director of the JCRC of Greater Philadelphia.
7. "Linked Donations? Political Contributions from Pro-Israel PACs Suggest Coordination," *The Wall Street Journal*, June 24, 1987.
8. Robert Kuttner, "Unholy Alliance," *The New Republic*, May 26, 1986, p. 2.
9. Bertram H. Gold, *New Realities in American Jewish Life*, Keynote address, 74th annual meeting of the American Jewish Committee, May 15, 1980, p. 19.
10. Earl Raab, "The End of Jewish Community Relations?" *The Journal of Jewish Communal Service*, 54 (Winter 1977), p. 107.

13

Sources of Jewish Charitable Giving: Incentives and Barriers

Arnold Dashefsky

The charitable giving behavior of the Jews is a subject that sparks dramatic headlines in the periodic literature. For example, in the past decade we have read with profound interest about "The Crisis in Jewish Philanthropy," "Does Jewish Philanthropy Have a Future?", and "Will the Well Run Dry? The Future of Jewish Giving in America."[1] These have appeared at a period roughly coinciding with the decade of the 1980s, when American politics has been dominated by the attempts of the executive branch of government to shift responsibility for some social and welfare functions of the federal authority to the private domain of religious and other organizations. Indeed, issues related to charities in other countries have made front-page news in the general press, suggesting the possibility that this direction may not simply be confined to the United States.[2] Yet, to what extent and on what basis do people in the private sector respond to the challenge of supporting philanthropic work and welfare activities by contributing to charities beyond their own religious congregations?

We do not know the answer to this question. A recent nationwide study prepared by Hodgkinson and Weitzman found that 75 percent of Protestants gave to religious charities, compared to 71 percent of Catholics. They concluded that "the survey results did not show a clear relationship between giving to religion and giving to other charities. What it did show was that those who were very involved in their church or synagogue gave more generously to religious charities."[3]

A Canadian study in progress found that 51 percent of Protestants and a similar proportion of Catholics (49 percent) made religious donations. As in the U.S. findings, a correlation between religiosity and religious giving was uncovered.[4] But a national British survey of charitable behavior, for example, failed to examine religious differences at all.[5] While some research is just beginning to include religion in national surveys on respondents' charitable giving, do we know anything about their motivations?

Presumably, this should be the kind of question for which a social scientific answer might readily be available. Indeed, social psychology has developed an area of inquiry called "prosocial behavior," which, according to one recent textbook definition, "involves acts that benefit other people—ways of responding to other people that are sympathetic, cooperative, helpful, rescuing, comforting, and giving."[6] A familiar part of the literature that examines such altruistic behavior, however, derives from research on bystander intervention spawned by the failure of at least thirty-eight eyewitnesses to respond to the murder of Kitty Genovese in New York City in 1964. Much less study is devoted to that form of prosocial behavior referred to as "donating," or "the act of making a gift or contribution, usually to a charity."[7] This subject is only briefly discussed, if at all, in recent social psychology textbooks.[8]

Much of the extant literature on explaining why people do or do not engage in charitable behavior focuses on the immediate context of the interpersonal situation between the donor and the recipient or the solicitor. For example, Reece[9] has defined philanthropic behavior as involving the voluntary transferring of economic goods to an organization or individual. The donor makes the decision to give or not based on a whole range of preconceived attitudes and values which may be influenced by the way he or she is approached. The less an institution speaks of its own needs and the more it emphasizes the tangible or intangible benefits received from such contributions, the more successful the campaign. Thus, researchers have focused on such diverse dimensions of charitable giving as the giver's perception of giving,[10] the solicitation context,[11] and gender differences.[12] The literature, however, focuses more on situational factors affecting giving behavior.

In truth, a substantial portion of this social science literature tends to be derived more from the psychological tradition.[13] An excellent review of the sociological literature, however, is provided by Galaskiewicz,[14] who presented a variety of sociological and anthropological accounts of the role of gifts and gift-giving in society. Relying on a "nominalist" theoretical framework, he concludes that selective incentives provide the basis for sustaining such gifts. This theoretical orientation is rooted in the dominant Western conception that the motivation for particular individual behaviors is simply the maximization of personal self-interest. According to this approach, an ethic of communitarianism does not appear to play a role in the motivation for the giving of gifts of charity. Both psychologically oriented studies, such as those focusing on situational factors, and sociologically oriented studies, emphasizing rational self-interest, fail to reveal a potentially more profound basis for such charitable activity that may be rooted in the process of socialization to a set of norms and values favoring such acts.

A somewhat different direction to the study of helping behavior is based on a "normative approach." Berkowitz and Connor[15] found experimental support for the "norm of social responsibility"; i.e., the more people are dependent on others, the more they will receive help. Similarly, Gouldner[16] defined the "norm of reciprocity" as based on the notion that the more people have been helped by others, the more help they should give in return.

Jewish Charitable Giving

Indeed, some research does focus on the normative requirement or community responsibility of donating or giving charity. Dashefsky and Lazerwitz[17] reported that 64 percent of respondents in the National Jewish Population Survey claimed to have given to their last local United Jewish Appeal Campaign. Tobin and Lipsman,[18] relying on more recent data for eight metropolitan areas, found the proportion claiming to contribute to Jewish causes ranging from a low of 63 percent in Miami to a high of 79 percent in Rochester. This empirical literature on Jewish charitable giving has focused on the normative demand for *tzedakah* (literally justice, not charity)[19] and the associated changes that have taken place in the Jewish community.

It has often been noted that Jews are disproportionately generous to charitable causes both in the Jewish and general communities, even controlling for income differences among religious and ethnic groups.

> Although Jews represent less than 3% of the total population in America they give about $500 million a year to UJA. This is in contrast to over 32 million Americans of all faiths including Jews who give about $1.5 billion annually to United Way. These figures are impressive because it means a community representing less than 3% of the total U.S. population raises for UJA 33% of the dollars that Americans generally contribute to the United Fund.[20]

As noted above, 64 percent of respondents claimed to have given to their local UJA or Federation campaign, and a similar proportion of 63 percent claimed to have given to their local community (non-Jewish) welfare fund drive.[21] Nevertheless, no comparative data appear to exist documenting the proportions of adherents of all faiths who give to their own religious causes or to other general charities above and beyond contributions to their own church, synagogue, or temple. Indeed, the amount of sociological research on the phenomenon of charitable giving seems very limited, with only one entry under "charity" in the *Cumulative Index of Sociology Journals*.[22] An investigation of the personal, professional, or ideological reasons as to why this is so goes beyond the scope of this article. Maimonides, acknowledged as the greatest medieval Jewish philosopher, taught that charity is obligatory, even for the poor, but that the highest level of giving was to create conditions such that the poor would not need charity. It is within this kind of historical normative order that a body of research has emerged focusing on charitable giving in the Jewish community.

Cohen,[23] for example, analyzed two surveys carried out in 1965 and 1975 in the Jewish community of Boston and found that the younger generation was less likely to be involved in Jewish community philanthropy. Furthermore, in his research, Heilman[24] documented the way in which charitable giving was a ritualized behavior that was part of the daily lives of the Orthodox congregation he studied.

In addition, an impressive number of Jewish population surveys have been carried out since the early 1970s, including such recent diverse community studies as Denver,[25] Hartford,[26] and Philadelphia.[27] They, however, have not probed deeply into the complexity of motivations for charity.[28] Taken together with the National Jewish Population Survey, it is noted that those who were most likely to contribute possessed a greater degree of Jewish identification based on synagogue attendance, Jewish educational background, and the like.[29]

To repeat, these surveys do not reveal in any great detail the motivations, both incentives and barriers, for such philanthropy. As a recent social scientific inquiry to better understand the charitable behavior of the Jews stated,

> The literature on Jewish philanthropic behavior is very thin. We suspect that a reasonable social scientific bibliography dealing with Jewish philanthropic behavior could be printed on one not terribly large page. As to our disciplinary field, sociology, there too we have found little dealing with charitable giving . . . We are operating then in largely unknown territory, borrowing theoretical insights from cognate areas, with little in the way of a cognitive map to lead us.[30]

It is hoped that the research reported in this chapter begins to fill that gap by examining this issue within the normative context of helping behavior; i.e., the extent to which norms such as those of social responsibility or reciprocity are operating. Adherence to these norms is indicative of individuals' relationships to their society and of their support for "whatever sense of moral order exists in that society."[31]

Data and Methods

Survey research, of necessity, requires reaching a large number of respondents to gather brief responses in a relatively short period of time. Such an approach usually does not permit the researcher to probe more deeply into the incentives and barriers to a particular type of behavior. Therefore, this study is based upon a purposive sample of seventy-two persons.[32] Unlike a random sample, in which every person in a population is assigned an equal probability of inclusion, a purposive sample intentionally includes categories of persons who represent the social types of maximum interest to a research project. In this study, the individuals selected (described below) were drawn from different regions of the country as well as from varying concentrations of city/suburban residence. This selection process was designed to focus on areas and individuals where it is assumed that the greatest opportunities for additional giving lies. They include two in the Sun Belt, Texas and Florida, which have received large numbers of Jewish migrants in recent years. In addition, two areas in the Frost Belt were studied, New York and southern New England, both of which have populations living in the central cities as well as a growing suburban dispersion of population.[33]

Of the seventy-two respondents that were interviewed, forty-two came from New York, and the other thirty were roughly evenly divided among Texas, Florida, and New England.[34] In addition, respondents were divided into three categories based on the assumption supported by the National Jewish Population Survey that Jewish identification and organizational involvement were directly related to contributing to the campaign (see table 13.1). These categories included:

(1) Donors: Givers (generally $500 or more) to United Jewish Appeal (UJA) and synagogue members and/or members of two or more Jewish organizations;[35]
(2) Nondonors: Nongivers to UJA who were synagogue members and/or members of two or more Jewish organizations; and
(3) Unaffiliated: Nongivers to UJA who were neither members of a synagogue nor two or more Jewish organizations.

TABLE 13.1. Categories of Jewish Associational Involvement: Synagogue/Jewish Organizational Membership and Giving to UJA

	Organizational Membership	
Giving	+	−
+	Donors (N = 24)	*
−	Non-donors (N = 24)	Unaffiliated (N = 24)

*Giving to UJA in the absence of synagogue or Jewish organizational membership is regarded as rare.

The interview consisted of over 100 questions and covered a variety of standard demographic and social characteristics (e.g., age, sex, marital status, employment, generation, number of children, residence, income, and necessary expenditures). In addition, a wide range of Jewish background characteristics was studied (e.g., synagogue membership, synagogue attendance, denominational preference, organizational involvement, and Jewish education). The major portion of the interview probed actual behavior and attitudes with respect to charitable giving (e.g., how much given, to whom given, decisionmaking in giving, degree of satisfaction in giving) as well as orientations toward UJA/Federation (e.g., motivations, inhibitions, preferred method of solicitation, involvement with UJA/Federation, and possible stimuli to giving). The interview concluded with a series of questions dealing with the respondents' knowledge and experience of Israel and anti-Semitism.[36] It is the purpose of this research to explore why the more marginal groups of Jews do not give.

It is important, however, to emphasize that *these seventy-two cases studied are not a representative sample of any sector of American Jewry.* Thus, the *findings constitute the basis for plausible hypotheses to be tested subsequently on a representative sample of Americans.* The purpose of presenting these data from a small sample is to locate these individuals in the larger mass of American Jewry, and to offer some insights as to the direction future research might take.

Comparison of Perceived Incentives and Barriers for the Three Groups

The Donors represent the Jewish community's "good givers." The Nondonors share with the Donors the characteristic of Jewish organizational membership and would therefore be expected to give to the UJA, but do not. The Unaffiliated represents an uninvolved group, which, according to some, is unreachable.

In a separate analysis,[37] the findings of this small sample were compared to those reported for the National Jewish population Survey on a variety of social, economic, and religious characteristics. The findings revealed that those who had children, were self-employed, had more Jewish education, were frequent synagogue attenders, and had more Jewish and general organizational involvements were more likely to contribute to the UJA. Such evidence is consistent with that of other researchers. For example, Cohen's study,[38] based on data gathered in Boston, found an increasing impact from 1965 to 1975 of Jewish activities on charitable giving. A study in Israel found that religious Israeli Jews were significantly more charitable than the secular subjects studied.[39]

While the individuals specially interviewed for this study are not statistically representative of the entire American Jewish community, they are illustrative of the patterns of affiliation with UJA and Jewish organizational life—or the lack of it. How, then, do the three groups of individuals (Donors, Nondonors, and Unaffiliated) view their relationship to the organized Jewish community with respect to contributing to UJA? What do they perceive as incentives for and barriers to giving?

Table 13.2 summarizes the findings in regard to the relationship of the three groups toward their perceived incentives for the barriers against contributing to UJA. Seven sets of factors were examined to see whether they could act as such incentives or barriers. They included the following[40]:

(1) Being Jewish,
(2) Israel,
(3) Anti-Semitism,
(4) UJA image,
(5) Giving readiness,
(6) Solicitation context,
(7) Financial situation.

TABLE 13.2. Orientations Toward Giving: Perceived Incentives and Barriers to Giving for Donors, Non-Donors, and Unaffiliated

	Giving Valence	
Level of Affiliation	**Perceived Incentives (+)**	**Perceived Barriers (−)**
	A	B
Donors	(1) Being Jewish: Identifying with Jewish community, Jewish organizations, Judaism, and moral obligation (Mitzvah) of Tzedakah (2) Israel: Trips and missions build identification with Israel (3) Anti-Semitism: Personal knowledge of Holocaust and awareness of anti-Semitism	(4) UJA Image/Structure: Elitist, wealthy, old (no room for young leadership), catering to big givers, exploitation of federation professional, Women's Division, don't know

(5) Giving Readiness: Parent
gave or relative benefits from
UJA services

(6) Solicitation Context: Charismatic speaker, inspirational professional, solicitation training, informational presentation, peer-group approval	(6) Solicitation Context: Public pledging, dinners, face-to-face, back-of-bus, phone, hard-sell techniques.
(7) Financial Situation: Reduction in inflation	(7) Financial Situation: Other financial obligations (Synagogue)

C	D
Non-donors (1) Being Jewish: Identifying with Jewish community, Jewish organizations, Judaism, and moral obligations (Mitzvah) of Tzedakah	
(2) Israel: Trips and missions build identification with Israel	
(3) Anti-Semitism: Awareness	
(4) UJA Image/Structure: Need to know, cut out administrative middle-man	(4) UJA Image/Structure: Establishment, wealthy, old, distant, invisible, not relevant, Women's Division, don't know, don't rock the boat
(6) Solicitation Context: Emotional appeal, personal friend	(6) Solicitation Context: Public pledging, dinners, face-to-face, phone
	(7) Financial Situation: No money, other financial obligations (JCC, Synagogue)

E	F
Un-affiliated (1) Being Jewish: Moral obligation, sense of responsibility	(1) Being Jewish: Not interested in religious organizations, lack of Jewish identity, estrangement from religious life/Jewish culture
(2) Israel: Emergency situation or crisis, identification or concern with Israel	(2) Israel: Policies of Israeli government
(3) Anti-Semitism: Awareness	
	(4) UJA Image/Structure: Lack of knowledge of the UJA, not knowing what one's contribution actually does,

	wealthy sponsorship
(6) Solicitation Context: Emotional appeal, sense of duty, personal contact	(6) Solicitation Context: Phone calls, dinners, meetings, face-to-face, hard-sell techniques.
(7) Financial Situation: Invest personal time in a cause rather than money.	(7) Financial Situation: Economic times are difficult, unable to afford contribution.

According to these findings, any one factor could serve as a stimulus toward increasing the incentive to giving or raising the barrier to it. For example, respondents in the Donors group perceived the "UJA image/structure" as a potential barrier to giving, even though they gave. Likewise, members of the Unaffiliated group saw the "UJA image/structure" as a real barrier to their giving. No one in these groups reported "UJA image/structure" as an incentive to giving. Nevertheless, among the Nondonors a certain "UJA image or structure" was perceived both as an incentive or barrier to giving for that group. Of course, at the time of the research, that positive perception was not as evident as the negative one since members of this group were still Nondonors.

Incentives and Barriers of the Donors

Of the seven different sets of factors identified, we found that three could operate to produce perceived barriers toward giving to UJA even for the Donors. For example, some of the images of UJA held by the Donors included: elitist, wealthy, old (no room for young leadership), catering to big givers, exploitation of federation professionals, having a Women's Division, or not familiar with UJA. Of course, many of these negative descriptions could also have been given by the Unaffiliated or the Nondonors. As one Donor from Texas suggested:

> The problem I sometimes have is not understanding how the process is supposed to work in terms of decision . . . I made one pledge. Then someone asked what about the women's division. My wife checked, and the pledge that I had made didn't count for that . . .

Another Donor from New York perceived UJA as distant and put it this way: "It's also a sense of something large and not connected to us."

Occasionally a negative description emerges that could have come only from an insider, such as this observation about the treatment of the professional workers from a woman in New England:

I think it's the nature of the beast. I think to work at a Jewish communal service organization like that and get paid bubkas "peanuts" and work with people who are dealing with millions and trillions of dollars—the whole volunteer versus professional psychology is absolutely wicked to deal with. I think a lot of the volunteers expect because the communal service worker is getting paid that they are, therefore, a servant of some kind. There is very much that attitude which bothers me terribly. I think they take terrible abuse. I can understand why someone who is very dynamic, wonderful, exciting, and inspirational would not want to stay in that kind of job and shouldn't. I get caught up in all that—sorry.

Another area that turned up as a barrier to the Donors was the solicitation context. Even in this group there were objections to one form of solicitation or another, such as public pledging, dinners, face-to-face or back-of-bus techniques phone calls, or hard sells. As one man ventured, "I would dislike it if someone asked me to stand up at a meeting unless I agreed to it. Generally, I don't like a meeting where they are announcing gifts in groups."

Another Donor objected to door-to-door solicitation: "I don't like a guy coming to me and tell(ing) me you owe me more than last year, and arguing with me as they have done." And another observed:

It's okay if you want to get the fifty wealthiest guys in the community and let them throw dollars at each other; but if you are taking someone who is just starting out and he's at a dinner where everyone is pledging $1,000 and he had about $25 or $50 in mind, (then) I'm not going to go to anymore dinners.

A final area of barriers that we found for the Donors dealt with their financial situation. Usually, this took the form of conflicts between commitments to other Jewish institutions, such as the synagogue, and the UJA Campaign. As one man commented:

We cut back on UJA to make up for the synagogue (Building Fund) last year. We were kicked out of the computer for too much charitable deductions, and we have to go down there with all our receipts and canceled checks.

Finally, here is the observation of a committed contributor lamenting her situation:

We are becoming somewhat disenchanted with the fact that we sometimes feel that we are the only ones who were giving to the tune that we were giving, and when you find that nobody else is carrying the burden as heavily as you are, you stop and think what is wrong with me. Why am I so charitable and nobody else is? We cut back because we needed the money for something else (synagogue).

Nevertheless, these Donors gave, in some cases with extreme generosity, to their local campaign. What prompted them to give? They gave largely, as we said before, for Jewish reasons.

As one New Yorker stated, "I support Jewish institutions because I feel they are my protectors." Another was quoted as saying, "we are proud of the continuity of the past of the Jews who have preceded us, and we have to live up to their heritage, and we have to leave something to our children."

Finally, one woman from New England saw her contributions as an element in her affirming her Judaism in a broad sense:

> I'm trying to think of a realistic kind of education for the entire Jewish population of what it means to be a Jew that is not only to spend a day in the synagogue and pray . . . There is a distinction in this country between social Judaism and religious Judaism. The two go hand in hand . . . (and) I mean a whole lot more than tzedakah. I mean active participation. . . . There is a distinction between social means and religious means, and I think Jews have an obligation to both.

In some instances, a particular Jewish experience was a motivating point for giving, as in one Texan's participation on a Federation-sponsored mission to Israel. This is how he reacted to it:

> The mission was the turning point. . . . Going to Israel has always been a dream . . . I have seen the needs. I have to do it. For me, it's a Jewish responsibility. . . . The trip to Israel really made me understand what it all meant. I felt dignity while I was there. Something touched very deeply within me. Perhaps, I didn't know it was even there.

Sometimes there is a twin focus to the concerns of individuals—Israel and anti-Semitism or the Holocaust. As one New Englander said, "There are two things that keep us up at night: that is the security of Israel and having just read or heard something about the Holocaust."

A New Yorker was very concerned about the situation of Soviet Jewry: "If you knew more Jews would get out of Russia because of your contributions . . . you certainly would give more money."

Indeed, in some instances the individuals reported feeling that some particular incident related to Israel or anti-Semitism was an especially powerful or peak experience:

> I was standing outside of the delivery room with G. [Holocaust survivor] . . . and they brought the baby [G.'s grandchild] . . . into the nursery. And G. and her friend started talking in Yiddish about how they never in all those days in the camps ever

thought they would live long enough to see their grandchildren and to stand there and share the experience of a grandchild being born, I mean . . . (choked with emotion) . . . IT CAN'T HAPPEN AGAIN, EVER!

Finally, for some individuals an additional motivating factor was their readiness to give, which resulted from their being socialized into a family oriented toward contributing to the UJA Campaign. As one New Yorker observed, "If there had to be any distinction that I had to make between givers and nongivers, it would be to see what the parents did."

Perhaps, it was best summarized in this way by one Floridian:

> I came from a very modest family. It made me feel good to be giving to the Jewish Federation. It was something I was taught to be charitable. My mother and grandmother never turned anyone away. They came from an Orthodox family. To be able to be charitable made me feel good.

Does this evidence support the norm of reciprocity? In discussing motivational factors, respondents did not generally view their contributions as a quid pro quo for their receiving previous help. There is some indirect evidence for the norm of social responsibility in that it might be argued that the more Israel is seen as dependent on American Jews, the more people feel a need to contribute. Perhaps a more comprehensive explanation exists in what we might dub the "norm of social cohesion." By this is meant the following: the more people feel integrated into a particular subcommunity, the more likely they are to aid members or causes of their sub-community perceived as in need of charitable contributions.

Incentives and Barriers of the Nondonors

For the Nondonors, we found the same three general sets of factors operating as perceived barriers to giving as for the Donors. The difference was that the latter did not permit their perceptions to block their actions. Let us examine the situation of the Nondonors to see why they did not respond similarly.

One level of barriers reflected the problem of the image and structure of UJA. The variety of negative images and perceptions was great. As one New Yorker said, "I get a sense from people that work there, and from my own perception (which may or may not be correct), that there is inefficiency in the staff and too much money goes in ways that aren't productive."

Another objected:

There is nothing really visible (of UJA) except for the phone calls. You never hear what happens if they made $100,000 last year. They have to show the Jewish community (what it does). . . . People have to see something tangible.

One Floridian was very blunt. He said, "The leadership is basically a bunch of old crotchety men who have retired and have nothing else to do but sit around and meet and hassle around the same issues." Another was disturbed by the concept of the Women's Division. She said: "They are not in touch with what the young Jewish woman sees and perceives . . . and they don't care."

In another instance, one Texan saw the local Federation not being sufficiently active:

I'm an old activist of a person. In college, I was very active mobilizing efforts for Soviet Jews. I had the feeling many times that the UJA decision-making processes are stodgy. They don't want to rock boats. Many times, in order to accomplish things that need to be accomplished, they should go out on a limb a little; and they are unwilling to do that.

One New Yorker was opposed to the merger of the Israel Campaign of UJA with the Federation Campaign for local needs:

I don't think the merger of the Federation and UJA was a particularly good idea. You had two very (in my mind) dissimilar organizations. Federation was an organization that supported Jewish activities in this general area, whether it was hospitals, community centers, old age homes. UJA is a support for Israeli organizations. Now the idea was that the same people basically give to both organizations, and therefore, a merging of the two would make one gift. I don't think that Federation-type activity has been helped by that particular merger. I feel that the Federation has been dominated more by UJA people than by Federation people, and it probably has lessened my sympathy with the organization as a whole.[41]

Another New Yorker volunteered this piece of advice: "UJA could get to me if I knew it wasn't a computerized business that makes me a number. I see UJA as a big, massive business."

Finally, another man thought of the local Federation as less interested in cultivating potential young leaders than in coddling older big givers. He was rather frank in his statement:

To get the Federation board to agree to subsidize a young leadership commission took months of political hassling around. To get the Federation to spend $40,000 to lease a boat and bring on a caterer to have a handful of people give initial gifts which total $400,000—that they don't think twice about.

A second level of barriers reflected the concerns with solicitation techniques. One respondent from Florida stated:

> I think the oral appeal affected me very early as a young man, or perhaps a teenager, in the synagogue High Holiday Services—the bidding for Torah honors. It was rather revolting, and I suppose that has carried with me.

A New Yorker was also upset about solicitation techniques: "I can't set aside my personal offense at UJA methodology. I find it extraordinarily offensive. I think what one gives is between himself and their maker and not a matter of public consumption. . . . "

Finally, a third level of perceived barriers reflected the competitive strains of giving on the respondents' financial situation. One man from Florida was most interested in contributing to an agency that appeared to give him the most "bang for the buck."

> [I] would rather give [my] money to . . . a programmatic agency rather than fundraising . . . you give to Federation once a year, fundraising time . . . but the JCC is a year-round program. It's not as politically motivated. If things have to be done, they get done. They don't squander hours and hours debating an issue and making a mountain out of a molehill.

Another woman was interested in relevance. As she saw it, "People don't see the direct personal relevance in their everyday lives. To join a Temple is more related to their own practical family living. UJA doesn't bear on this family living."

Another person saw the synagogue as the basis of a local communal identity as a Jew and, therefore, the practical necessity of supporting it. He said:

> The synagogue is our top priority because we feel it is very important to maintain a visible, viable focal point in the community for having some support for Jewish traditions in a secular society, particularly in the public schools.

One New Yorker was rather introspective about the problem of giving money:

> In some respects, money is always a problem in giving, and I guess there is always that feeling of I should have given more; but that's only a feeling of my own compulsiveness and my own personality so that it is an unsatisfying experience.

Another New Yorker felt frustrated in giving: "What prevents people from giving? A feeling that no amount is really enough."

Another person saw himself as philanthropic—and by the level of his reported contributions he was, but he did not see how UJA represented a potential beneficiary of his largess. This is how he put it:

> I'm philanthropic by nature, generally, and sometimes I'm concerned whether I have the ability to give as much as I would like. . . . Once I've committed myself it's just such a wonderful feeling, and that's the way I feel with the contributions I've made to the [humanitarian] project; and I'll go on to say as far as the contributions we've made to our Temple, I feel equally rewarded that I have done that.

For persons who do give and are involved in the UJA Campaign, it must be difficult—even painful—to hear people who are generous and contributing individuals subjectively and objectively not willing or able to include UJA in their circle of giving. Perhaps this is because these individuals do not feel deeply about themselves as Jews. Other evidence showed that the differences in Jewish identification were greatest comparing the Donors to the Unaffiliated rather than to the Nondonors.[42] What then are the incentives to giving perceived by the Nondonors?

In many ways these individuals seemed responsive to the same Jewish concerns as the Donors. The Nondonors generally felt a fairly strong sense of Jewish identification and even of the role of charitable giving in that sense of being Jewish. As one Texan said, "I am Jewish and believe in being responsible for my community." Israel also played a role in their readiness to give. A Florida man suggested, "If I didn't like what I saw happening to Israel, I would definitely give more money." So what would encourage them to give? One level of incentives for giving perceived by the Nondonors is the Jewish level. As one individual said, "Contributing to Jewish-oriented causes is more rewarding than others because of cultural, religious perceived ties." Indeed, the Nondonors are concerned about Israel:

> Money that goes specifically to help Israeli society in any way would be helpful. Anything that raises money to defend Israel strikes me as the most important organization. Israel is not only essential to all Jewish life, but it is essential to the future of Jewish life.

Another said: "If they [the American government] don't support Israel, we have to. So the more negative the government is, the more positive and supportive of Israel we are."

In some instances, UJA is not perceived as the most appropriate vehicle to help Israel: "I would be far more interested in being charitable to an organization that is essentially Israeli in its nature and not created, conceptualized, whatever, from outside Israel."

Another type of incentive was the need for more information about UJA. As one woman suggested, "If we knew about the specifics [of UJA] in more detail [we would give] . . . [We do] give [to our synagogue] because of our Jewish heritage."

Another person seemed to suggest that the right kind of information could become an incentive for giving. He said:

> Maybe there is an image problem. If it were better known what activities were available in our bedroom communities, . . . We would support to a greater extent these activities . . . more activities that would involve the family.

In the area of the solicitation context, individuals offered suggestions as to what approaches might serve as incentives to giving for them and persons like themselves. One man from Florida did not like the high-pressure approach:

> Giving contributions . . . is basically a private matter. . . . [There should be] no requirement to give them despite a very professional and very slick approach. . . . If you want to go home and think about it, you should have every right to do so.

Another felt that the appeal in the middle of a crisis was the best incentive to giving. When asked under what circumstances would people be most likely to give, he replied:

> Wartime appeal when there is a crisis . . . because it's an emotional appeal. To say you have to support Israel when most people haven't been there, . . . They have never come in contact with the Israeli culture, the historical background, never stood at the wall.

A New Yorker suggested that an approach by the right person might work: "If someone you know asks you to give to something that is important to him, you do. It has to do with respecting his sense of value by requesting for a specific project."

One is tempted to conclude that even though the Nondonors have a good sense of Jewish identification, they are more selfish or less emotionally sensitive to the needs of their fellow Jews. This would seem unwarranted. Rather, it appears that the overriding reason such people are not contributing to the UJA Campaign is because they do not see what their giving does for them.

Their dollars may do something for someone else in a far-off location, but, they ask, what does it do for their immediate local needs as Jews? Thus, the Nondonors represent the "locals," whereas the Donors may be referred to as the "cosmopolitans." This is so because the latter have a broader view of their Jewish identification tied to the unity of worldwide Jewry (*am ehad*—one people—as the UJA slogan goes).

On the basis of this evidence, it may be specified that the norm of social cohesion applies more strongly to those individuals who are cosmopolitan rather than local in their orientation. Thus, while the Donors took a broader view of their obligations to the larger community and, hence, were more cosmopolitan, the Nondonors took a narrower view and saw their obligations as more limited to their immediate local community.

Incentives and Barriers of the Unaffiliated

The Unaffiliated differ significantly from the other two groups in their Jewish characteristics. They have the least Jewish education; they are most likely to have no denominational preference (or something other than Orthodox, Conservative, or Reform), and they have the lowest level of synagogue attendance.[43] Hence, it is not surprising that a major barrier to their giving to UJA is their lack of Jewish identity. As one New Yorker said simply, "I feel no real identity." Another stated, "I don't feel a personal involvement as I would with some of the other things that people ask me to contribute to." A New Englander put it this way:

> It is essentially a story of ineffective Jewish upbringing; partly the result of parents who were, of course, Jewish but not deeply committed, and were not able to give me any sense of inward identification with Judaism at home.

Finally, another New Yorker indicated his estrangement from Jewish life: "UJA is not part of my circle. . . . If I were involved with Jewish religious life, I think I would contribute. . . . I am completely estranged from that."

A related barrier was the respondents' perceptions of Israel. As one New Englander said:

> " . . . the UJA/Federation money, to my understanding, goes to Israel and as firm a supporter as I am to the people of Israel, I think some of the money goes to finance some of the 'crazy' things the government of Israel is doing."

Another put it this way: "I suspect that Israeli politics have become very central in determining how much people give or don't give. That could simply

be a projection of what is on my own mind: the very recent aggressiveness.
. . ."

At another level of concern was the familiar problem expressed by Donors
and Nondonors as well—the image or structure of UJA. One New Yorker
voiced a recurrent theme: "I don't understand the structure of Jewish charities.
I don't know what UJA does." Another wondered: "I don't know how much
money goes to run the organization, and how much gets paid to fundraisers,
and how much actually filters down to charity after bureaucracy gets through
with it." Finally, another New Yorker seemed more hostile: "Does my contributing to UJA foster the very forces in Jewish life that I am against? That's my
real concern. Am I giving to the enemy so to speak."

A New England resident suggested: "One reason people don't give is that
they don't know anything about it. It is not high on their priority list." Another
said:

> People of my age have left—and I feel in distressing numbers—due to a communica-
> tion problem, or what I suspect that part of it is a matter of image sales, and I'm not
> sure the organization communicates very well with the assimilated Jews such as
> myself who nonetheless consider themselves Jews.

A third level of barriers reflected concerns with solicitation techniques. One
New Yorker offered the following statement: "I don't want someone pushing
the button on my door or the telephone. I tend to be turned off by that. It's a
sales pitch, like anything else, like selling soap." Another complained: "It's the
pressure part that I don't like, more than anything else. You are being asked to
make a decision too quickly. Someone is using their personal relationship with
me for reasons other than their relationship with me."

Another kind of barrier related to solicitation was voiced by a New England
woman: "[They] consistently refer to women by their husband's name. It made
me totally angry, despite the fact that she may have accomplished a great deal. I
would hope that they would have a consciousness of the contemporary
woman."

A New England man objected to the pressure of solicitation: "I personally
resent anyone telling me I have to give, and I think part of the good feeling of
giving is wanting to give, and I would not get that if someone said I had to unless
it was a dire emergency."

Finally, for some individuals there was the financial barrier, as one Florida
man said: "People just don't have the money; it's getting increasingly more
difficult to make ends meet. When you're struggling to keep your head above
water, it makes it a littler harder to think outside of your immediate circle."

Despite the fact that the Unaffiliated group had a lower level of Jewish identification, their sense of being Jewish generally remained alive, as we indicated earlier. As one New Yorker said, "No matter what is going on in our life, good, bad, whatever, we have always felt a definite responsibility." Another was very concerned about the plight of Soviet Jewry: "I would love to know how I could contribute to their welfare in anyway . . . I'm most conscious of those Jews in danger."

In another instance, anti-Semitism was seen as a motivating factor: "If I begin to perceive anti-Semitism as a real threat, I would once again begin to give to Jewish causes a lot more liberally than I am now."

In addition, some of these Unaffiliated individuals were also very concerned about Israel—especially if they perceived an emergency: "If, God forbid, there was going to be a war tomorrow and Israel needed planes or something, then obviously we would do everything we could to help." Another affirmed: "I would feel a commitment to help preserve the state of Israel." Indeed, some individuals may contribute but only during wartime: "I suppose the UJA appeal at that time perhaps gave me a sense of satisfaction that I did something. It brought home a lot of memories. It brought to mind a lot of things that I feel I contribute in terms of Israel." The implication of these findings is the need to first cultivate that sense of Jewishness, however vaguely defined.

Some individuals saw the need for a certain type of solicitation context: One Floridian said: "It's more nonthreatening for you to talk to a personal contact, someone you might know, than if someone knocks at the door."

A New England resident suggested a similar theme of solicitation by the "image maker" or "significant other," the person influential in shaping the thinking of the solicited person:

> If I got a letter addressed to me from (the prime minister of Israel) asking me for money, I would probably find it hard to turn down. If someone of personal importance . . . you would be hard pressed to turn it down. Not from the mass mailing, no, like from Reader's Digest, but if something was impressed upon me as being of great need I would give it considerable consideration.

Another type of incentive mentioned by one of the Unaffiliated was the possibility of offering a nonmonetary contribution. Perhaps this was more consistent with the financial situation of the individual: "I am more inclined to spend time, rather than money, for causes I believe in."

In sum, the Unaffiliated shared with the Donors and Nondonors similar concerns about the barriers they perceived to their contributing to UJA with respect to its image or structure and solicitation techniques. Where they differed significantly from the Donors and Nondonors was in the barrier that their lower level of Jewish identification posed. In respect to incentives for giving, they perceived that certain Jewish concerns might arouse their consciousness toward charitable giving, such as Israel or anti-Semitism. Without further cultivation of their sense of Jewishness, these charitable gifts might only be forthcoming from some in an emergency situation. Thus, the evidence suggests that the norm of social cohesion applies more strongly to those individuals (Donors and, to a lesser extent, Nondonors) who have a stronger personal identity as community members than those who have a weaker personal identity (Unaffiliated).

Notes

1. Eliezer David Jaffee, "The Crisis in Jewish Philanthropy," *TIKKUN* 4 (September–October 1987), pp. 27–31, 90; Milton Goldin, "Does Jewish Philanthropy Have a Future? *Midstream* 24 (November 1983), pp. 22–24; and Paul Ritterband and Steven M. Cohen, "Will the Well Run Dry? The Future of Jewish Giving in America," Response 12 (Summer 1979, pp. 9–17.

2. See, for example, Felicity Barringer, *The New York Times*, December 25, 1987, and David Brown, "We Will Not Hand Out Free Beef, Say Charities," (London) *British Sunday Telegraph* January 3, 1988.

3. Virginia Ann Hodgkinson and Murray S. Weitzman, *The Charitable Behavior of Americans* (Washington, D.C.: Independent Sector, 1986), p. 41.

4. Linda Mollenhauer, personal letter (December 18, 1987).

5. Susan K. E. Saxon-Harrold and Jill Carter, *The Charitable Behavior of the British People* (Tonbridge, Kent: Charities Aid Foundation, 1987).

6. James W. Vander Zanden, *Social Psychology, 3rd edition* (New York: Random House, 1984), p. 273.

7. Vander Zanden, *Social Psychology*, p. 274.

8. See, for example, Jeffrey H. Goldstein, *Social Psychology* (New York: Academic Press, 1980); Arnold S. Kahn, ed., *Social Psychology* (Dubuque, IA: W. C. Brown Publishers, 1984); and Cookie White Stephan and Walter G. Stephan, *Two Social Psychologies* (Homewood, IL: Dorsey Press, 1985).

9. William R. Reece, "Charitable Contributions—New Evidence on Household Behavior," *American Economic Review* 69 (March 1979), pp. 142–51.

10. James Gregory Lord, "Marketing Nonprofits," *Grantsmanship News* 9 (1981), pp. 53–57.

11. See, for example, P. L. Benson, and V. Catt, "Soliciting Charity Contributions—Parlance of Asking for Money," *Journal of Applied Social Psychology* 8 (January–March 1978), pp. 84–95; and Peter H. Reingen, "Inducing Compliance with a Donation Request," *Journal of Social Psychology* 106 (December 1978), pp. 281–82.

12. See, for example, M. B. Harris, S. M. Benson, and C. L. Hall, "The Effects of Confession on Altruism," *Journal of Social Psychology* 96 (August 1975), pp. 187–92; and Benson and Catt, "Soliciting Charity Contributions—Parlance of Asking for Money," pp. 84–96.

13. See, for example, the bibliographic review of A. Miren Gonzalez and Philip Tetlock, *A Literature Review of Altruism and Helping Behavior*, Yale University Program on Non-Profit Organizations, New Haven, CT, undated.

14. Joseph Galaskiewicz, *Social Organization of an Urban Grants Economy* (Orlando: Academic Press, 1985).

15. Leonard Berkowitz and William H. Connor, "Success, Failure, and Social Responsibility," *Journal of Personality and Social Psychology* 4 (December 1966), pp. 664–9.

16. Alvin W. Gouldner, "The Norm of Reciprocity: A Preliminary Statement," *American Sociological Review* 25 (April 1960), pp. 161–78.

17. Arnold Dashefsky and Bernard Lazerwitz, *Why Don't They Give? Determinants of Jewish Charitable Giving* (Storrs, CT: University of Connecticut Mimeographed, 1983).

18. Gary A. Tobin and Julie A. Lipsman, "A Compendium of Jewish Demographic Studies," in Steven M. Cohen, Jonathan S. Woocher, and Bruce A. Phillips, eds., *Perspectives in Jewish Population Research* (Boulder, CO: Westview Press, 1984), pp. 137–66.

19. Charity comes from the Latin, *caritas*, meaning love. Charity has a connotation in English of philanthropy, which derives from the Greek, *phila*, meaning love, and *anthropos*, meaning humankind. Essentially it reflects the Christian message emphasizing the need to love and care for others, borrowed out of the original Judaic context. By contrast, *tzedakah comes from the Hebrew root tzadok*, which yields the words *tzedek*, justice, and *tzadik*, a righteous person. Thus, *tzedakah* is the righteous action of people seeking justice, as compared to charity, which implies loving people and caring for others. If a person does not feel love, he or she will find it difficult to care for others and to act charitably. In the Jewish tradition, however, doing or giving *tzedakah* is required whether or not the person feels love or caring for the other. It is a religious requirement or commandment, a *mitzvah* to be fulfilled. See Danny Siegel, *Gym Shoes and Irises* (Spring Valley, NY: Townhouse Press, 1982) and Jacob Neusner, *Tzedakah: Can Jewish Philanthropy Buy Jewish Survival?* (Chappaqua, NY: Rossel Books, 1982).

20. Arnold Dashefsky, "Orientations Toward Jewish Charitable Giving," in Nahum M. Waldman, ed., *Community and Culture* (Philadelphia: Gratz College Seth Press, 1987), p. 19.

21. Dashefsky and Lazerwitz, *Why Don't They Give?*

22. Judith C. Lantz, *Cumulative Index of Sociology Journals 1971–1985* (Washington: American Sociological Association, 1987).

23. Steven M. Cohen, "Trends in Jewish Philanthropy," *American Jewish Yearbook* 80 (1979), pp. 29–51.

24. Samuel C. Heilman, "The Gift of Alms: Face to Face Giving Among Orthodox Jews," *Urban Life and Culture*, 3 (January 1975), pp. 371–95.

25. Bruce A. Phillips and Eleanor P. Judd, *Denver Jewish Population Study* (Denver: Allied Jewish Federation of Denver, 1981).

26. Mark Abrahamson, *A Study of the Greater Hartford Jewish Population* (West Hartford, CT: Greater Hartford Jewish Federation, 1982).

27. William Yancey and Ira Goldstein, *The Jewish Population Study of Greater Philadelphia* (Philadelphia: Federation of Jewish Agencies of Greater Philadelphia, 1985).

28. See Tobin and Lipsman, "A Compendium of Jewish Demographic Studies," pp. 162–4.

29. Dashefsky and Lazerwitz, *Why Don't They Give?*

30. Richard Silberstein, Jonathan Rabinowitz, Paul Ritterband, and Barry Kosmin, *Giving to Jewish Philanthropic Causes: A Preliminary Reconnaissance* (New York: North American Jewish Data Bank Reprint Series, No. 2, 1987), p. 1.
31. David J. Cheal, "The Social Dimensions of Gift Behavior," *Journal of Social and Personal Relationships* 3 (1986), p. 423.
32. Actually, interviews were carried out with seventy-nine individuals, but seven cases were excluded because they did not fit the general criteria established. These individuals were referred by various local Federation representatives and were interviewed using a screening interview schedule. Those individuals not possessing the appropriate criteria were subsequently not interviewed. While some members of the Nondonor or Unaffiliated group may have given at an earlier point in time, they were not considered current or recent donors.
33. See Dashefsky, "Orientations toward Jewish Charitable Giving," for an earlier account of the sample selection.
34. The sample is disproportionately composed of New Yorkers because it represents the largest single pool of those not contributing to UJA or Federation: 40 percent of them do not claim giving to UJA or a Federation compared to 36 percent nationwide. See Dashefsky and Lazerwitz, *Why Don't They Give?*
35. Since donors interviewed generally gave gifts of $500 or more, they were viewed by UJA officials as "significant" or "good givers."
36. The interview schedule underwent a series of changes, so that five different versions were developed during the period from November 1981 until March 1982. The majority of the interviews, those from New York and New England, used Version 5 of the schedule; and the others utilized the slightly different Version 4. A small group of individuals was interviewed using Version 6 for a focus-group approach, in which closed-ended questions were filled out in a questionnaire, and the open-ended questions were asked in the interview.
37. See Dashefsky and Lazerwitz, *Why Don't They Give?*
38. Cohen, "Trends in Jewish Philanthropy."
39. Yoel Yinon and Irit Sharon, "Similarity in Religiousness of the Solicitor, the Potential Helper, and the Recipient as Determinants of Donating Behavior," *Journal of Applied Social Psychology* 15 (1985), pp. 726–34.
40. These seven themes were derived from the interviews through the questions suggested by UJA professionals and consultants as potentially the most revealing. The themes are not presented ordinarily.
41. In most urban communities, the Federation conducts one unified campaign for major Jewish charities both nationally and locally. Generally, the greatest single beneficiary of that fundraising effort is the United Jewish Appeal, which collects money on behalf of welfare agencies in Israel. In New York, UJA and Federation were separate entities for a long period of time.
42. See Dashefsky and Lazerwitz, *Why Don't They Give?*
43. See Bernard Lazerwitz and Michael Harrison, "A Comparison of Denominational Identification and Membership," *Journal for the Scientific Study of Religion*, 19 (December 1980), p. 336, for the importance of denominational identification in Jewish identification.
This article is derived from a research report prepared for and funded by the United Jewish Appeal (directed by Arnold Dashefsky and Bernard Lazerwitz, with the assistance of Dana Kline) and originally produced by The Center For Judaic Studies and Contemporary Jewish Life at The University of Connecticut, Storrs, Connecti-

cut. Thanks are due to the Department of Developmental Services and New Gifts of the United Jewish Appeal, National Director, Barry Judelman, and National Program Director, Neal Hurwitz, for permission to use these data. Special thanks are owed to Mark Abrahamson, Steven M. Cohen, Dana Kline, Bernard Lazerwitz, and Egon Mayer for their advice and aid during the course of the research, as well as to Celeste Machado, Rachelle Rosenberg, and David Zeligson, who served as student research assistants. I am also much indebted to David O. Moberg, who offered numerous, helpful suggestions in reviewing the manuscript, and to Alan Davidson, for editorial assistance. Last, but not least, special appreciation is extended to Linda Snyder for setting up the interviews and typing the rought draft, and to Shelly Korba and Carolee Tollefson for typing the final drafts of the manuscript.

IV

San Francisco and Earl Raab

14

"There's No City Like San Francisco"

Earl Raab

"There is no city like San Francisco," say the Jews of the Golden Gate with some conviction. But they say it in two different ways. Some say it happily, with an expansive smile. Others say it drily, and sadly shake their heads. As is usually the case in such matters, both are probably right.

The almost universal experience of any visitor to San Francisco is nostalgia-at-first-sight. This is the kind of reaction normally reserved for small villages tucked away on some by-road in a farming country, with an ancient pitcher pump in the square, a population of about five hundred, an atmosphere of more or less live-witted serenity—and a single national origin and cultural heredity. San Francisco's population is three quarters of a million. It is the commercial and banking center of the West. It is a polyglot city that has been heavily infiltrated by a dozen nationalities. Withal, there is no mistaking its village air of friendly order and homogeneity.

There is the pitcher pump, in the form of the rheumatic old cable cars. There is the serenity, in good measure: wide sidewalks; greens and flower banks, and little flower stands on every third corner; streets that dip and bob like a merry roller coaster; and a population that rushes only when it has some place to go.

Of course, San Francisco considers itself a sophisticated and lively town ("Bagdad on the Bay"), but there are few physical evidences of upstart vulgarity and self-conscious bohemianism that mark many modern American metropoli. Thomas Mann (in concert with others) has called San Francisco the most continental city in the country.

San Francisco is a genteel city. San Francisco is a poised city. San Francisco knows where it's been and where it's going.

Confronted with it, what East-weary mortal can resist nostalgia?

And what Jew will not sigh just a little longer than the rest?

229

There are fifty-five thousand Jews in San Francisco, and not even the historic traces of a ghetto. There is a Jewish community that has been called, with reason, the wealthiest, per capita, in the country. There is, at the same time, a startling poverty of anti-Semitic tradition. San Francisco, for cities of its size, is the nation's "white spot" of anti-Jewish prejudice.

In near-top-level social and country clubs there is Jewish membership, and even charter membership. Gentlemen's agreements are quite uncommon in its quality residential sections, old or new. In filling public and quasi-public posts, there seems to be no trace of a policy of exclusion or "quota" or even discriminatory hesitation. At times, Jewish citizens have concurrently held the presidencies of the Chamber of Commerce, the Community Chest, the Board of Education, Art, Fire, and Harbor Commissions, and many other appointive and elective posts; it is a situation that cannot be duplicated in any other city with a six percent Jewish concentration.

Of course, "anti-Semitism" is not a word without meaning in San Francisco. The Jewish Survey and B'nai B'rith Community Committee handle anti-defamation matters, and across its desk every day the usual reports pass in a light but steady flow. An employment agency has cards that are marked "No J's," or "Blonds only." Some private cooperative housing ventures won't include Jews. A sidewalk altercation where someone turns out to be not only a "damned —" but a "damned Jewish —."

Under the impact of Hitler, a Nazi Bund and a "Friends of Germany" were formed in the city. In the large Italian population, there was a backwash of admiration for Mussolini's Fascism. While these organizations have disappeared without even an underground trace, the people who joined them, it must be assumed, are still around. So are upwards of a hundred thousand newcomers from the Midwest and the South, who came to the city to work and live during the last war.

There are, then, steady incidences of employment discrimination and petty uglinesses, but they are relatively infrequent and without pervasive quality; a pattern more of scattered anti-Semitism than of any policies, regulations, or encased habit. Professional anti-Semitism has never been a paying proposition in San Francisco. Efforts in that direction have always been short-lived. The tip-off is that the latrine-wall type of anti-Semitic literature that has turned up in San Francisco has been datelined Chicago and Los Angeles, and mailed in.

So far as the city and its institutions are concerned, the Jew is a first-class citizen. It may well be that he can live in San Francisco with a greater degree of personal dignity than in any other large city in the country.

The attractive face of San Francisco, and the attractive status of the Jewish community within it, have common causes. The histories of the city and of its Jewish community have developed together along a shared course.

In 1848, San Francisco was a mule-stop. When gold was cried, the West exploded, and San Francisco became the center of new wealth and of wealth-seekers, Jews were there with the first wave. They were in the main immigrants from Germany, although there were many from England, France, and Alsace-Lorraine. The second surge of Jewish pioneers in the early 1850s contained some East Europeans. They came the hard ways, the only ways, across the hazardous continent or over the Isthmus. During the High Holy Days of 1849, services were held in a tent on the old Embarcadero near the waterfront.

While the mass of the forty-niners went scrabbling into the hills for gold, there were surer fortunes to be made in the city. One Jewish immigrant landed with his baggage in 1849 and immediately invested a hundred dollars in stationery, which he sold in front of a hotel at 500 percent profit. After a short interlude of playing a piano in a honky-tonk for an ounce of gold and a "grab" (literally a handful) of silver, he bought a store and began buying trunks from gold speculators anxious to get into the hills. Selling these again, he made five or six thousand dollars in seven or eight weeks. Soon, dozens of boxlike little stores were set up by his fellow Jews along the sprawling streets, heaped with hard-to-get clothing and merchandise shipped by friends and relatives in the East.

Other Jews played a part in the creation of the financial institutions on which San Francisco's economy was to rest. They became bankers, money brokers, exchange dealers. Names like Davidson, Priest, Dyer, Glazier, and Wormser were identified with the giant financial transactions that became necessary with Europe and with the East. The London, Paris, and American bank was founded by the Lazards. The Seligmans helped create the Anglo-American bank. The directorates of a half-dozen other mushrooming banks bore Jewish names. Jews became leading realty brokers, founders of engineering enterprises, and manipulators of the grain exchange. They were in on the ground floor of a speculative venture that swelled to fantastic and permanent proportions, and they made fantastic and permanent fortunes in the process. They also helped construct the basic economy of the new community of San Francisco. One of the differences between a "Shylock" and a "financial genius" is, after all, the size of his enterprise.

Some of these Jewish immigrants brought with them uncommon strains of culture, education, and qualities of leadership, and many plunged immediately into civic life. Samuel Marx was made United States Appraiser of the Port of San Francisco in 1851, and Joseph Shannon was County Treasurer in the same year. In 1852, Elkan Heydenfeldt and Isaac Cardozo were members of the state legislature, and Heydenfeldt was also Chief Justice of the state Supreme Court from 1852 to 1857.

In 1851, the San Francisco *Herald* struck the note of respect that was to be characteristic in generations to follow: "The Israelites constitute a numerous and intelligent class of our citizens and conduct themselves with great propriety and decorum. They are industrious and enterprising and make worthy members of our community."

From the beginning, the Jews were conspicuous for their sense of community. The first two welfare organizations in San Francisco were set up by Jews. In 1850, the Eureka Benevolent Society was organized to help the needy, and it still exists as the Jewish Family Service. As the little clothing stands turned into large department stores, and the money counters into financial empires, the Jews—feeling an understandable kinship with the city—began to make large monetary contributions to the general community life.

This tradition, as well as that of civic participation, has persisted. A startling number of the pools, parks, libraries, museums, and halls that are available to the public at large bear familiar Jewish names. Many institutions that are administered under Jewish agency auspices are nonsectarian in character (such as the Maimonides Hospital for chronic ailments, which serves a specific community need). Even the more private support of the cultural institutions of the city by the Jews has been too frequent to escape public attention—the music critic of the *Chronicle* reported that he had been informed that about 40 percent of the deficit of the San Francisco symphony orchestra is written off by three Jewish families.

The fact is that the Jews in San Francisco have never been cast in the role of "intruder." This was historically impossible. There was no aristocracy in California in 1849. There was only a ragtag gang of money-hungry pioneers of heterogeneous origins, welded together into a "frontier brotherhood" community. As the "first families" became incrusted, they did so necessarily in amalgam with the "first families" of the Jewish community.

The Jews aside, San Francisco has maintained a degree of tolerance for minority groups that has not obtained in other cities along the coast. One is prompted to speculate on the reasons for this, not only partially to explain the relationship between San Francisco and its Jewish community, but also to explain something of the nature of the Jewish community itself.

San Francisco has not had a serious boom since 1849. It was built on California gold and Nevada silver, and settled down as a financial and commercial center. It has never changed its basic character. The great industrial eruptions in the West—with their accompanying invasions of "barbarian hordes" from the East, the Midwest, and the South, and their extensions of eastern power and influence—that have boomed and burst cities like Los Angeles and Oakland, in the main bypassed San Francisco, and were reflected only in its increased prosperity as a financial center. Indeed, San Francisco is physically incapable of much expansion along industrial or population lines. It is a compact city, bounded on three sides by water, and on the other by a number of small communities jealous of their identity. It has been estimated that, just by virtue of physical limitations, San Francisco's top population would be around a million. As a matter of fact, the artificial surge in population that San Francisco experienced as a result of wartime activity has dissipated.

San Francisco is a middle-class, white-collar city. (It has the highest average percentage of office-building occupancy and the greatest telephone density in the country.) It is also a city whose top social and economic layers have remained fairly well preserved. As a result it has a conservative cast, with accompanying overtones of unblurred tradition and general *noblesse oblige*. (To be sure, it has also had a rather violent labor history—notably the general strike of 1934. But since San Francisco is not, like Detroit, a city of industries with a large industrial working class, its labor history has had surprisingly little effect upon the "tone" of living.)

All this has worked, of course, to preserve undisturbed the status of the Jew in the community. It has also worked to preserve the internal structure and character of the Jewish community itself. The Jewish population has increased, along with the general population, not by spectacular leaps, but by normal accretion. And the Jews attracted to San Francisco have generally been those who would not tend to disrupt the community's basic character. There have never been, for instance, the job opportunities that would encourage a mass influx of Eastern Europeans of the first generation.

There are many who claim, however, that the favorable position of the Jew in San Francisco is not just a derivative of the history and nature of the city, but also of the "historical position" and "astute leadership" of the old Jewish families who have maintained their identity and influence over several generations. This claim certainly has some truth. On the other hand, it is also true that out of this "historical position" and "astute leadership" by the older Jewish families there has developed a deep-rooted set of conflicts and a Jewish community on the verge of schism.

This schism is not so notable for its actual violence or disruptive effect, or for the number of people involved, as it is for its symptomatic quality and its implications for American Jewry in general. The history of the conflict is not just a petty scrap for power (which it sometimes has all the earmarks of being), or a local fight for "democracy," or an ideological dispute on this or that specific; but it seems ultimately a reflection of sharp differences in approaching the fundamental problems of Jewish identity in America.

San Francisco witnessed the dramatic enactment of this conflict. But there had long been people who felt privately or semiprivately that the Jewish community was "moribund," that Jewish life as such was "marginal," that the organs of Jewish expression in the city were muffled and misdirected, that

Jewish community organizations were not representative, that leadership needed changing.

When these critics talked about the "leadership," they knew exactly whom they meant: certain members of the old and influential families who held their rein firmly on community organizational life, and particularly on such agencies as the Survey Committee, which long served as the *de facto* public-relations body for the Jewish community. But when they talked about "autocracy," they were not always clear as to exactly why, if the dissidents were in large number, no remedial action was ever effectively attempted. The explanations ran variously that: the leadership was entrenched; the leadership had the money and the facilities; the atmosphere was "such as to smother" any creative activity; the body of the community was mired in a long tradition of disinterest in Jewish matters; they themselves had developed no effective leadership. Always, however, for a full explanation, it seemed necessary to add a mysterious ingredient, sometimes referred to as the San Francisco "x" factor. (Someone postulated that if a half-dozen Jews of similar background, Jewish intensity, and ideology, were settled three in Los Angeles and three in San Francisco, they would be found to be very different groups in outlook and activity after five years.)

The fact is that it took nothing less than the catalysts of Hitler and the state of Israel to bring the latent elements to a boil.

In 1943, when the extraordinary horrors of Nazi genocide in Eastern Europe reached a publicity peak, mass meetings were conducted everywhere in this country. In San Francisco, preliminary deliberations stretched over two months. A modest conference was at first suggested and it became clear that the "traditional leadership" as such was reluctant to sponsor a mass political meeting of an obtrusively Jewish nature that had no precedent in the city's history. A provisional committee was formed, and a call was sent out for representatives. A reported fifty-three organizations responded. A prominent section of the traditional leadership, including the Survey Committee, refused to participate, personally or organizationally. On June 17, 1943, at the Civic Auditorium, more than ten thousand people packed the hall to hear Thomas Mann, Eddie Cantor, and others.

Shortly afterwards, two prominent Russian Jews, Solomon Michoels and Itzik Feffer (the latter was later "liquidated"), were sent to this country by the Soviet Union, then our "staunch ally," to "bind up the American Jews into one antifascist bloc in common with the Russian Jews." They were received by public dignitaries and by Jewish communities at large meetings throughout the nation. Again, and with the Soviet stigma lending them added conviction, the "traditional leadership" declined to lend support to a mass San Francisco reception. Under the same sponsorship as the previous meeting, the Civic

Auditorium was again filled to capacity on August 31, this time for the two Russians.

The impact of these successes, and the emergence of some earnest young men of leadership caliber, led to a round of discussions and conferences on the possibility of reconstituting organizational life in the community. A United Council was formed by the "new coalition" of organizations to provide some channel for "representative community expression." This left the community in deep breach. A number of dismayed individuals immediately pressed for a compromise between the two camps. Several of the United Council groups were thrown into turmoil, and there ensued a brief period of labyrinthine political activity out of which the United Council emerged an abortion. One of their larger groups had seceded; conciliation was the apparent order of the day, the United Council was ditched, and the compromise Association of Jewish Organizations (AJO) was formed, in full convention, to include all the elements of the community.

But when the smoke cleared, the AJO was revealed as an organ of traditional policy and of traditional leadership, and the cries of "aristocracy" and "no representation" were undiminished in vigor.

There is a lot of political over-the-fencing about if and why and how the AJO is "undemocratic by constitution and intent." (Example: Should the Welfare Fund have representation, as it now does, for every one hundred twenty-five members, giving it a balance of power, although there is no voting constituency and the delegates are appointed "from the top"; if not, what about the people who would not otherwise be represented and, "Where would you get a hall big enough to hold a vote of the Fund membership anyway?")

And there is some question of how the "opposition," claiming to represent the "popular" sentiment, having been a coalition of fifty-three separate groups, and having pulled in audiences of ten thousand people at the occasion of their mass meetings, could not exercise enough control in open convention to scotch the "undemocratic" provisions of the AJO in the first place. Answers of "sinister influence," "inequality of leadership," discouragement at the demise of the United Council, probably must be supplemented by some consideration of the San Francisco "x" factor.

But the central fact was that against the first major attempt to unseat them, the Old Guard firmly maintained their role as the community leadership.

In 1948, a picket line was set up in front of the British consulate to protest the British refusal to allow debarkation of refugees in Palestine. The Survey Committee promptly dispatched a letter of apology to the consulate, disavowing the demonstration. A representative of the irate picketers wrote a letter to the public press, disavowing the apology.

In the fall of 1949, several "Where Do You Stand" and "You Are Not in Exile" anti-Zionist advertisements were paid for by the American Council for

Judaism and run in the press. The Survey Committee tried to dissuade the Council from this step, offering to publish, in lieu of the ads, a brief statement of policy under the name of the Survey Committee. The Council, however, felt that their ads should run, which they did. The Survey Committee published its own statement anyway, "in the interests of Jewish public relations in San Francisco." This statement embodied an attack on Ben Gurion and the late Daniel Frisch for remarks that they had made concerning the responsibilities of American Jews to Israel.

This incident again brought to a boil those people who felt that the Survey Committee was, in effect, acting as the public voice for the entire community, and, in this capacity, misrepresenting the community to itself and to the world at large. (The Survey Committee calls itself "the duly organized and recognized agency for public relations in the community.")

Out of this later occurrence, delegates from forty-odd organizations in the community elected a working committee of about a dozen to discuss again the problem of community organizational life. This committee is functioning currently, although not in what might be called a violently activist atmosphere. (Remember the "x" factor.) In support of its claim of being neutral in ideological questions, the Survey Committee made a balancing statement about the disruptive character of the Council ads, but this has not had any visible ameliorative effects.

Whatever the various merits or demerits of the contending parties in the present situation, partisan polemic should not be allowed to obscure the Jewish concern of the Old Guard. The leadership, as such, had an earnest sense of its patrician responsibilities to the Jewish community, in which it had great pride. It wore, with firm dignity the mantle of authority that had been handed down and feels that, as against "outsiders" and "newcomers," it understood the traditions and peculiar necessities of the local scene.

To say, as many did, that its component members were fearful of anti-Semitism, was to say merely that they are Jews. To say that out of this fearfulness they would not be averse to a withering away of the Jewish community as such, was untrue: they spent too much time, money, and sincerity on the preservation of that community. To say that they subscribed to the "craven" theory that "Jews out of sight are Jews out of mind" was untenable: they did not follow the logic of that pattern. A report of the Richmond Jews (*Commentary*, December 1949) that "they hardly ever ran for public office, and frowned on other Jews who did. They just didn't think a Jew should put himself forward." In San Francisco, they run for office, and they put themselves forward prominently as citizens of the city.

"The leadership," one of its spokesmen said, "has never acted out of fear or truckling. Quite on the contrary, it has always shown particular courage of conviction in following a line of thought . . . " That line of thought is really a kind of political philosophy for special groups in an American community: they should not unnecessarily duplicate civic functions, nor intrude on the community with their internal problems, nor, for their own sake, engage in public relations activities that will unnecessarily offend the general community.

Of course, the leadership's definition of "good public relations" had always been shaded by their general political complexion, which as of 1950 was naturally conservative and often strongly Republican. (It is now, 1989, largely Democratic, ed.) "Mass meetings and mass pressure," they insist, "can serve no useful function in San Francisco, and can only militate against the group that uses them."

The leadership pointed to its successful technique in handling anti-Semitic incidents as a blueprint for proper public relations behavior: "Once we have the facts, we contact the offender in man-to-man fashion—the American way. We explain the danger of prejudice, the unfairness of indicting a whole group, the harm it can do to a free American society."

A local radio station once broadcast the program of a well-known anti-Semite. A movement developed to prevail on all the Jewish clients of the station to cancel their advertising. The Survey Committee quelled this movement, and, instead, called the proprietor of the radio station who, after discussion, canceled the contract.

"I'm canceling this program," the station owner said, "because you came to me in a decent way and presented a decent argument. Had you moved in by threatening my business, I'd have fought you all the way."

When a bus driver used offensive language, the Committee called quietly on the personnel manager; when the temples were smeared with Columbian slogans, and the culprit's membership in a local church was traced by a private detective, they approached the priest; when a real estate concern acted out a discriminatory policy, they met with the owners in conferences lasting more than a year before convincing them, in all logic, of the error of their way.

There can be no question but that this kind of diplomatic approach to anti-Semitism in-the-fact worked effectively in San Francisco.

As for the internal life of the Jewish community, the leadership thought of itself largely in institutional terms and is proud of its accomplishments. Certainly, in general, there was no look of impoverishment as of 1949 or 1989. The orphans' home, equipped with cottages and "mothers," was a showpiece, generously endowed. The residence home for Jewish working girls was complete with all the extracurricular facilities that might be desired. There still is a home for the aged that has been described as a "veritable hotel." The Community Center is huge, thriving, and unstintingly equipped.

Critics (some of whom grew up in the East) certainly have had no quarrel with these activities so far as they go—but they felt they do not go far enough.

They felt that the leadership (and community thinking) had been too exclusively concerned with considerations of a public-relations policy, on the one hand, and of a welfare community on the other. They felt that there had been too much "local Jewish community" in the thinking and not enough Judaism. They felt that the leadership had dispatched its responsibility as far as it saw them, but that it had a minimal concept, of a Jewish community life. Finally, many of them believed that this minimal concept, no matter how sumptuously attended, would inevitably lead to the self-annihilation of the Jewish community.

These critics pointed to the disparity between the tremendous sums generally spent on philanthropic projects and the almost negligible amounts allotted to such projects Jewish education. They also deplored the paucity of activity directed towards underlining the historical mission of Judaism and the historico-mystical ties that bind Jewry to Jewry everywhere.

What they were, in fact, pointing up, objecting to, and being frightened by, is the apparent trend of a large (and the particularly "San Franciscan") section of the community, and its leadership, to slip away from the traditional moorings of Jewish life, to loosen its Jewish roots, and, in the process, eventually to blur and devitalize Judaism itself.

This kind of trend, insofar as it is a by-product of Americanization, had its evidences all over the country, but nowhere else did it involve such a large portion of the Jewish population or have such a dominating influence. Nowhere had it had such a fertile field to develop in its "laboratory" form. Nowhere had it kept such clearly defined lines or been less obscured by "recent generation" leavening. Indeed, such leavening served, more than anything else in recent years, to point up "the trend."

In defining the various segments of the Jewish community, the synagogues serve as the most convenient and the most accurate (although always approximate) focuses. Temples Emanu-El and Sherith Israel have the largest congregations in the city, a combined total of about twenty-five hundred members. They are Reform temples, and both had their origins in the pioneer year of 1849. (There is some disagreement about which was first.)

In these congregations all the lay leaders and the famed "leadership" of the community are found (when they can be found in any congregation). Temple Emanu-El has the preponderant number of first-family and wealthy-family names in the community. Its social character has remained more stable, having acquired less of the foreign (to San Francisco) element, and fewer of the "nouveaux." Symptomatically, almost all of the local members of the American Council for Judaism were affiliated with Emanu-El, almost none with Sherith Israel. One rabbi said: "Just as America will be the last citadel of capitalism, so Temple Emanu-El will be the last citadel of the kind of thing that Isaac M. Wise and Elka Cohen and Voorsanger stood for."

In general, the diminution of ceremonial intensity in religious life that has characterized the Jew (and the Christian) in America, is particularly noticeable in San Francisco. And there has been a general (not official) stretching of the Reform philosophy at its most radical points. Some of the city's religious leaders once felt that many of those who have maintained their affiliations with the temple could very well be happy in a church of different proportions; a church that would be named, say, the American Mosaic (or Monotheistic) church where people who believed in Moses' One God could convene to make their simple devotions, renew their faith in the moral tone of life, and where their children could attend Sunday school.

"Sunday school" is, indeed, a problem. Parents who have lived apart from any formal religious affiliation all their adult life (and, of course, in San Francisco, in a "mixed" neighborhood) are suddenly faced with growing children who desire to attend the neighborhood Sunday school (Baptist or whatever) along with the other children. Parents are continually approaching their rabbis with this problem, and even where long traveling distances are involved, are anxious to have their children receive Jewish Sunday school education. An interest in the drama of religion inevitably captures some of the children, and there is the recurrent spectacle of children demanding of flabbergasted parents that candles be lit on Friday night.

Culturally, this segment of the population has lost its basic contact with the historical language and literature of Judaism. Hebrew education is barely existent. The European accent is, of course, completely gone. One of the more prominent members of the community told this story: At a private affair he was attending in Los Angeles, a number of men around the table burst into strange song. "What in the world are they singing?" he asked. He was astonished to hear that they were singing Yiddish songs. That sort of thing, he said (by way of describing the temper of the city) could never have happened in San Francisco, or at least in that large part with which he was acquainted. It says a great deal that shortly after the American Council for Judaism was formed in 1943, fourteen hundred of its twenty-five hundred national members were San Franciscans. (The local membership has since disappeared.)

The rate of intermarriage is greater in San Francisco than any place else in the country. This is an inevitable result of the relative freedom of social movement. One old-timer named, offhand, children of five rabbis who intermarried in the past. It is only necessary to read the social pages of the press over the months to get a comparative index.

The really significant fact about all these various aspects of Jewish life in San Francisco is, by and large, the naturalness and matter-of-factness of their development. They are not marked by evidences of self-hatred, anti-Semitism, fear, hysteria, or other minority neuroses. This is emphasized rather than confuted by the few cases of individuals in the community who follow the more obvious and self-betraying pattern of overvehement and overemotional "150 percent, Americanism." It is the normal temper of San Francisco's old-line Jews, however deviant their behavior from old Jewish patterns, to accept their Jewishness, their deviations, and their Americanism as matters of course, without conscious design, without a special sense of urgency, without schizoid complications. This is underlined by the way they go about their business, the way they engage in civic affairs, conduct their social affairs, or talk about their Jewishness. However, it may be elsewhere, and whatever its implications for Judaism, it is necessary to recognize that in San Francisco, by and large, the features of the Jewish community are those of an adjusted Jewry, not of a maladjusted Jewry full of jitters and tensions. To many, the "adjustment" threatens much that lies near to the heart of traditional Judaism. And there is a real problem here—the problem of best integrating the old into the new. Perhaps San Francisco does not represent the ideal integration. But who, in the glass houses of other American Jewish communities, will cast the first stone?

And it is worth remembering that so far as it concerns the majority of San Francisco's older Jewish families, the most remarkable fact of San Francisco is not the vanishing (or shrinking) Jew, but on the contrary, the insistent Jew—the Jew who insists on being a San Francisco Jew despite the historical (and geographical) distance from his ethnic origins, the thorough Americanization, the complete lack of ghettoization, the social mobility, the freedom of wealth, the mutations in religious thought, and the relative isolation and absence of pressures.

This may seem strange in an area where the sentiment is strong that "Jews are members of a religion and nothing more." But one man said: "Of course I'm a Jew. I'm a Jew by religion. Is a Jew not religious because he doesn't go to temple every Friday night?" There is an overwhelming emphasis on the ethical texture, which men like this feel is unique to, and inherent in, the Jewish religion: *rachmones* or a deep-felt (not just formal or ideological) compassion for fellow men. This, along with a personal devotion to One God, they feel is the essence of the Jewish religion, and they know they are Jews because they feel it and live by it and believe in it.

Yet, on the occasion of Israel's fight for independence and its constitution as a nation, many of San Francisco's anti-Zionists were profoundly affected, and the tone of the whole community shifted perceptibly. As a matter of fact there has been recently in the "integrated circles" an intensification of religious life, as there has been in the rest of the country. This has been reflected in temple attendance and activity. And of the recently installed rabbi at Temple Emanu-El, one of the Conservative-Orthodox rabbis in town said: "He is, if anything, a more intense Jew than I am."

There are also two fair-sized Conservative congregations in town—one of which can still understand an address in Yiddish—and a scattering of Orthodox. Influenced by the same historical circumstances as the older settlers, but on a smaller scale, these people generally consider themselves integrated civically and socially into San Francisco. There is little evidence of intermarriage in their ranks, but there is a tendency for them, with the accumulation of time of residence, position, and influence, to move over to Sherith Israel, the next step on the ladder to Emanu-El. And some of those who maintain their affiliation elsewhere have liked to send their children to temple Sunday school so that, as one rabbi said, "little Sarah might grow up with and catch the eye of some little San Francisco scion."

There is, community-wide, a relatively small synagogue attendance and— compared with other large cities—a relatively light preoccupation with Jewish affairs at large. (Although, again in pattern, the Welfare Fund in San Francisco has had the reputation of having a higher percentage of contributors in relation to the population than any city but Boston.) One member of the community seriously offered as a partial explanation of the generally limited amount of synagogue activity the fact that San Francisco had such fine weather that people weren't so disposed to go to meetings or services. But considering the climate of Israel, or at the very least Los Angeles, it would seem that the predisposition to apathy owes less to the temperature of the air than to the tone of the community.

The vocal critics of the present leadership of San Francisco's Jewish community are centered mainly around several hundred people who feel strongly about traditional Judaism and world Jewish affairs. They aren't interested in excommunicating those whose personal Judaism has taken a different turn ("They are mostly good men. They have done fine things here. But because of their background they are out of step with Jewish life. A Jewish community cannot flourish without its traditions, its historical and cultural references . . . ") so much as they are interested in making their own influence felt, sponsoring activity along more traditionally religious and more Zionist lines. They feel that a different leadership would give a different, "more specifically Jewish," complexion to the community, and this is what they hope to achieve.

The "Old Guard," for its part, is not anxious to relinquish any more of the office of leadership than it has to. It is clear that they feel that it is not they who are "out of step" but their critics, who fail to recognize that Jewish life must mean something different to third-generation American Jews from what it did to their ancestors in the ghettos of Europe.

"Majority" is cried on both sides but there has been no counting of noses. (In any case, most of the noses of the community wouldn't be twitching excitedly in any direction.) At this point, "unity of expression" does not seem possible or, by any democratic standards, desirable.

The over-all character of San Francisco's community seems to be in for some "pendulum" change, however slight and however temporary. But come what may, the bulk of the Jews of San Francisco, neither vanished nor concerned with themselves as laboratory specimens, will merely thank the Lord that in whatever fashion they find it necessary to practice their Judaism, they are doing it in San Francisco.

This article was first published in *Commentary* 10 (October 1950).

15

The Pope Comes to San Francisco: An Anatomy of Jewish Communal Response to a Political Crisis

David Biale and Fred Rosenbaum

Introduction

The visit of Pope John Paul II to the United States in September 1987, less than three months after he had received accused Nazi war criminal Kurt Waldheim, provoked a major crisis in community relations for the Jews of the San Francisco Bay Area. This crisis is of general interest not only because it focused acute attention on Jewish–Christian relations, but also because it proved to be a symbolic crucible for how the Jewish community shapes policy towards an unexpected situation. In this case, as opposed to issues around Israel, Soviet Jewry, or anti-Semitism in the United States, Jewish communal policy was by no means clear cut. On the one hand, ancient hostility and suspicion of Christians remained; on the other, strong local alliances between Christians and Jews, the lack of official religious anti-Semitism, and, in the case of Catholics, the positive legacy of Vatican II all counterbalanced old hostilities. Because there is great ambiguity in how Jews feel about Christians today, the community did not have ready a collective response to the Pope's reception of Waldheim and therefore struggled to develop such a policy as events unfolded. We thus have an excellent case study of Jewish communal response to a new situation and an opportunity to evaluate the dynamics of decision-making within the community.

Our attention in this chapter is directed not toward the response of national Jewish organizations to the Pope, but toward the response of one community, that of the San Francisco Bay Area. Because John Paul II was scheduled to visit

San Francisco as part of his national tour, the local community became deeply involved in deciding how to express itself directly to the Pope. Many local elements were not content to leave Jewish diplomacy to the representatives of national Jewish organizations, but instead sought local initiatives. Indeed, some of these elements argued that the very unrepresentative nature of national Jewish organizations left many Jews without an adequate voice to express their anger and outrage at the Pope's reception of Waldheim. What emerged was a tension between the responses of national Jewish organizations and local initiatives. The desire for a local response was a reflection, in some ways, of the lack of a truly centralized and representative Jewish governing structure in the United States.

San Francisco represents a fascinating case study for several specific reasons. Although small protests against the Pope did take place in Miami and Los Angeles (the protest in Los Angeles was actually on about the same scale as in San Francisco), in no other city did the process leading up to demonstrations against the Pope become so acrimonious and develop such symbolic import. In no other city did the issue engage the organizations of the Jewish community to such a degree, and in no other city did it produce such a diverse spectrum of political expressions. It is fair to say that only in this community did the Pope's reception of Waldheim polarize and politicize the community.

It is especially striking that this struggle developed in San Francisco, long considered one of the most assimilated Jewish communities in North America, and not in one of the cities visited by the Pope with a highly visible Jewish population. Why was it that only in this community did a militant response develop against the Vatican, a response that also sought to challenge the established leadership of the organized community? Was it, perhaps, the very image of the communal leadership as assimilated and as particularly close to the Catholic elite of the city that engendered such a strong reaction?

In addition, the crisis revealed that the active Jewish community of the Bay Area was much larger and more diverse than the organized community. The sentiments of this larger community, influenced, in part, by the strong culture of protest that characterizes the Bay Area, were often very different from those of the establishment organizations.

The struggle in the Bay Area over who would control the community's response and what that response would be uncovered underlying tensions within the community. These tensions tell us much about the nature of the internal politics of the Jewish community; they also have much to tell us about the symbolic language in which the Jewish community conducts its business.

In the pages that follow, we first present a chronology of events from the point of view of the organs of the established Jewish community, in particular the Jewish Community Relations Council (JCRC). We then turn to an examination of the roles of key players in the political drama who came from outside the establishment: *Tikkun Magazine* and the Holocaust survivor community. In the next section, we consider the response of the rabbinate. We conclude with some reflections on the larger meaning of this case study of Jewish communal relations.

Community Organizations

Although the Pope met Waldheim on June 25, 1987, half a month transpired before the San Francisco Jewish community realized the nature and magnitude of the political crisis it faced. On July 10, the *Northern California Jewish Bulletin*, with a circulation of 23,500 and the only Jewish weekly in the area, launched the issue that would be its major news story for the next ten weeks. The *Bulletin* was to keep the issue alive by giving a forum to a variety of voices at a time when some establishment organizations would have preferred to ignore the controversy. *Bulletin* editor and publisher Marc Klein had not shied away from controversial copy since coming to San Francisco in 1984, and his extensive coverage of the community's response to the Pope's visit would be a further indication of his independence, despite the fact of a large subvention from the local Federation. The gadfly role that the newspaper played suggests how Jewish newspapers can open up the political life of the community by giving a forum to elements outside of the establishment and by creating issues that might otherwise be buried.

The initial article, written by News Editor Peggy Isaak Gluck, in a sense created the controversy by focusing on Mayor Dianne Feinstein's plans to hold a fundraising dinner for the papal visit on July 23 in her home. Mayor Feinstein herself represented the singular character of the Jewish elite of this area: half Jewish by birth, raised as a Catholic but married to a Jew, the mayor found herself caught between the desire to defend Jewish interests and an equal desire not to offend the Catholic population. On the one hand, the mayor hosted the fundraising dinner that was to generate much controversy. But she also wrote and signed a number of letters to the Catholic Church protesting the reception of Waldheim.

In addition to the mayor and her husband, the article named five prominent Jewish leaders on the fundraising committee and included brief remarks from four of them defending their continued willingness to serve. One, the hotel magnate and real estate developer, Melvin Swig, was known for his leadership in the Federation and his generous support for Jewish causes abroad. But Swig, like the mayor, was also tied to the Catholic community by strong personal and philanthropic ties. In particular, Swig served as chair of the Board of Trustees of the University of San Francisco, a Jesuit institution, and had fostered the creation of a Jewish studies program there.

Gluck's article mentioned a letter expressing Jewish concerns over the Waldheim meeting sent by the JCRC president Andrew Colvin to the Papal nuncio in Washington, D.C., and revealed that a meeting had taken place on June 27 between the Archbishop of San Francisco, John Quinn, and several local Jewish organizational heads. But Gluck's piece also included a rough outline of plans to protest against the Pope being made outside the Jewish establishment. Specifically rejecting meetings or letters as "not the answer," Michael Lerner, the editor of the left-wing *Tikkun* magazine, went on to call for "massive" demonstrations in the streets, in order to transcend American Jewry's "orgy of civility," a phrase he would repeat frequently throughout the crisis.

The leadership of the JCRC was deeply angered and troubled by Lerner's plans and the publicity he was receiving not only in the *Bulletin*, but also in shorter articles in the mass-circulation dailies. The JCRC's director, Rita Semel was worried that a militant demonstration would harm the excellent relations between Jews and Catholics that had been built painstakingly over the decades. Moreover, she and several of her leading lay people had concerns that the media would be unable to distinguish the Jewish protest from the loud and irreverent demonstration sure to be mounted by the city's disaffected homosexual population.

Semel was appalled to learn, only after the fact, of a press conference Lerner held outside St. Mary's Cathedral on July 15. Accompanied by Carol Ruth Silver, a liberal member of the San Francisco Board of Supervisors, he asked the Archdiocese for the Cathedral itself in which to hold a teach-in the night of the Pope's visit. A long telephone conversation with the mayor, livid over Lerner's plans to picket her house at the time of the fundraising dinner, served to convince Semel that Lerner needed to be contained at all costs. Semel and other JCRC leaders were loath to give a forum to Lerner, whom they regarded as a "loose cannon," with no ties to any recognized organization. Semel and others saw Lerner not as the representative of a Jewish organization, but as a self-promoter trying to sell magazines.

This perception raised the larger question of what constitutes a Jewish organization. This is a central question for community relations councils, which claim to be umbrella institutions made up of all organizations within the Jewish community. Yet, it is clear that some groups are regarded as within the pale while others are not. For example, a bitter battle was waged in the Community Relations Council in Seattle over whether to admit the New Jewish Agenda, a left-wing Jewish organization, to membership in the Council. The group's request for membership was defeated by an overwhelming majority. Although Lerner's *Tikkun* was not an organization with a membership, some of the same reluctance to expand the "umbrella" of the JCRC characterized the response to Lerner in San Francisco.

An additional charge made by Semel and others against Lerner was that he was an "outside agitator" who had crossed the Bay from Oakland (where *Tikkun* is published) to intrude himself for opportunisitc reasons into the delicate fabric of Jewish–Catholic relations in San Francisco. This particular charge was wrapped up in the peculiar historical demography of the Bay Area Jewish community, in which the much wealthier and more assimilated San Francisco community, dominated originally by German Jews, at times finds itself at odds with the East Bay community, with far fewer of the old pioneer families. Like the tensions between Manhattan and Brooklyn, the San Francisco–East Bay divide molded some of the mutual perceptions.

Although Semel reluctantly allowed Lerner's wife, Nan Fink, the publisher of *Tikkun*, to attend the first of the JCRC planning meetings, she refused to involve the editor himself in any part of the process of framing Bay Area Jewry's response to the Pope. At all subsequent meetings, *Tikkun* was not represented.

The first phase in the crisis culminated with the fundraising dinner at the mayor's house. As a result of personal appeals by a number of influential members of the community, all of the prominent Jews on the fundraising community withdrew. Melvin Swig did so publicly, making his views known in the *San Francisco Chronicle* and on local television. Not a single Jew, with the exception of the mayor and her husband, attended the dinner. One prominent Jew returned his invitation with the words "you've got to be kidding." Others rejected appeals for money from the Archdiocese's fundraisers. It had become clear that the wealthy Jewish elite of the city, despite its strong personal ties to the Catholic community, had formed a consensus to boycott the Pope's visit. Although it is unclear exactly how this change in opinion took place, it is likely that activists in the JCRC as well as all the publicity played the major roles in persuading these wealthy Jews to abandon the Catholics.

Despite the Jewish withdrawal from the fundraising dinner, the event was picketed by about fifty Jews, perhaps half of them Holocaust survivors, including Dr. Michael Thaler, president of the Holocaust Center of Northern California. Thaler and Lerner, who was also present with a small contingent, exchanged words with the mayor and her husband on the front porch of the mayor's home. Local television stations covered the confrontation, but the protestors were dismayed at the next morning's *San Francisco Chronicle*, which gave more than equal billing to the outrageously costumed homosexuals and prostitutes who demonstrated at the same time. This article was to be an omen for the press coverage during the Pope's visit itself.

On August 3, the JCRC held a second meeting, attended by Thaler, who gave a provocative speech and pushed the group toward a more militant position. Indeed, even before the meeting, the JCRC had prepared a declaration expressing dismay at the Pope's "unqualified reception of Waldheim," and urged the

Church to further Holocaust education and recognize the state of Israel. Those at the meeting ceremoniously signed the declaration, and it was soon endorsed by the mayor and circulated both locally and by community relations councils in the other cities on John Paul II's tour.

The more militant tone at this meeting was also the result of a pastoral letter written by Archbishop John Quinn and circulated at the meeting. The Archbishop took a defensive tone in which he justified the Pope's reception of Waldheim, the lack of recognition of Israel, and Vatican actions during the Holocaust. Taken altogether, all these arguments added up in the eyes of the Jewish leaders to a refusal to understand why the Jewish community felt so strongly. As opposed to other Catholic leaders elsewhere who had deplored the reception of Waldheim, Quinn's apology for the Pope poured oil on the fire locally. It is possible that a different letter might have had a more conciliatory effect, at least on the mainstream leadership.

The participants at the JCRC meeting agreed on a number of activities, including a vigil and educational forums, and encouraged the JCRC to advertise and help plan a series of community events. Although the gathering broke up without taking a position on the appropriateness of militant demonstrations, it was widely felt that no Jewish response, short of violence, should be repudiated by other Jews. Those at the meeting persuaded the JCRC to remove a statement explicitly disapproving demonstrations in the streets that had initially appeared on its set of guidelines on the issue.

In late August and early September, John Paul II made several attempts to mollify the American Jewish community, including a letter on the Holocaust to Archbishop May of St. Louis and meetings with Jewish leaders in Castel Gandolfo in Italy and, later, in Miami on the first leg of his U.S. tour. Although these gestures were welcomed locally by Andrew Colvin of the JCRC, they were roundly condemned by Lerner, Thaler, and other community figures. Two long articles in the *Bulletin* on the Miami meeting starkly revealed the sharp differences of opinion that had emerged between the Jews of the Bay Area and the national Jewish leadership. One piece, by the Jewish Telegraphic Agency, was headlined "Miami papal meeting called success by Jewish leaders," while a local article bore the title "Pope's message miffs local Jews."

When the Pope arrived on September 17, he was greeted by a JCRC declaration, which was presented to the Archdiocese with 3,000 signatures and half-page advertisements, with pictures of Holocaust victims, in the morning and afternoon dailies. Eight major events were held by Jewish organizations in the week of the papal visit, including five teach-ins or educational forums, two vigils (a shiva at St. and a JCRC-sponsored gathering at the Holocaust memorial) and the *Tikkun* demonstration. All of the community events except Lerner's teach-in and demonstration were advertised by the JCRC.

Despite the generally high quality of these events, the combined attendance at all of them numbered a little over a thousand, far fewer than came to a single rally for Soviet Jewry held the following month. Could this, then, have been a case in which leaders (including those outside the establishment) created an issue that did not strike a chord among the bulk of the over 200,000 Jews of the Bay Area? While sentiments were undoubtedly strong over the Pope's reception of Waldheim, they were not strong enough to turn out thousands for a street demonstration or teach-ins.

The *Bulletin* devoted much of its September 25 issue to an evaluation of the effectiveness of the prior week's protests, and included Andrew Colvin's conclusion that "the community came together as one in sentiment on (the Pope's visit) but allowed different elements to express the sentiment in different ways." In fact, there was deep disunity and even rancor at times, not only between those who wanted a strong protest and those who did not, but also among the militants themselves.

The JCRC acted as a force for unity only in part. While early in the process it tried to "keep the lid on," as one of its executives put it, and insure a very measured and restrained response, it was later flexible enough to adopt a more activist position when pressed by other segments of the community, most notably Holocaust survivors. It expended much energy in excluding the "outsider" Lerner from participating in the official decision-making process, but could not prevent him, as the subject of an enormous amount of attention in the press, from playing a highly visible role during the entire crisis.

The ability of dissident elements in the Jewish community to turn to the general press is a reality of Jewish life in late twentieth-century America, and it is unrealistic of official community relations organizations to try to prevent it. Indeed, the essence of Jewish political life today is based on use of the general media, as is manifested by the way the various political factions in the Jewish community turn to the press either to support or criticize Israel.

With the exception of Lerner, however, the JCRC had embarked by the end of July on a course of coordinating, advertising, and even subsidizing a large array of events. Yet it lost the initiative at the outset by failing to identify the significance of the issue and the necessity to provide clear leadership even in the role of a facilitator.

Tikkun Magazine

As we have seen, the singular developments that took place in San Francisco owed a great deal to the activities of two groups: *Tikkun* magazine and the Holocaust survivor community. *Tikkun* magazine was established in 1986 as a national journal of progressive political and cultural opinion with a specifically Jewish orientation. In its initial advertising, *Tikkun* posed as a liberal alternative to the neoconservative *Commentary* magazine. *Tikkun*'s editor, Michael Lerner, was a veteran of the New Left, having served as one of the founders of Students for a Democratic Society and as an editor of the now-defunct *Ramparts* magazine. Lerner, now in his mid-forties, had been a well-known figure on the Left in the Bay Area for the last two decades, but *Tikkun* represented his first major Jewish enterprise.

Several months before the Pope received Waldheim, Lerner had planned to use the September 1987 issue of *Tikkun* to confront the Pope on a host of general social and political issues. This issue was timed to coincide with the Pope's visit to the United States, and Lerner planned to encourage Jews to join with others in demonstrations against the Pope. The general argument he planned was that the Catholic Church's positions on abortion, birth control, and so forth have an impact on American politics and, therefore, Jews, as American citizens, have a stake in Vatican dogma. At this point, no specifically Jewish issue seemed involved with the Pope's upcoming visit.

The Waldheim Affair did not instigate Lerner's plan to call for demonstrations against the Pope, but it did change his whole emphasis. Now the issue became primarily a Jewish one. From the outset, Lerner envisioned a street demonstration. He later appended a teach-in. With his press conference in front of St. Mary's Cathedral, Lerner succeeded in bringing the issue to public attention before any other Jewish group mobilized to consider its response. Lerner's moves, which were well reported in the press, immediately drew attention to the role of *Tikkun*, and gave Lerner control of the issue; the organized Jewish community found itself on the defensive.

Lerner made it clear from the outset that he regarded the organized Jewish community, because of its close ties to the Catholic elite in San Francisco, as unwilling to take a principled stand on the Pope. In Lerner's view, the question of how to respond to the Pope pitted the "Jewish monied elite" against militants. The Jewish establishment was, by definition, incapable of taking a bold position on the issue, and no coalition with mainstream Jewish groups was worth considering. This was to be his position in editorials, advertisements, and speeches, and would introduce an element of polarization that might otherwise have been lacking. Thus, as a result of a virtual mutual ban, neither the JCRC nor *Tikkun* was willing to coordinate its activities with the other.

The isolation of *Tikkun* was a result of a Jewish community policy, but it was an isolation that *Tikkun* welcomed, for it fit neatly into the ideological baggage that Lerner brought with him. This baggage included a particular view of *Tikkun* that went far beyond what is usually associated with a magazine or journal of opinion. Lerner had set out to do more than establish a journal; his goal was to create a political and cultural movement. He believed that liberal and progressive groups in the Jewish community have been politically and intellectually disenfranchised: they do not find representation in Jewish organizations, and they do not have a voice in the media. He wished not only to make *Tikkun* that voice, but also to mobilize the constituency of *Tikkun* for political purposes. The Pope's visit was his first opportunity to step outside of the magazine and lead this constituency. His action introduced to the Jewish community a new concept, one that was, by definition, based on rejection of the "organized" community.

Why was this issue so important for Lerner? Why did the editor of a new magazine, burdened with deadlines and enormous financial expenses, choose to devote several months and considerable resources (estimated in the vicinity of $20,000–25,000) on a demonstration against the Pope? Several factors, in our judgment, led to this virtual obsession.

First, Lerner saw the issue of the Pope and Waldheim as an excellent opportunity for *Tikkun* to establish its Jewish credentials. The June issue of *Tikkun* was devoted to the twentieth anniversary of Israel's occupation of the West Bank and Gaza. His radical position against the occupation opened up *Tikkun* to criticism for undermining Jewish interests. By leading the attack on the Pope, he felt that *Tikkun* could legitimate its criticisms of Israel. Thus, one advertisement proclaimed: "The Catholic Church has been responsible for the deaths of more Jews than the PLO." Why, then, it went on, was the leadership of the Jewish community unwilling to meet with PLO leaders while it found no difficulty in meeting with the Pope? *Tikkun*'s advertisements for the demonstration adopted a shrill nationalist tone that must have surprised many of its left-wing readers, as well as conflicting with the more balanced tone of the magazine itself.

More importantly, because Lerner believed that the Jewish community would not dare to antagonize the Catholic Church, and because he rejected the efforts of national Jewish representatives at dialogue with the Vatican, the issue became for him the symbol of a fight against a corrupt establishment. Both the rhetoric and the tactics he adopted were borrowed directly from the experience of the 1960s. For instance, one advertisement taken out in the *East Bay Express* proclaimed: "Passivity in the face of Papal Power? Oppose the Orgy of Servility."

More specifically, Lerner found an impetus to advance a theory of Diaspora Jewish power. The accommodationist posture of Diaspora Jewish leaders throughout the Middle Ages had culminated in the scandal of the Jewish Councils during the Holocaust. Israel had taught the Jewish people that it must stand up for itself. If it is illegitimate for Jews to express their righteous anger against the Pope, then they had might as well move to Israel. In other words, only by demonstrating against the Pope, the traditional symbol of Gentile authority, could Lerner justify living in the Diaspora. An attack on the Jewish establishment was a necessary corollary to a demonstration against the Pope:

both symbols of authority had to be rejected in order to carve out an assertive Jewish presence in America.

For Lerner, the issue of the Pope thus became symbolically overlaid with his career of struggle against establishments and, particularly, the American Jewish establishment. This explains why what was an issue of restrained passion for most American Jews became for him an obsession. It also explains his absolute need to stake out *Tikkun*'s position over and against that of the Jewish community—even those elements that agreed with him—to insist on *Tikkun*'s total leadership, and to deny that the community was capable of anything but a "wimpy" response, as he put it.

In the final analysis, it is hard to judge whether Lerner's claim to speak for a voiceless constituency in the Jewish world was correct. It is likely that the anger he expressed at the Pope did represent what many Jews felt, although it is not clear that they saw him as the only voice presenting this position. What is more certain is that few were willing to respond to his call for a street demonstration: only a few hundred people showed up the night of the Pope's visit, and of the four hundred or so at the teach-in, a substantial number were either from the homosexual demonstration or were members of the First Unitarian church, where the teach-in took place. Notably missing were the liberal Jewish professionals and intellectuals who form the backbone of *Tikkun*'s readership. But even if Lerner failed to turn his magazine into a political movement around the Pope's visit, he did serve as one of the important catalysts in creating the unique response of the San Francisco community.

Holocaust Survivors

A second, and, in our view, even more important, catalyst in the Bay Area was the Holocaust survivor community. As opposed to *Tikkun*, the survivors were included in the deliberations of the JCRC and played a critical role in maneuvering that body to take a more militant position than it might have otherwise. The survivors who took the most militant stance, like *Tikkun*, considered themselves outsiders and repeatedly leveled severe criticisms against the perceived community leaders—both lay and professional—for undue timidity. As in the case of *Tikkun*, this perceived outsider status and the sense of militancy it engendered were important in setting the tone in responses to the Pope's visit.

It must first be noted that the survivor community is split between a number of groups, and the underlying tensions between these groups were brought to the surface by the Pope's visit. One group, the Holocaust Remembrance Committee, is an official committee of the JCRC. Led by William Lowenberg, a prominent real estate developer and member of the United States Holocaust Commission, this committee met very early on and decided on a stance of "dignified silence" in response to the Pope's visit. Lowenberg argued in meetings of the JCRC for ignoring the Pope entirely. This position was regarded by more militant elements as essentially a sell-out. In fact, however, our sources in the Catholic Archdiocese informed us that the boycott by Jews invited to the mass in Candlestick Park (the equivalent of Lowenberg's "dignified silence") made more of an impression on the local Church than did the street demonstrations.

A sociological analysis of the Committee on Remembrance would probably show that this group represented those survivors who had become relatively wealthy and well integrated in American society. The second group of Holocaust survivors, which took the more militant stance, was perhaps less economically successful and assimilated. This group was composed mainly of survivors active in the Holocaust Center of Northern California, which operates a small library and study center. The board of directors held a meeting of their own on July 28 to which a few observers were invited, notably Rita Semel of the JCRC. At this meeting, the survivors argued for a strong, militant response to the Pope's visit and castigated the JCRC for its alleged passivity. Although the JCRC had played a small role in the creation of the Holocaust Center, its members felt that the "downtown Jews" paid little attention to their interests. The group decided on a variety of activities, including large ads in the *Chronicle* and *Examiner* on the day of the Pope's visit, a shiva at St. Mary's Cathedral, and demonstrations along the papal route.

It was also clear to those who attended this meeting that this survivor group was operating quite independently of *Tikkun*, and although they merged their efforts at the time of the Pope's visit, the survivors had little in common with Michael Lerner's efforts. Indeed, politically, the leaders of the survivor group lean more toward the right-wing in American and Jewish politics (especially with regard to Israel) than toward the left.

Once again, we are struck by the question why it was in San Francisco and not in any other city that Holocaust survivors took such a militant position. In Los Angeles, which has a much larger survivor community, survivors did not organize a demonstration; rather, it was the children of survivors who instigated the demonstration that did take place. Although sentiments within the survivor community in Los Angeles were undoubtedly as great, they did not lead to the same activism as in San Francisco.

One explanation must lie in an observation we have already made: that the San Francisco survivors, particularly in the Holocaust Center, felt alienated from the Jewish community establishment, and this sense of alienation impelled them toward greater militancy on the occasion of this unique opportunity. Had they felt themselves already central to communal policy-making—as did William Lowenberg, a former president of the San Francisco Jewish Federation—they might have taken a more moderate position.

An additional factor, as was the case with *Tikkun*, was the particular personality of the central figure in the group. In the case of the Holocaust Center survivors, this was Michael Thaler, a survivor from Poland and presently a professor of pediatrics at the University of California at San Francisco. Thaler was relatively unknown in the Jewish community before the summer of 1987, but he made an extremely strong impression in all the forums in which he appeared. Articulate, and motivated by a clear ideological position, he offered a sharper analysis and more coherent program than any of the other participants in policy-making meetings. In essence, Thaler argued that the Pope's reception of Waldheim was a symbolic turning point and that San Francisco Jews bore a responsibility to the whole Jewish world. Thaler emphasized in particular that by establishing churches and convents at Nazi death camps in Poland, the Church was trying to erase the singular suffering of the Jews. But not only was the memory of the Holocaust at stake, for anti-Semitism in countries like Austria was on the rise, but the Pope had aligned himself with these forces by receiving Waldheim. Thaler gave the impression that these events were for him the most important crisis facing the Diaspora Jewish community since the Holocaust. His tactical position was, if anything, more militant than that of Michael Lerner, and he even publicly considered the possibility of civil disobedience during the Pope's visit.

Thaler's own biography may help in understanding why he took such a militant stance while many other survivors, as upset as they undoubtedly were at the legitimation of Waldheim, appeared less impassioned. Born in 1934 near Lvov, Poland, Thaler was hidden as a child during the Holocaust by a Catholic family, under whose influence he espoused to Catholicism. He was forced to leave this refuge several times as a result of denunciations by collaborators, including the village priest. He remained a devout Catholic until after the liberation, but had returned to Judaism well before his bar mitzvah in 1947 in a displaced-persons camp.

Without entering into a psychological analysis, for which we do not possess sufficient information, it is clear that Thaler's personal relationship to Catholicism, and particularly to Polish Catholicism, must be very complex. Saved by Catholics but also witness to the anti-Semitic streak in Polish Catholicism, it is likely that his experience must have played a role in his obsession with the Polish Pope.

Under Thaler's leadership, the Holocaust survivors pushed the JCRC toward a more militant position. Although that body never formally endorsed the survivors' demonstration in front of St. Mary's Cathedral or their shiva vigil in front of the Cathedral, it did cooperate with them on an advertisement in the *San Francisco Chronicle* and on a vigil at the Holocaust Memorial. It is unlikely that the JCRC would have taken as public a position as it did without the constant agitation by the survivors. In addition, the president and executive director of the San Francisco Jewish Federation issued a joint "personal statement" of support for the survivors' demonstrations.

In early September, Thaler arranged a meeting with Archbishop Quinn, which was attended by two other survivors as well as Rabbi Robert Kirschner of Temple Emanu-El. The survivors presented their personal stories to the Catholic leader, who appeared to be profoundly moved. Group pictures were taken, and Thaler declared afterwards that the meeting had been a total success. But Thaler was less interested in defusing the situation than in presenting the survivors' point of view. The Archbishop, for his part, was distressed that the meeting with the survivors did not result in a cancellation of plans for demonstrations. Here was a clear instance of the totally different perceptions and expectations of the two sides.

Thaler's evaluation of this meeting as a success was based on his belief that survivors are the only Jews who can communicate Jewish concerns about the Holocaust directly to the Church. He must have felt that this meeting contrasted favorably with what he considered the servile meetings of national Jewish leaders with the Pope in Italy and Miami. Here was a concept of the Holocaust survivors as the true leaders and spokespersons for the American Jewish community.

The role that the survivors played in formulating community policy points out what a force they have become in Jewish politics. Although we have argued that part of their militancy came from a feeling of exclusion, once they participated in policy-making meetings their presence could not be ignored. Their argument, which, at times, was even made explicitly, was that American Jews had abandoned them during the Holocaust and that the community should not do so again. The joint statement by the president and executive director of the San Francisco Federation echoed Thaler's plea at the JCRC meeting of August 3: "The survivors of the Holocaust stood alone once. They must never stand alone again."

Guilt on the part of American Jews about their behavior during the Holocaust, rightly or wrongly, has given the survivors increasingly a more central voice, which they certainly did not have up until a decade ago. The very fact that Elie Wiesel is the closest to an official spokesperson that the Jewish community has also points out how important survivors are in American Jewish life. Whether this development ultimately is healthy for rational policy-making is a question we do not propose to answer, but became clear in the events we are describing that it is a factor that needs to be recognized.

The Bay Area Rabbinate

One of the most striking aspects of the crisis was the lack of involvement of the area's rabbis, approximately a hundred men and women who, in the past, had played a much more visible role in regard to such issues as Soviet Jewry, Israel, and the Holocaust. One reason for their conspicuous absence was certainly the timing of Waldheim's visit to the Vatican—late June—which coincided with the beginning of the vacation period for most congregational rabbis. Moreover, the hectic days preceding John Paul II's visit to the city on September 17 came just before Rosh Hashanah, the busiest time of year for most rabbis.

Yet there were other, more important factors at work as well. Rabbi Malcolm Sparer, Executive Director of the Northern California Board of Rabbis, might have been expected to urge a tough responsa to the papal visit. Instead, Sparer took a conciliatory position, largely due to his friendship with the Archbishop, the closest of any Jewish leader in the city, which remained unharmed even by Quinn's pastoral letter of July 29. After consulting with other Jewish leaders, Sparer did refuse the invitation of the Archdiocese to appear in a videotaped greeting to the Pope, to be played prior to the papal mass in Candlestick Park (an event boycotted totally by those Jews invited to attend). But if he would not greet the Pope, Sparer was more staunchly opposed to protesting the leader of the Catholic Church. He was even more incensed by plans to picket the mayor's house during the fundraising dinner, arguing on the basis of Jewish law that a person's home should remain private. Sparer was clearly concerned, as were many other rabbis, that interfaith relations would be severely damaged by a militant response to the Pope.

A number of rabbis devoted High Holiday sermons to the issue, but, with one notable exception (to be discussed below), none played a role in shaping the community's response to the Pope. A meeting of the East Bay Council of Rabbis on August 17 revealed a dearth of strong feelings on the issue and the lack of a prepared response. The Pope's reception of Waldheim and the whole question of how to relate to the Vatican over such matters clearly did not fall within the prior ideological or theological commitments of these rabbis; like many others in the Jewish community, they were taken by surprise and were not prepared to grapple with an unexpected crisis.

For one local rabbi, however, the occasion of the Pope's visit proved to be the greatest crisis of his decade in the rabbinate—in his own words, "something seismic." Because this chapter of the story is so dramatic and symbolic of the tensions within the community, we shall devote some attention to it. Robert Kirschner, still in his mid-thirties, had become the senior rabbi at San Francisco's largest and oldest congregation, Temple Emanu-El, only a year earlier, having served for four years in the posts of assistant and, later, associate rabbi. The editor and translator of a volume of rabbinic responsa during the Holocaust, and a doctoral candidate at University of California at Berkeley, Kirschner's mastery of classical and modern Hebrew texts distinguished him as one of the leading intellects among the Reform movement's younger generation.

During the High Holidays of 1986, his outspoken sermons on the AIDS epidemic demonstrated his willingness to face difficult and controversial issues from the pulpit.

Kirschner was also a member of the national editorial board of *Tikkun*, despite serious objections from a handful of leading Emanu-El congregants. Early in 1987, the rabbi himself had expressed misgivings about the "shrill" tone of the periodical, but he still held Michael Lerner and the journal in high esteem. Yet Lerner did not succeed in his initial attempt to enlist Kirschner in the cause of a militant protest to the Pope's visit. Like Sparer, Kirschner enjoyed warm relations with the Archbishop, who had sat on the bimah during his installation the previous summer, and who, in April 1987, had participated in an interfaith Holocaust Day service held in the cathedral. Kirschner, along with other Jewish leaders, had attended a private meeting with Quinn at the beginning of the crisis in which the Archbishop indicated that he would convey Jewish concerns to the Vatican. Kirschner had even spoken to the Archbishop a year earlier about asking the Pope to speak at Temple Emanu-El. Kirschner clearly saw himself as a link in the tradition of ecumenism at the synagogue, the stance taken by each of the ten rabbis who preceded him since the founding of the congregation in Gold Rush times. It seemed to the rabbi that Lerner's theatrical plans were simply inappropriate and possibly counterproductive.

Within a few short weeks, Kirschner would rethink his position and emerge as one of the most forceful voices of protest. While Lerner's tenacity played an important role in his thinking, Michael Thaler, an Emanu-El congregant, was even more decisive for Kirschner. His own scholarly work on the Holocaust made him feel that although he did not come from a family of survivors, he could not desert these people if they chose to demonstrate publicly.

Moreover, Kirschner's faith in ecumenism was crushed on July 29 when he read Quinn's pastoral letter. He felt as if Quinn had betrayed him personally by defending the Pope's reception of Waldheim and praising the role of Pope Pius XII during the Holocaust. Kirschner would later convey directly to Quinn his "deep, personal disappointment" at the time of the meeting between the Holocaust survivors and the Archbishop.

The rabbi also came to the conclusion, over the strong objections of Rita Semel, that Emanu-El's large sanctuary would be the appropriate site for Lerner's teach-in, thus making it a truly communitywide event. But on this point he backed down after a phone call from JCRC President Andrew Colvin, another of his congregants. Still, Kirschner cooperated with Lerner in two important respects: he agreed not to hold a competing meeting even at Emanu-El and, more importantly, accepted the invitation to speak at the *Tikkun* teach-in at the Unitarian Church.

To be sure, Kirschner was not pleased with the format of that event, and he actually walked out on the long, rambling talk by the irreverent *Examiner* columnist Warren Hinckle, who had been asked at the last minute to open the program. But he returned to deliver a blistering attack on the anti-Judaism of the Catholic Church, and read his own translation of a bitter poem by the Hebrew poet Uri Zvi Greenberg, *Under the Tooth of the Plough*, a searing indictment of Gentile insensitivity to the murder of the Eastern European Jews.

Kirschner's mood in these days was one of increasing anger at the non-Jewish world and at those in the Jewish community, like his rabbinical colleagues, who seemed to him strangely quiet at what he regarded as a crucial historical moment. At an interfaith forum at the Graduate Theological Union in Berkeley, he appeared angry and aggressive to the largely Christian audience, a stance quite uncharacteristic of him previously.

Kirschner's anger peaked five days after the Pope left San Francisco, on the eve of Rosh Hashanah. Before two separate services of nearly 4,000 people, he repeated the address he had given to Lerner's teach-in, demanding "a new beginning, a true departure from (the) 2,000-year litany of sorrows" that Jews had suffered at the hands of the Church. He drew a parallel between the credibility that Pius IX had conferred upon Hitler with the Concordat of 1933 and the legitimizing of Waldheim more than fifty years later by John Paul II. He concluded in a tone approaching belligerence:

> Let the Church at least understand: the people of Israel lives—not in shadow, not in degradation, but in our own place in the sun. We recognize your beliefs—but not as the fulfillment of ours. We grant you respect—but not at the price of ours. We welcome your friendship—but not if it means betraying the memory of six million Jews, who have already been betrayed enough.

The sermon drew applause, a rarity during a worship service, and the response that followed was extraordinary. For many of the congregants, much like the rabbi himself, it had a cathartic effect, releasing feelings of rage that had been bottled up for many weeks. In the next few days, Kirschner received ninety letters expressing appreciation for the sermon, a number of them from among the community's most influential lay leaders.

Amidst all of the praise, Kirschner felt increasingly uneasy about the sermon and came to the judgment that it had constituted the most serious mistake of his entire rabbinate, and that he had betrayed his calling and himself. Carried away by the current of anger, he felt that he had neglected the unique role of his congregation in fostering interfaith relations. On a more personal level, he was "devastated" when he realized how deeply his sermon had hurt dozens of intermarried couples in the synagogue that evening. Kirschner wept when he learned of a specific case in which a Catholic woman, accompanying her Jewish husband to the temple for the first time, became distraught upon hearing the sermon and, convinced that Jews regularly preach hatred of Christianity, vowed never to return to the synagogue again. Other mixed couples put letters under his office door, informing him, in several instances, that his remarks had driven a wedge between husband and wife.

Convinced that he had to attempt to right the wrong he had committed, Kirschner chose Kol Nidre, the eve of Yom Kippur, to apologize to his congregation. Although many would later speak of the unusual sermon as a "retraction," in actuality, Kirschner did not take back any of the arguments he had made ten days earlier about the Church's persecution of the Jews. His main theme was that his sermon on Rosh Hashanah had not been "offered in the proper spirit":

> What should have been spoken in love was spoken in anger. What should have been said in hope was said with bitterness. For this error, I . . . have come back to the very same place to ask the Holy One, blessed be He, for His forgiveness, and you for yours.

He reflected eloquently upon anger as "a symptom, not a cure," and added:

> When anger runs too deep, it singes the borders of the heart. When it runs too deep for too long, it burns out the lining of the soul.

The reaction to this address was largely negative. Although a number of congregants were impressed with the rabbi's courage, many felt that he had simply recanted his earlier assertation, and unfounded rumors had him capitulating to pressure from the Temple's Board of Directors. In particular, many Holocaust survivors were angered at the second sermon, and two shouted insults at him outside the Temple on Yom Kippur day. Kirschner's office received over two hundred letters of disapproval during the next two months.

The intensity of Kirschner's response to the Pope's visit, although atypical among the rabbis, reveals the powerful emotional symbolism generated during the crisis. The full circle he traveled personally from ecumenism to defense of Jewish memory and back to ecumenism symbolizes the profound tensions between tolerance and exclusiveness that characterize Jewish identity in an open society. Kirschner's oscillation between these two poles reflects the struggle that the community as a whole underwent in response to the Pope's reception of Waldheim, and accurately captures the ambivalence with which Jews who are conscious of their history must necessarily feel in confronting contemporary Christianity.

Conclusion

At the beginning of this chapter we asked why it was that only in San Francisco did the Pope's visit become a crisis in Jewish community relations. In light of the analysis we have presented, two general answers can be suggested. First, the Bay Area is one of the most politically liberal centers in the country and, although the Jewish protest against the Pope brought together people from all parts of the political spectrum, a liberal culture of protest is perhaps more deep-rooted here than anywhere else. Although many Jews had no wish to be associated with the much noisier demonstrations of homosexuals and lesbians, both actions were products of the tradition of political demonstrations that is virtually unique to this area.

In addition to this culture of protest, certain structural peculiarities of the Bay Area Jewish community made it particularly vulnerable to the kind of polarization by determined individuals that we have described. Rightly or wrongly, the San Francisco community is perceived as governed by a small, very wealthy, highly assimilated elite. A large proportion of the annual fund of the Jewish Federation is given by a small number of families, some of which go back to the days of the Gold Rush. In no other community is this elite so intermarried, especially with Catholics. Although our research on this issue suggests that the views of this elite were not as accommodationist as the militants believed, this prevailing image of the leadership was critical in mobilizing the protest. Both the circle around *Tikkun* and the Holocaust survivors saw themselves as outsiders battling an unrepresentative communal establishment.

While it is difficult to assess the claim that the established Jewish organizations do not represent the community, it is worth noting that a recent demographic study of the Bay Area Jewish community discovered that the number of Jews in the region may be around 225,000, or some 50 percent more than had been believed. In other words, there are large numbers of unaffiliated Jews who were essentially unknown to the Jewish establishment. While many of these Jews are undoubtedly even more assimilated than the organized community, it is also likely that some fraction of them do not find their Jewish identity expressed by the existing organizations. Yet, it would be hard to argue that any of the active forces in the Pope controversy spoke for these unaffiliated Jews. It was more the perception than the proven reality of an isolated leadership that motivated those demanding militant action.

The crisis revealed a fundamental contradiction in the self-conception of the Jewish Community Relations Council as the organ that represents the community to the non-Jewish world. The JCRC holds that it can only speak when there is a communal consensus. Since such a consensus is rarely present, what kind of effective leadership can such a body provide in a political crisis? Perhaps the whole concept of consensus needs to be replaced by a concept of democratic decision-making in which all parties debate the merits of a particular policy and the majority sets the direction.

Clearly, such a democratic notion of a Jewish communal council—a structure found in some Jewish communities in Europe—would require a more inclusive approach to dissident elements. Such groups would have to be given equal rights of representation so that the council would not merely reflect the points of view of the Federation leadership (that is, those who fund the philanthropic activities of the community). In this model, the JCRC would become the highest deliberative body of the community rather than a public-relations arm of the Federation.

The crisis around the Pope's reception of Kurt Waldheim was essentially a product of historical memory. In Jewish eyes, Waldheim represented the quintessential unrepentant Nazi who denied his role in the greatest crime in human history and contended that he was "only doing his duty." By receiving and appearing to condone him, the Pope conjured up associations for Jews of the perceived silence of Pope Pius XII during World War II toward Nazi war crimes. In brief, then, the Waldheim affair seemed to many Jews to be a symbolic reenactment of events nearly half a century ago.

It was on the level of symbolic memory rather than in terms of present-day policy that the drama unfolded in the Bay Area. From the point of view of contemporary Jewish–Catholic relations, the question of Vatican recognition of Israel is perhaps a more pressing concern, but, although this issue was introduced into Jewish grievances against the Vatican, it was really the Holocaust that played the central role. It was almost as if those who had failed to make their voices heard during World War II (or were not alive then to have done so) saw the controversy over Waldheim as a chance to make amends for past silence and passivity.

Perhaps it is no surprise that this controversy occurred when it did. Not only has consciousness of the Holocaust become much greater in recent years (partly as a result of the vocal role of survivors), but, in particular, the question of whether American Jews could have done more has been given increasing attention. American Jewish guilt and anger at the Allied governments (and the Vatican) have become important emotions alongside hatred of the Nazis themselves. The displacement of anger, from Waldheim to the Pope, was symbolic of this subtle shift.

The sense for some that the Jewish response to the Pope and to Waldheim was a replay of the Holocaust undoubtedly distorted perceptions. For instance, some of the accusations against the JCRC and other Jewish leaders by the militants hinted that the "moderate" leadership was behaving with the same accommodationist passivity as the American Jewish leadership did during World War II. Even more extreme was the unspoken suggestion that this moderation was similar to the lack of militancy on the part of the Jewish Councils under the Nazis. Some of the responses by the Jewish leadership may have been molded by just these historical associations and the desire to behave differently. Thus, all parties were captives of a discourse produced by Jewish memories of the Holocaust.

The response to the Pope's reception of Waldheim suggests that the American Jewish community needs to discuss more openly just what role the memory of the Holocaust will play in policy decisions, especially in relation to the non-Jewish world. The line between exploiting guilt and creating legitimate empathy is a fine one, and it may be too much to expect that it can be maintained, especially given the increasing role of survivors in shaping the cultural ethos of American Judaism.

That the struggle between the memory of the Holocaust and the realities of contemporary Jewish policy took place most explicitly in San Francisco tells us much about the nature of the Jewish community today. Perhaps it is no longer appropriate to speak of an assimilated Jewish culture, for even in this most assimilated of communities, Jewish self-interest, in the form of sensitivity to historical memory, plays a major role. The very fluidity of this community, a result of its lack of roots in a traditional Jewish community, allowed new, militant forces to assert themselves. How the organized Jewish community responds to these forces will shape the future of internal Jewish politics and relations with the larger world.

Note

The authors both took an active role in the events discussed here. David Biale was involved in the early discussions in *Tikkun Magazine* and later organized a Jewish–Catholic forum at the Graduate Theological Union. He took part in meetings of the San Francisco JCRC. Fred Rosenbaum also took part in these latter meetings and spoke in a number of forums in San Francisco and Berkeley. Despite the authors' intimate involvement, which led to their taking certain positions, they have nevertheless tried to present the various sides with as a great a degree of objectivity as possible.

16

Earl Raab in the Community

William Becker

It is particularly important to write about "Earl Raab in the Community," my assigned topic, because Earl gave so much to the general community—to the broader agenda, broader than specifically Jewish concerns. There was, however, no conflict in Earl's mind since he believed and taught, over and over again, that what strengthened democracy in America as a whole, in the general community, was good for Jews; that the Jewish community had a basic stake in the degree to which democratic rights and practices existed for all. The most important, but not only, arena for this effort was the civil rights campaign of the 1950s and 1960s.

Along with the principle that democracy is the basic good, Earl, as assistant director of the San Francisco Jewish Relations Council, expanded and developed the thesis that there existed the "totalitarian personality." People thus affected tended to be not only anti-Semetic, anti-black, antiimmigrant, but also antiwelfare, anti–United Nations, anti–mental health programs, antiequality in education, antiseparation of church and state. If affirmative action had any image at that time, these right-wingers certainly would have been anti–affirmative action. It was a clean approach, oversimplified perhaps, but the opinion polls supported this general analysis. It made it easier to identify the enemy, and, I think, made a contribution to broadening the coalition, which made progress of civil rights necessary and possible. It also increased the attitude of caring, and lessened the spirit of meanness. The totalitarian personalities have their own composite enemy. Witness the statement of the host of a radio talk show called "Aryan Nations Hour." He blamed its cancellation on a "Marxist, liberal, homosexual, Zionist coalition." For these right-wing extremists, Jews have almost always been a part of the evil empire.

Today it is harder to identify the enemy. I suspect, however, that some hard research might reveal similar kinds of patterns, not necessarily the same patterns. Many on the far right are ashamed to admit to an objection to equal opportunity.

Part of the essential broad coalition used in California, and later nationally, was the labor movement. Trade unions fully supported every civil rights legislative effort in the 1950s and 1960s in California. In putting together these efforts, Raab was important: He was not bitten by the antilabor virus that hit so many within the liberal community. The importance of this involvement with labor went beyond the achievement of antidiscrimination legislation to the still-unsolved problem area of economic achievement and well-being. The guarantees of nondiscrimination, even equal opportunity, did not, in themselves, mean that the disadvantaged would prosper, or that there would be no underclass of poor in this richest of nations. Unions had and do concern themselves with the economic foundation of life for those who get into the system, including many who are not members; that is, their pressure for higher minimum-wage laws.

Raab's help to the farm-workers union in 1951–1952 was at a different level. This was not really helping labor, but helping the most disadvantaged. Against some strongly placed indifference, he put together a citizen's committee to put out a newsletter on farm workers and the union's problems. Some of the reluctance to help on the part of liberal academics may have been because the first conciliator of California, who tried to bring together parties (that is collective bargaining) in a 1950 cotton strike, was relieved of his position as a state employee. Raab made a viable committee nonetheless.

Indeed, according to Raab, just as the Jewish community does not exist in a vacuum, neither does the issue of human rights or those in the United States affected by the progress of civil rights. So the community agenda had to be broad, in the fullest sense. For example, mental health, as a community program, took much of Raab's time first as activist, then as president of the San Francisco Mental Health Association. Mentally ill people need help, not solely for themselves, but for those close to them, and for the community at large. I think he saw the totalitarian personality afflicted with a large degree of paranoia, which was a danger to the community, and which mental health programs might alleviate. One successful end result demonstrated by mental health activists was in keeping the communist operators from getting any foothold in this broadly supported movement.

One success of these efforts was the establishment of community-based mental health programs, which legitimized the closing of most hospitals for the mentally ill, however, this action did not result in programs in the communities effective at helping most of the discharged ill; from this action has come some of our urban homeless.

The United Nations was also a cause that was supported by Earl Raab; hence, the involvement in the American Association for the United Nations. In this effort, other members of "the coalition" were drawn from the National Association for the Advancement of Colored Peoples (NAACP) and from unions. Over the years, the United Nations has become an area of more complicated policy for people of good will, liberal and conservative alike. But there may be a new window of opportunity; perhaps more hard bargaining in the Security Council (where the power to act lies) will increasingly be emphasized and not lost in the rhetoric of the Assembly. If this proves to be a possibility, a more broadly based discussion of the policy issues will certainly be needed. We will need many Earl Raabs out there to make possible the reasoned discussion that is necessary.

Of course, the broadly defined church–state issues, were an important part of Raab's community agenda. Separation of church from state required ongoing involvement. With the coalition approach, the Jewish community seldom, if ever, confronted this issue alone; there are, after all, many religious orders which have a self-interest as well as a broad constitutional concern for preventing the imposition of a state religion. Because America decided at its origin to make room for all religions, some religions that have developed want others to conform, and have been uneasy with our extreme pluralism. The issues are raised continually: prayer in school, crosses on government property, creationism versus evolutionism. Creationism still generates heated debates versus the theory of evolution, and the continuation of this issue is a tribute to the openness of our society, and to the persistence of a continuing, far-right syndrome. In fact, only recently the governor of Arizona reminded a Jewish audience that, in the United States, "Jesus Christ is the lord of the land." More serious is the evolving political content of reconstructionist preachers, who state the following; Ruling should be done by a spiritual elite, not by the majority; democracy has failed; one man, one vote is a threat to the world; and the source of law is not the Supreme Court or elected officials, but God. Fortunately, many evangelical teachers do not agree with this. It becomes clear that the agenda presented by Raab thirty years ago still needs to be addressed.

The civil rights arena, however, is what absorbed the largest portion of Raab's considerable commitment to the general community and to the health of democracy in practice. Raab was a leader in the organization of the coalition, which broke the ground for legislation in the 1950s and 1960s, as a board member of the California Commission for Fair Practices. He became a commissioner of the San Francisco Human Rights Commission, and served for over twelve years. He became most prominent as a teacher and counselor and was often called upon by both private and public agencies involved in the agenda or problem of civil rights.

Civil rights activities first concentrated on a concern for the problems of black Americans. As the 1960s and 1970s unfolded, other minority groups also needed and received attention, especially in multiethnic California. In fact, at one point (around 1970), the San Francisco Human Rights Commission was working with Samoans, Koreans, native Americans, and Filipinos, as well as the older communities of black, Latin American, Chinese, and Japanese residents. The standing joke at that point was that when all the alleged population statistics were added up, the city had a total population of over two million, rather than the 750,000 as recorded by the census. It was the organization of the black community, however, that energized the campaigns, the first of which was for civil rights legislation, for antipoverty programs, and political/electoral success. The NAACP, along with the Jewish agencies, understood the importance of coalition efforts, and recruited the other minority communities, religious leaders, and the trade union movement into the campaigns for Fair Employment Practices, public accommodation, and fair-housing laws. In helping put together and retain the many and diverse forces, Raab was an essential player. What evolved was not just a coalition for specific legislation, but, by the mid 1950s, a movement that made FEPC a win-or-lose issue in the state Senate races of 1958, and a prominent plank in the platform of Edmund G. Pat Brown, who became governor in 1959. Opposition to FEPC in earlier sessions played a roll in the defeat of four senators in 1958.

The Jewish legislative agenda of the 1950s in California was dominated by civil rights concerns. Church–state issues, religious practices, such as kosher slaughtering, were also there, but the broad civil rights agenda was what galvanized Jewish organizations into greater involvement in legislation issues. It was this agenda that also turned their attention to act upon a broad spectrum of outside community concerns.

Even as the laws were passed—first, in a few states, then nationally, following the civil rights protests of the 1960s—each of us was reminded that the centuries-old legacy of racism and its resulting discrimination had created problems, some of which could not be solved by the antidiscriminatory legislation that was enacted. This became equally true of the judicial interpretation of the law being promulgated over time by the courts. Many cases of discrimination are not filed, and the case-by-case processing of discrimination complaints ended only some of the discriminatory practices. Some complaints could not be proved, especially given the time lag between the report of an act and the full-scale investigation. Some complaints were frivolous, aimed at harassing a respondent. Because some complaints could be proved, restitution in some form was possible. But even when a complaint was proved, the conditions that led to the complaint might still exist.

There were many problems among those left out of the mainstream, even as opportunities opened up. They were not prepared by education or training for jobs. They were uninformed about the labor market as to which jobs were available, how to get them, and the preparation needed. They were inexperienced in work habits, English language, work-place idioms, and work vocabulary. To be able to compete required some extra help for many of those liberated from overt discrimination.

Out of this grew the need and demand for what came to be called "affirmative action," a term which became more and more confused and abused with each passing year. It required, as we began to know by 1962, a conscious concern for race, gender, nationality—not simple color blindness. This required counting and keeping records of numbers as well as procedures. [Once you GET into numbers, the attack on alleged quotas begins.] Yet, there clearly is a vast difference between counting and requiring the fulfillment of a quota, no matter what. [To confuse this is to be deliberately dishonest.] The issue of quotas needs to be dealt with clearly, on its own playing field.

In practice, numbers could be and were used primarily to measure the direction of change, if any, and the degree of problem, if any. They were sometimes attached to "goals and timetables," but for most practitioners, the direction and degree of change—in the ethnic composition of a work force—was the dominant use of the numbers. Past numbers were important in describing the patterns of practice in more formal approaches, especially if they might lead to litigation.

What could one infer from numbers? Underrepresentation? This is where affirmative action comes in. Recruitment is an obvious need, especially to provide the first examples in a particular work place or job category. But recruitment implies that people are prepared; if they are not, affirmative action makes an effort to get them prepared. However, this may be a big order. Ideally, employers should work with the schools closely, so that the students know what they need to learn; if they do learn this material, the company representative they spoke with will offer them a chance at a job. Unfortunately, that ideal is seldom achieved. An easier way out is to commit cooperation in hiring to special community-based training organizations, such as those that developed out of the antipoverty programs. Earl Raab made a major contribution to this stage of affirmative action, first as the major drafter of San Francisco's first antipoverty program application, then by working with some of these community training organizations, and, finally, as Human Rights Commissioner.

Civil service selection procedures create difficult problems, which bother many people who must work with them. Some of Earl Raab's most frustrating experiences before, during, and after serving as a Human Rights Commissioner were counseling with government officials on their personnel problems. The difficulties in civil-service selection systems are made, on balance, neither greater nor smaller by affirmative action. They do point out, however, that a simplistic worship of the concept of "merit" as the argument against affirmative action leaves much to be desired. It is difficult to measure or even identify merit in many situations.

San Francisco operated its civil service lists using the "rule of one"—the department had to hire the person at the top of the list. The state originally had a "rule of three"—hire one of the first three on the list. As the weaknesses in the exam/selection procedure became more evident, the state began to hire from the qualified "poll" of eligibles. Perhaps giving such greater latitude of choice to the hiring department, plus greater ease of discharge in the probation period, are the methods to use on behalf of both effective programs and affirmative action.

Apprenticeship, and the integration thereof, presented a different challenge to Raab, the Human Rights Commissioner. It involved another significant institution: organized labor, plus a considerable involvement of government, both in the administration of apprenticeship (to protect apprentices from exploitation in its origin) and in how government let contracts for which skilled workers are required. Government obviously cannot be party to an exclusionary system. In addition, government funds should be spent in such a way that all people have a chance to earn a portion of these funds through work, regardless of race, religion, or sex. This is an extremely complicated field with different rules, traditions, power centers, and combinations of these for each craft. In some cases, the employer makes the basic decision; in others, the union decides; in still others, the apprenticeship apparatus decides.

Employers, however, decide whether to hire any apprentices. Union contracts generally set top limits on the number who can be hired in ratio to journeymen. Hiring traditionally has been promoted on a voluntary basis. In California, the employment of apprentices was required on all state-related contracts. This was both to provide a larger base of skilled workers, so essential to healthy economic growth, and to weaken the argument against affirmative action in that there weren't that many calls for apprentices. In San Francisco, an ordinance required the contractors to implement an affirmative-action program with the Human Rights Commission, a program based on hiring more apprentices, and ensuring that this greater number was representative of the ethnic population of the city as long as the supply made that possible.

To create the supply of minority apprentices, the Human Rights Commission in the Raab tradition, negotiated with the unions and employers most involved—not only the empowering ordinance, but also the implementing institutions. This created an Apprenticeship Opportunities Foundation, which had a federally funded staff to recruit applicants and tutor them in basic math, trade technology, tool names (which children of craftsmen absorbed from their parents in the normal course of growing up, exam-taking, and dates of exams.

It was at this point that the issue of equal opportunity for women became an issue of public policy. Prohibition of discrimination had been added to all the laws, but the resistance was greater than most had experienced on the race, religion, and national origin front. (Unfortunately, in some areas of work, resistance is still great.) Women were unable to aspire to many jobs, not just apprenticeships. Commissioner Raab supported the funding of a program to recruit and tutor women for apprenticeships. Apprenticeship committees could be held responsible if women did not apply and were reasonably prepared for their selection process. With cooperation from some contractors and some unions, this outreach program was modestly successful.

The women's broad agenda received increasing attention. One result was a considerable increase in the number of women appointees in the cities and the state. Mayors and governors tapped into the broadest pool of talent available— all people. The most deliberate and significant effort was that of California Governor Jerry Brown, who projected women into all kinds of government in the administration and the judiciary.

That women have been able to increase their earning from $0.60 per man's dollar (which was the practice for years) to $0.70 is progress. That it is still only $0.70 is an indication of how much further we have to go, and how much resistance still exists. I suspect that if the progress in government were taken out of the measuring system, the progress in the private sector would be modest indeed.

In some situations, affirmative action evolved into a simplistic quota approach, especially as enforcement agencies relied increasingly on litigation. Courts, after all, could mandate quotas. The hostility to the quota approach came, in part, from a reaffirmation of merit; partially from the extension of affirmative action beyond the Italian plumber apprentices to the graduate schools; and, in part, from an understandable concern for the exclusionary impact on individuals who had not themselves been party to discrimination. However, the argument deteriorated into an attack on affirmative action in general.

It is against this background that a statement defining affirmative action was drafted by Raab for the Human Rights Commission in 1973. In it he spelled out the essentials of the approach for affirmative action; recruitment (with community help); training and trainee classifications; review of selection criteria and procedures, and relevancy of standards; counting. In reference to quotas, he said, "Hiring and promotion quotas are not to be used routinely, but only when there has been a clear refusal on the part of an employer to apply affirmative action programs in good faith. The failure to reach number goals is not prima facie evidence of the failure of good faith, but may be an important clue to the substantive failure of the affirmative action program." His statement also said, "Quotas are not a program, but, at best, a strategy of last resort. They do not find people, prepare people, or match people to job requirements, or job requirements to job needs."

One of the sadder aspects of the imposition of quotas by some courts (the only institutions that can legally require them) is the degree to which they often result in little change. They did not find people or prepare people. It was and is difficult for an external agency to know enough about the details of a hiring and promotion system to be able to anticipate every problem. It is also often convenient for a respondent to be able to "blame" the court and, in the process, take no responsibility for what needs to be done. Nondiscrimination is not enough. But when a sincere effort is made to examine (and change, where necessary) the selection process, a more integrated work place almost always results.

The fair-housing front was a simpler, although much more controversial, issue. It did not, except in large projects, involve affirmative action. It did run counter to the "home-is-the-castle" ideal. The history of conscious realtor, developer, and lender discrimination was, however, all too clear to allow Raab to run away from the problem. Laws were passed. Despite the setback in California, with the vote on Proposition 14, the courts sustained the law. The involvement of thousands of people against Proposition 14 in 1964 was a significant event in the history of civil rights activity based on mass participation. It contributed to the practice of integration. Raab was a leader in that citizen effort. The laws in this field have had a real impact on the practices of realtors, developers, and lenders, and this affects large-scale patterns affirmatively. The impacted concentrations of the black poor in inner-city government projects is not, however, much changed by these efforts.

School integration, although based on the Supreme Court's decisions, has, in many ways, been the most difficult area for progress. Our nation's schools have been turning out graduates, often poorly educated, often unequally prepared for the contest ahead. The answer to this problem emphasized integration through busing. In some respects, busing became the only remedy courts felt able to impose. There were initially, in fact, few others, even discussed.

Support for busing was based, in part, on the 1966 Coleman Report, an exhausting study of 737 pages plus an additional 548 tables. He found that children of disadvantaged backgrounds (regardless of race) benefited from integration with advantaged students (regardless of race). He also reported that the latter group were not harmed by such integration, if they remained in the majority. Most important, the Coleman Report created a baseline that required all future discussion of our schools to be concerned with their output and their results.

The big problem with busing is that it results in the flight of many "advantaged" students from the public schools. They go to private schools, parochial schools, or to outlying school districts, by moving if necessary. Many of the "busing" districts have experienced this; a few have not.

Alternatives to busing have continued to be studied, even as Raab and other civil rights advocates still support busing as the only tool available for integration. Less accepted alternatives include magnet schools, educational parks, a voucher system, neighborhood/district control of schools, and remedial education programs. Magnet schools exist in many cities as college-preparatory high schools, and they are often the best places to teach. But they tend to cream off the student population (the advantaged students) needed as lever in any integration program. It is also very difficult to get school districts to create other magnet schools. If every school is a magnet in some field, this system could help integration. If not, it primarily helps those interested in the few magnet schools that exist, not, in itself, an unimportant or unhealthy end. A few magnet schools also keep many superior students in the public schools. But they do not result in much integration. Educational parks have the disadvantage of being costly and of concentrating students in large numbers although most believe that the small-sized schools and classes are better. Mixing age levels on one campus also draws criticism.

Although the goal of integrated schools remains unfulfilled, the efforts to attain it have focused attentions on such depressing facts as dropout rates, test scores, the gap between black and Hispanic test scores and white test scores, comparative expenditures, comparative disciplinary procedures, and other measures of an educational institution's effectiveness and fairness.

Language handicap issues in the 1960s and 1970s are a separate matter, different from, even opposed to integration. Greater separation of the language-minority students are sometimes sought by their community organizations. In fact, at one point Human Rights Commissioner Raab was faced with the demand of major groups in the Spanish- and Chinese-speaking communities for separate schools based on the language spoken at home. The case for this was based on the desire to preserve the culture, and the greater ability to teach subject matter in the "native tongue." Segregation, the most extreme approach to bilingual education was only one of the many different problems the demand created. Where bilingual education done poorly, it results in a flight to English language classes by families who have a choice.

Given Raab's committment to a pluralist society, one in which the different cultural communities are encouraged to maintain identity, he also pressed for more and better bilingual education. He believes that integration and cultural pluralism are both important for our democracy.

He and his fellow commissioners understood how vast difference in cultural origins affect propensity to learn. Those from cultures that emphasized and revered education (Chinese, Jewish, Japanese) approach the classroom with a different mind-set than those whose forebears lacked these orientations.

In the 1980s, pressure for all-out bilingual education declined partly out of the sheer size and diversity of the language-handicapped numbers, which made the job much more costly and more difficult, even as the need increased. The emphasis shifted back to teaching English as a Second Language. I am told by educators that today, students who have achieved some basic competency in English are shifted out of their separated classes into the regular classes.

The anti-poverty programs followed on the heels of the civil rights struggles because of the realization that the disadvantaged required government actions to overcome the results of discrimination. They were generalized affirmative action. Earl Raab was the chief drafter of San Francisco's program proposal to the federal agencies.

The separate-schools approach was rejected, as the opposite of integration. Integrationists, in general, are convinced that the free public school is a major contributor to the acculturation and assimilation of millions of immigrants to America. Hispanic educators have argued against the segregated schools of Texas, New Mexico, and California. They have been against them, not only because they are often inferior schools, but because they did not provide the impetus toward acculturation. The shift in emphasis among Latin-American educators and organizations, towards separation, came with the development of the Chicano movement in the 1960s. Its emphasis has been on cultural pride, not integration.

Language-handicaps emerged as a major problem, as the vast numbers of immigrants (both legal and illegal) from Mexico (especially), and also from Central and South American countries, Puerto Rico, China, Korea, the Phillipines, and Vietnam increased. Clearly, new residents have to know English; the health of our democracy is improved if society helps them do so.

Educators have argued all sides of these issues over the years. The point most often made to support a bilingual approach is that, if well done, the language-minority students will not fall behind their grade level in subjects such as history, math, and science, if these are taught in their native tongue. Ideally, this approach should take place in integrated classrooms, where bilingual teachers teach both language groups concurrently. This approach, however, requires more highly skilled bilingual teachers than are available. He also served as consultant to the California government on welfare programs. He has continued this concern for alleviating the subculture of poverty to the present. For example, in a 1987 talk to a national Jewish organization, he called on the Jewish community to renew its will to tackle poverty and its subculture at the local level, and, in so doing, to stimulate the general community into action. He pointed to "two institutional settings in which, as a society, we have some access to the children and to the families that are involved": the school system and the welfare system. He concluded: "But the hard fact is that these ethnic concentrations of social disorganization exist today, an artifact of our society. It will not melt at all in the forseeable future, much less with deliberate speed without this kind of systematic affirmative action. And as far as the Jewish community is concerned, it is a civil rights problem, it is our problem."

The war against poverty has obviously not been won. The income gains made by the large minority middle class, especially of two-income, two-parent families, is undermined by the more impacted concentrations of poor. By many measures, the problems are gargantuan, and in some cases growing—for blacks, the high school drop-out rate in some inner cities approaches 50 percent. The percentage of black high school graduates who go on to college is only 26 percent (against a white 37 percent) down from 33 percent in 1976. A 1984 census study found the median black household net worth of $3,397 to be only one-eleventh of the white median. We could continue with statistics. We have much yet to do and we need Raab's continuing effort.

Before and after his term as Human Rights Commissioner, Earl Raab worked to involve the community. He chaired a Civil Rights Clearing House, which brought together most of the ethnic communities. He organized discussions between some that were in conflict with each other. To work in this area, requires a tremendous commitment to the democratic ideal, great staying-power, and an open-minded understanding of the day-to-day process. This Raab had. This he gave.

Index

DATE DUE

DHUW   MAR   REC'D